THE HISTORY OF CRIME AND CRIMINAL JUSTICE SERIES

Five Centuries *of* Violence

in Finland and the Baltic Area

Heikki Ylikangas,
Petri Karonen, and
Martti Lehti

With a Foreword by Eric H. Monkkonen

OHIO STATE UNIVERSITY PRESS
Columbus

Originally published in 1998 by the History of Criminality Research Project,
Academy of Finland, Helsinki

Library of Congress Cataloging-in-Publication Data
Ylikangas, Heikki.
Five centuries of violence in Finland and the Baltic Area / Heikki Ylikangas, Petri Karonen, and Martti Lehti ; with a foreword by Eric H. Monkkonen.
p. cm. — (The history of crime and criminal justice series)
Originally published: Helsinki : History of Criminality Research Project, Academy of Finland, 1998.
Includes bibliographical references and index.
ISBN 0-8142-0860-6 (alk. paper) — ISBN 0-8142-5062-9 (pbk. : alk. paper)
1. Violent crimes—Finland—History. 2. Violent crimes—Sweden—History. 3. Homicide—Estonia—History. I. Karonen, Petri. II. Lehti, Martti. III. Title. IV. Series.
HV7015.5 .Y48 2000
364.94897—dc21
00-057468

Text and cover design by Gary Gore.
Type set in Berkeley by G&S Typesetters, Inc.
Printed by Thomson-Shore, Inc.

The paper used in this publication
meets the minimum requirements of the American National
Standard for Information Sciences—Permanence of Paper
for Printed Library Materials. ANSI Z39.48-1992.

9 8 7 6 5 4 3 2 1

Contents

Foreword

ERIC H. MONKKONEN

Most Americans associate Nordic countries with peace, tranquillity, civility, high living standards, and generally progressive social arrangements. It is this very quality which also gets Nordic countries rejected as policy models because they are too peaceful. What happens there is too remote and too easy compared with the harsh American world. That is, the very difference between them and us seems to preclude comparative understanding.

The contents of this book should help reverse all these thoughts: Sweden and Finland were once quite violent, and their Baltic neighbor Estonia has late twentieth-century homicide rates that parallel those of America's cities. Lacking urban decay, even lacking cities of any size, early modern Finland had rural traditions of knife fighting and has suffered aggressive male violence in ways as grimly predictable as in the late twentieth-century United States. In both Sweden and Finland, cities led social pacification, becoming less violent before the countryside. Contemporary Estonia has, on the other hand, high violence rates within its Russian population, rates which point to enormous social gulfs in a country that Americans would see as homogeneous and "white."

The excavation of these differences and change over time is as interesting as the differences themselves. The contributors to this book give enough sense of their archival methods and materials to cause surprise. These profoundly rural places in hard climates populated by peasant farmers and woodcutters, with tiny cities no larger than what we would call villages today, all had record keeping of quality better than the contemporary world's nonindustrial nations. The simple survival of these peoples is impressive: that the records were written and maintained is truly fortunate.

What we can learn from this book addresses issues of policy and history. For policy, it makes clear that personal violence can lodge like a virus in many host organisms: that although American violence is a unique problem in some ways, it is not due to some peculiar set of conditions limited to America. Multiple causes have the same violent outcomes: rather than attacking root causes, violence control should attack the much more specific proximate causes—

whether it is the carrying of knives to wedding dances or the goading of soldiers to show male superiority through impulsive violence. From the historical point of view, we can see how Finland's experience can give hope; how entrenched traditions of personal violence can change; how history, like circumstance, is not destiny. For the United States, a long history of violence, of tolerant courts, of aggressive weapon brandishing, can in fact be turned around, just as it has been in Finland where cell phones are now as common as was the traditional *puukko*—a razor sharp knife familiar to Americans as the Rapala fishing knife.

This remarkable collection of articles advances our understanding of personal violence in the West in two ways. First, in his masterful overview, Heikki Ylikangas compresses two decades of scholarly research conducted in several languages from dozens of sites into an up-to-date synthesis and evaluation. In his initial dozen pages, Ylikangas has produced a compelling synthesis that masks his erudition and analytic work with disarming ease; this section should be read and reread for its insight and power. Second, all three contributors add new empirical knowledge about amounts and kinds of violence in a vast reach of time and space. Readers see how the interactions of church, state, and family shift in the early modern period to rearrange an angry and impulsively violent social world.

As a bonus, American readers meet, for the first time in the United States, three outstanding Finnish scholars.

Heikki Ylikangas, an imaginative and prolific senior scholar, is already widely known in Europe. A professor of Finnish and Scandinavian history at Helsinki University, Ylikangas is also currently a professor with the Academy of Finland's History of Criminality Research Project, of which this book is an early product. He has written on a variety of scholarly subjects, mostly in Finnish, Swedish, and German. He has also written three plays and a historical novel.

Petri Karonen, a faculty member at the University of Jyväskylä, has made his research cover what are now two nations by focusing on Sweden and one of its towns in what is now Finland.

Martti Lehti, a scholar at the History of Criminality Research Project, brings to the English-speaking world an extraordinary study of personal violence in Estonia, no doubt the first of its kind.

The extensive documentation in these articles makes a third contribution, with both primary and secondary citations constituting a thorough and up-to-date bibliography. In the lists of sources and published materials, the articles show both prodigious work and extensive knowledge. American scholars will appreciate the lists of citations as much as they do the substantive contributions themselves.

Readers of this book will discover lively and surprising discussions—whether on the fights between soldiers and townspeople in the seventeenth century, Finnish knife fighting, or the spate of violence in Estonia accompanying Russian immigration and the Soviet government policy of producing more vodka in bad economic times. Ylikangas's analysis of the knife fighting region and subcultures in Finland is fascinating: he delineates a region whose social practices evolved into stunning lethality. In this he provides an outstanding example of how a male fashion trend in weapons has outcomes far more serious than the meaning of the original trend.

Theoretical insights abound. Ylikangas shows how at the end of the sixteenth century the power of the family was broken, to be replaced by the state. Given how "the family" has an almost sacred sound to it today, we need this reminder of a world in which families were obligated to revenge their members against wrongs and, conversely, were required to pay the victims of offenses committed by their members. The result was social control via the family, but accompanied by recurrent feuds and retribution. Feuding, revenge, and self-protection, all of which could escalate and perpetuate violence, had to be wrested from the family by the state—a shift that one might associate with different social consequences than those demonstrated here. Karonen shows how in early seventeenth-century Stockholm the settlement of disputes by courts was adopted first by elites and then by the lower social orders. This clearly supports Norbert Elias's theory of the "civilizing process."

This book is a real treat. It gives us the benefits of the most timely historical scholarship in an easy and readable package. In the best way it combines the exotic with the mundane, the "world we have lost" with the world we are in.

Preface

This publication is an integral part of a research project dealing with historical criminology from an international perspective. The project is funded by the Academy of Finland, and in initial stages it received considerable support from the University of Helsinki. Of the contributors, Heikki Ylikangas and Martti Lehti are members of the project's research staff, and docent Petri Karonen of the University of Jyväskylä is one of the scholars associated with the project. Anu Koskivirta and Sari Forsström, whose doctorate research is being funded by the project, have compiled research material. Mirkka Lappalainen, who has recently completed her master's degree, has also collected material, and she is responsible for editing this work. Gerard McAlester accepted the demanding task of translating two articles. To all of these I offer my warmest thanks.

HEIKKI YLIKANGAS

CHAPTER 1

What Happened to Violence?

An Analysis of the Development of Violence from Medieval Times to the Early Modern Era Based on Finnish Source Material

HEIKKI YLIKANGAS

Translated by Gerard McAlester

The Main Line of Development of Violent Crime in England

FOR SOME TIME NOW, RELIABLE RESEARCH DATA HAVE shown that the level of violent crime (as recorded in judicial proceedings) was extremely high from the Middle Ages onward. Sample data describing the development of homicide in England from the thirteenth to the twentieth century show a falling curve, starting from a level of 20 homicides annually per 100,000 persons. And as late as the seventeenth century, the rate was still nearly 7. However, by 1900 there was less than 1 homicide a year per 100,000 inhabitants.[1]

What do these figures signify measured by present-day standards? The figures for the 1980s represent the general level in Western Europe today, but the early figures are staggeringly high. However, today's world does offer us examples of comparable homicide rates from both ends of the curve. In the industrial nations of Western Europe, the homicide rate is now 1 or 2 per year per 100,000 inhabitants. In Finland the rate is at least twice as high, while the highest rates in Europe are in the Baltic countries and in Russia (more than 20).

Equally high rates also exist in the largest cities of North America: in 1992, the rate for the whole of the United States was 9.9. Such rates are equivalent to the level existing in fourteenth-century England, that is, about 20 per 100,000 capita per annum. There are also high rates reported in present-day Poland, Hungary, and the Balkan countries, which are "only" around the Finnish level (3.6). In Bulgaria and Hungary, the rate is more than 4. Most Latin American countries also have a rate of more than 4, and in Brazil, Colombia, Mexico, and Puerto Rico it is more than 10. Of the Asian countries, Sri Lanka, Turkestan, and Uzbekistan have more than 4 homicides per year per 100,000 inhabitants.[2]

Thus homicide rates throughout the world today vary greatly. This in turn obliges us to examine the extent to which the curve describing the historical development in England is reliable and representative of a more general historical development or simply haphazard. The question is pertinent because the limited size of the samples and the shortness of the periods analyzed tend to increase the rates. Local and chronological fluctuations are considerable. Nevertheless, the Dutch scholar Pieter Spierenburg believes that the interpretations presented concerning the main trend are valid.[3]

Is Spierenburg correct? Apparently he is. His views are supported by research data on the development of violent crime elsewhere in Europe, which indicate that the direction of the curve describing the trend in England is not just a matter of chance.

The Development of Violence in Western and Northern Europe

The development of crime from the Middle Ages up to the present day in Western Europe seems to have been much the same as in England. Violence was rife during medieval times, but then it began to wane, probably in a fairly similar way to how violence declined in England.[4] The same is true of the Nordic countries, although the information available for them is sporadic, local, and mainly limited to the towns. This limitation, however, applies to all countries and makes it difficult to arrive at accurate estimates. In any case, Jörn Sandnes has registered about fifty homicides for Bergen (Norway) in the 1560s, at which time it was a fairly large port with six thousand inhabitants. This would raise the homicide rate for Bergen at that time right up to 80 per 100,000 capita per annum.[5] More reliable data are available from the Kingdom of Sweden-Finland than from Denmark-Norway because in Sweden, where there was no feudal system, a premodern state machinery evolved at a fairly early date, and from 1540 on it began to produce extensive series of source data, for example, in the form of judicial records (fine rolls). Additionally, for the towns as well as for a few rural areas there is information available from medieval times. The situation with regard to sources in this area is thus exceptionally good.

The studies made by Eva Österberg and Dag Lindström of a number of Swedish towns from the end of the fifteenth century to the early seventeenth reveal slightly better figures than those for Bergen in the 1560s. Even so, the degree of aggression in Swedish towns was huge. The rates are in the region of 30 to 40 homicides per 100,000 capita per annum. At the top of the list comes Vadstena with the shocking figure of 77.[6] Indirect evidence about the towns of Ribe and Helsingör in Denmark in the sixteenth century also point to a high rate of homicide. However, there are no exact figures available for Denmark.[7]

Grievous violence was, therefore, particularly common in the large ports of the Nordic countries at the end of the Middle Ages and the sixteenth century. The validity of the conclusions is undermined by the shortness of the periods and/or the limited areas investigated. If we take a large number of towns and long, uniform periods of time, we obtain figures that are lower. Petri Karonen has calculated the amounts of homicidal crime in Finnish towns (which were relatively small) in the sixteenth century and determined that between 1540 and 1599 there were on average 15 homicides a year to every 100,000 persons. For Finland the following rule seems to apply: the larger the town, the higher its homicide rate.[8]

Information about the rural areas in the Nordic countries is even more locally limited and diverse than it is for the towns. It seems, however, that the figures for the rural areas—at least at the end of the Middle Ages and the sixteenth century—are lower, indeed only half of those of the towns.[9] The rate is usually between 10 and 20 per 100,000 capita per annum. To mention one or two examples: in the judicial district of Långhundra in Sweden, the homicide rate rose to 14 between 1545 and 1560,[10] while in the Telemark-Agder region in Norway it was 17 between 1536 and 1571. Elsewhere in the Norwegian countryside, the level was lower.[11] With regard to Finland, there are some high rates for brief periods: 19.7 in the Province of Satakunta during the years 1550–52 and 25 in the Province of Tavastia (Häme) between 1506 and 1610.[12] The figures drop over longer periods of time. In the western part of the Province of Nyland (Uusimaa) in southern Finland in the 1550s, the homicide rate was 7 per year per 100,000 inhabitants.[13] The rate for Savo in the east is about 11 for the years 1559–65 and 4.4 for the period 1547–1616.[14] In Finland Proper (Varsinais-Suomi) in the southwest, the rate was 6.2 in the 1560s and 1570s, while in Ostrobothnia (Pohjanmaa) in the west it was only 3.[15] As far as Finland is concerned, therefore, it is difficult to come to any other conclusion than that in the sixteenth century violence was worse in the towns than it was in rural areas.

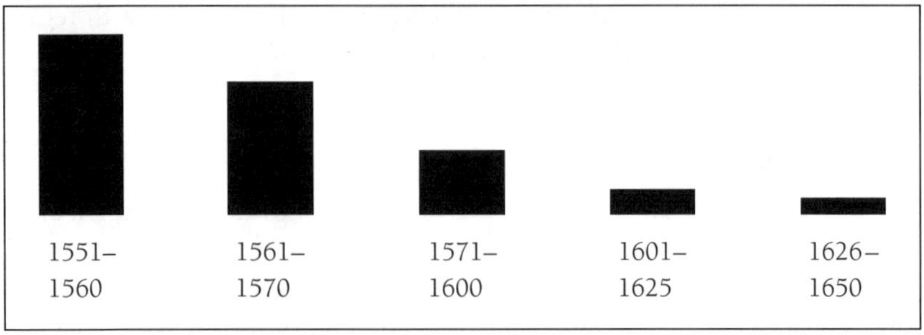

Fig. 1.1. Registered decrease in violence in the Greater Lohja area in relation to the population. The greatest decline took place during the period 1571–1625.

Locally, at the level of the province, let us say, violence in Finland seems to have been more common in remote areas than in more settled regions that had an established culture. Generally the dependent parishes were more violent than their mother parishes, the coast was more peaceful than inland regions, and violence smoldered longest in the eastern parts of the country.[16] Similar observations can be made about the other Nordic countries. The judicial district of Konga in Småland in Sweden still had an astounding annual homicide rate of 40 per 100,000 inhabitants as late as the seventeenth century.[17] In Norway the worst areas were the outlying Agder and Telemark regions.[18]

For all their limitations, these data show that violence was as common in the Nordic countries in the Middle Ages and the beginning of the modern era as it was in England at the same time. On the other hand, we have found little evidence pointing to the same kind of subsequent downward trend that was observable in the case of England. Nevertheless, there was a decline in violence in the Nordic countries, too, although interpretations regarding the time it began vary somewhat.[19] The process began in Finland in the sixteenth century.[20] A fall in violence, and serious violence in particular, from the sixteenth century to the beginning of the eighteenth is as evident here as it was in England and in France. For example, the annual rate of homicides per 100,000 persons in the Province of Tavastia in Finland between 1506 and 1510 was approximately 25, but between 1751 and 1776 it had fallen to only 2.6, a tenth of what it had previously been.[21] The same trend is even clearer in Sweden. According to the so-called population tables (a register of the total population, which when it started in 1749 was the first of its kind in the world; it also contained information about crimes of homicide), the overall homicide rate in Sweden for 1761–1850 was between 0.3 and 2.9 per 100,000 capita per annum (see fig. 1.2, below).[22] The situation in Finland in the mid-eighteenth century was very much the same as in Sweden.[23] The information available about Norway is less reliable, but there, too, the decline is both permanent and undeniable.[24]

The pacification process seems to have taken place from the coasts inland and from the more settled areas to the more remote regions. In the Provinces of Savo and Käkisalmi in the east of Finland, homicide was relatively common in the seventeenth century.[25] And even in the eighteenth century there were areas of eastern Finland where the homicide rate was still about seven or eight.[26] However, these exceptions do not change or upset the overall picture. The level of homicidal crime at the beginning and middle of the eighteenth century in all the Nordic countries was only a fraction—less than a tenth—of what it had been in medieval times and the sixteenth century.

Thus we conclude that the decline of gross violence from the Middle Ages up to the present century is not a phenomenon limited to a particular country but rather a feature common to the development of many European states. As such, it therefore requires an explanation that is not limited to any single country.

Explanations for the Decline in Violence

Norbert Elias's Theory of the Civilizing Process: For and Against

A number of broad macrolevel theories have been proposed. Because the rate of grievous violence was high in the Middle Ages and then tended to fall steadily down to the early years of the eighteenth century, since when it has not risen to any appreciable extent, there is a temptation to explain the phenomenon by means of anthropologically based theories. One such is the so-called theory of the civilizing process, which numerous scholars have used to explain the development. Among others, Lawrence Stone, Ted Robert Gurr, and Yves Castan turn to this theory, although Stone admits that the causal relationship is weak between the main postulates of the theory and the empirical evidence.[27] Most Nordic scholars of historical criminology (including Eva Österberg, Dag Lindström, Jan Sundin, Johan Söderberg, Jörn Sandnes, and Henrik Stevnsborg) also base their research on Elias's civilizing process theory. It is true, however, that their assertions have become somewhat more circumspect in recent years.[28] An explanation with similarities to the civilizing process theory was also favored by Finnish scholars of the older generation, especially Pentti Renvall.[29]

What then is the theory of the civilizing process? It was formulated by the German philosopher Norbert Elias in the late 1930s, although it was anticipated at a much earlier date in German developmental psychology. The main premise of Elias's theory is the fact, in itself indisputable, that in normal everyday life people tend to become peaceful and renounce violence. Elias understands this change as a psychic process (psychogenesis), behind which lie changes in society (sociogenesis). According to Elias, the process of pacification begins from the highest stratum of society (the court) and spreads from there down through the social scale until the whole of society has become pacified. The upper classes are the key to the change, followed by the middle and lower classes.[30] Gurr summarizes the process as follows: "The process is in essence a cultural one, and like most cultural change it had its origins in the changing values of social and intellectual élites."[31]

Until they are civilized, people are incapable of controlling their feelings and emotional behavior. After the civilizing process, they begin to behave in a peaceful, rational, and controlled manner.[32] However, Elias does not interpret the change as an autonomous anthropological process, as does, for example, Pentti Renvall with his distinction between natural peoples and civilized peoples.[33] According to Elias, the state plays a central role in this development.[34] The premodern state monopolized the use of violence and in this way forced its subjects to renounce it. People had to control their aggressions and instincts, or the state institutions would punish them.[35] "People are socialized to control and displace anger," states Gurr.[36]

These are the main features of the civilizing process theory. It explains many of the facts relating to excessive violence and its decline. Chronologically, the steepest drop in the curve—that which describes the decline at the end of the seventeenth century—accords fairly well with the growth of the premodern state. The change occurs roughly at the beginning of the Age of Autocracy (1680–1719) in Sweden.[37] By linking the described pacification process to the development of the state, one can also explain how the change became permanent. The state's hold on its subjects has not appreciably relaxed since it tightened in the seventeenth century. Indeed, it has been claimed that it is the forms of control that have changed rather than its intensity.[38] In assessing this claim one must, however, take into account the fact that punishments have become more lenient since the 1770s.[39]

Several research studies support this theory. The basic premises of the civilizing process theory provide an easy explanation for the fact that the more populous centers tended to become pacified before the outlying regions and the coastal areas before the interior.[40] This phenomenon exhibits *mutatis mutandis* the same hierarchical progression—a movement from a more developed level to a less developed one—that in Elias's theory takes place between the different social strata in society. Again, the fact that in Sweden the first manifestations of harsher state punishments (linked to Mosaic law) came into codified law from royal court ordinances also fits the picture.[41] In accordance with the civilizing process theory, the increase in the severity of sanctions, which reached its peak in the Nordic countries in the early seventeenth century, began in the court at the latest at the end of the 1560s; in other words, the harsher punishments first affected the court nobility, not the common people. This generalization is not undermined by the fact, supported by a wealth of evidence, that penal practice became stricter at a very early stage in the big cities.[42] The autonomous position of the cities made them in a way states within states. The same autonomy meant that it was in the towns that the centralization of power happened first. Thus the development in the towns does not conflict with the civilizing process theory—except insofar as violence was not easily eradicated from them despite the harsh punishments. However, the failure in this respect can probably be put down to a constant stream of migration that brought to the towns elements who had already fallen into criminal ways or who were otherwise inclined to a deviant way of life.[43] Thus the theory of the civilizing process does not necessarily fail in respect to the towns.

However, the theory is vitiated by a number of other, rather serious weaknesses. In the first place, it seems to contain a kind of tautology or circular argument: first, the practice of excessive violence is characterized as original uncontrolled behavior, and then uncontrolled emotional behavior is asserted to be the cause of violence. Second, if before the phase of civilization people's behavior was characterized by uncontrolled and impetuous excess, one would assume that they would have shown it particularly when they were confronted by naked violence. One would expect people with such a mentality to have immediately tried to slay anyone who had taken the life of their nearest and dearest or at least to have demanded the death penalty for the killer in court. As we shall see later, neither of these hypotheses holds true in the sixteenth century. Third, if we assume that the fundamental reason for pacification is the development of the state—the monopolization of violence under the authority of the state—how are we then to explain the fact that crimes of violence did not disappear altogether? Even today, there exist large areas of the world (Brazil, Colombia, Mexico, Zimbabwe) and even of Europe (the Baltic countries, Russia) where grievous violence is at the same level that it was in England during the Middle Ages.[44] This cannot be explained by regarding these countries as not yet having undergone the civilizing process, as new waves of violence have also come in abundance to countries that have indisputably undergone a process of pacification. This holds true of many developed European countries in light of events in the past few years.[45] Nor can the recent increase in violence be put down to organized crime alone, although the Mafia is certainly not without significance here. The Mafia would seem to offer a convenient explanation for high crime rates in both eastern Europe and South America as well as for the grim

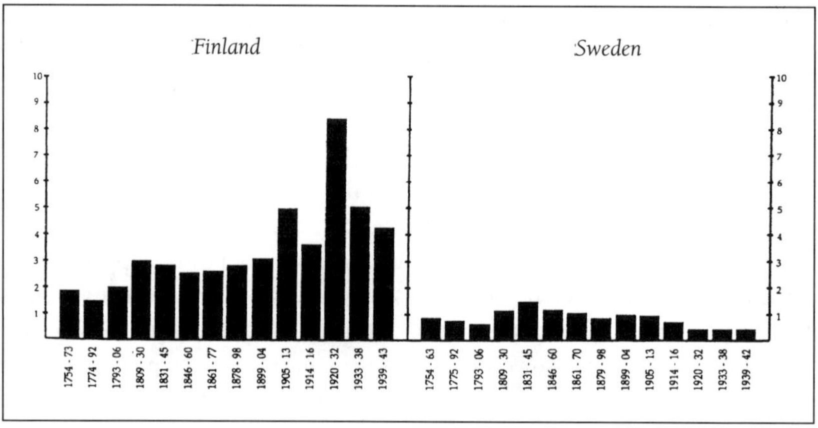

Fig. 1.2. Victims of violent crime per 100,000 capita in Sweden and Finland.
Source: Verkko 1949, 2.

homicide statistics of the cities of the United States—although admittedly these last have recently shown a slight decline. However, data about Estonia, a country in the clutches of a staggeringly high crime rate, show that only a fifth of all killings at the most can be attributed to organized crime; the remaining homicides amount to a rate of well over 15 per 100,000 inhabitants annually.[46]

Perhaps the clearest proof of the failure of the civilizing process theory can be found in the history of Finland: the level of violence and the development of violent crime in Finland do not correspond with the claims of the theory. As figure 1.2 indicates, from the 1750s on, for reasons that are not yet properly understood, the paths taken by Finland and Sweden diverged.[47] Generally speaking, despite slight fluctuations, homicidal crime steadily decreased in Sweden, while in Finland it increased almost as steadily.[48] Yet the two countries belonged to the same kingdom until 1809. By the 1920s, homicides in Finland reached a level of more than 8 per 100,000 persons annually.[49] This is of the same magnitude as the average rate in the Finnish countryside in the fourteenth century.

Finland provides another graphic argument against the civilizing process theory, albeit a local one, but one that at the time was both unique and exotic. Around 1790, homicidal crime began to increase sharply in one county of Finland, Southern Ostrobothnia, which at that time was the most important tar-producing area in the world. During the next hundred years or so, two thousand county residents were murdered. This is equivalent to approximately 10 lives per annum per 100,000 inhabitants. If one selects a narrower interval of time, say fifty years, and the worst affected parts of the region, one arrives at a figure of 50 to 60 homicides a year. This is of the same magnitude as the rate in the Middle Ages and the sixteenth century in the largest mercantile cities. The statistics for Southern Ostrobothnia do not begin to show a decline until midway through the 1880s. It should be noted that only a fraction of the killings can be attributed to organized crime.[50]

Both of these developments in violent crime in Finland conflict with the basic postulates of the civilizing process theory, and so do changes in the rate of violent crime in the past few years in western industrialized countries, particularly in countries that belonged to the former Communist bloc. Regarded from either of its principal standpoints—the anthropological or the state—the civilizing process theory does not stand up in this respect. The relationships between weak state administrations and the high crime rates in former Communist bloc countries is more complicated. Here, the theory of the civilizing process is in a certain sense relevant.

The problem can be clarified with a few apposite questions. If people changed emotionally in the seventeenth century, suppressed their impetuosity, and began to behave rationally, then—and this is the principal question—what was it that barbarized them anew? The upper classes? Clearly not, because the mutually corroborative evidence of numerous researches on various countries (Germany, France, Britain, Sweden, Finland) shows that since the fifteenth century, and even earlier in the case of the larger cities, crime has generally tended to be concentrated among the lower classes.[51] When crime increased in some places after the seventeenth century, it was certainly not inspired by the example and model of the elite.

Information gathered from Finnish local histories can shed some light on this matter. They tend to be summary and thus only roughly indicative, but they carry some probative force. The proportion of soldiers implicated in homicides (excluding infanticide) is low up to the period 1635–64, when it jumps to 18 percent (8 soldiers out of a total of 45 killers). The corresponding figure for the period 1665–99 is 21 percent (14 out of 67).[52]

Again, according to the civilizing process theory, all levels of society were equally violent before the seventeenth century. Society gradually became pacified from the top down. Empirical research does not necessarily support this hypothesis. In fact, it suggests something rather surprising: apart from the big cities, the most delinquent group in the Middle Ages was the upper class.

According to the Norwegian scholar Jörn Sandnes, the upper strata of society were overrepresented among the perpetrators of violence in Norway. Among those who were guilty of homicide and other forms of physical aggression were priests and *lagmenn* (officials with judicial and administrative authority over large areas, similar to the English sheriff), whose behavior presumably reflected

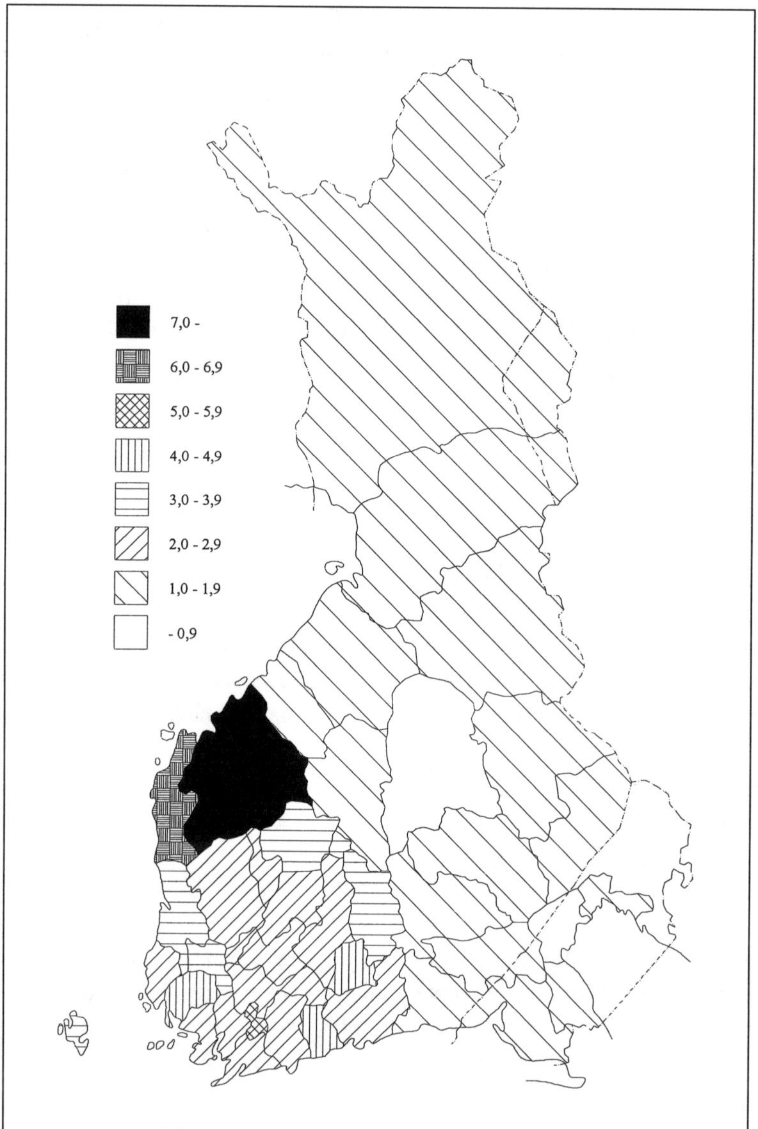

Map 1.1. Murdered adults per 100,000 capita of the average population in the Finnish countryside, 1816–65. *Source:* Ylikangas 1976b, 19.

their social origins, for until the seventeenth century most of them were descended from the nobility.[53] In Stockholm at the end of the Middle Ages and the beginning of the modern era, violent criminals included burghers and artisans and were not only members of the lower classes such as soldiers, apprentices, and hired hands, as was the case later.[54] As far as Finland is concerned, it has been shown that, at least in the mid-sixteenth century, the peasant jurors who owned the largest farms in the parishes committed more murders than ordinary peasants.[55] According to J. A. Sharpe, the representatives of the upper classes in England, the landed gentry, were more inclined to violence and brutality than the lower classes.[56] Other British scholars have come to the same conclusion.[57] It seems clear that the behavior of the English upper classes did not become more peaceful until the seventeenth century.

Such research indicates that before the seventeenth century extreme violence was characteristic of the upper and middle classes, and it was apparently only after 1600 that the situation changed and the perpetrators of violence gradually began to come from the lower classes.[58] Only the big cities constitute an exception to this rule and then only from the chronological point of view: the process took place in big cities at an earlier date than in rural areas.

The Nature of the Violence

These observations oblige us to make a wider and deeper analysis of the empirical material that is available. We must try to determine the nature of the violence when it was rife. Was it serious or petty, carried out by individuals or groups, committed in fights or in individual assaults?

The material available in the Nordic countries provides an opportunity to answer these questions that is not easily afforded elsewhere. The weakness of feudalism here made it possible to establish a machinery of state control at an exceptionally early stage. In Sweden there are the fine rolls, going back to 1540. The king received a third of all fines, and consequently the lists of fines imposed were appended to the Crown accounts. There are, in fact, sporadic data from the fine rolls from considerably earlier times. As far as the towns are concerned, the judgment books (*tänkeböcker*) exist from medieval times.[59] From the sixteenth century on, there are available a few judgment books, official records of proceedings in the lower courts which contained all cases that came before the courts, both civil and criminal, including those that ended in acquittal. From the beginning of the seventeenth century, there is a further significant improvement in the source situation. Courts of appeal began to be established in Sweden in 1615, and from then on there exist continuous series of judgment books. In Finland, the series constituted by the records of the lower courts begin in 1623, when the Turku Court of Appeal was established.[60] All in all, the source situation in Finland (which belonged to Sweden until 1809) is exceptionally good compared with that in central Europe, where the material is more sporadic as a result of the enduring particularism of the feudal system.[61] This then is reflected in the small size of the samples used in the research on violent crime in central Europe.

A comparative analysis of the sources in Finland has shown that, at least before the beginning of the seventeenth century, there is no significant difference between the fine rolls and the judgment books with regard to the information they provide about crime; in other words, the fine rolls also regularly contain entries about crimes that received punishments other than fines.[62]

Even so, the Finnish judicial sources are by no means complete even where they have in principle survived. This is because the sources for the history of criminality in Finland were also to some extent affected by the feudalism of central Europe. The fines were shared by the king, the court, and the plaintiff. The fief holder, however, might take the king's share of fines imposed on persons living in his fief, in which case there was nothing left for the bailiff to enter in the Crown accounts. As a result, these crimes do not appear in the records. This mainly reduces the value of the judicial sources in the years either side of 1600. The fine rolls contain at best limited references to homicidal crime, often without the names of the perpetrator and the victim. This is an indication of malfeasance. The situation improved markedly after the establishment of the Turku Court of Appeal in 1623.[63]

The quality of the sources and particularly the deficiencies mentioned above oblige one to inquire whether the decrease in violence observable in them was real or just the result of an increase in unrevealed crime. Before taking issue with this possibility, let us return to the question of the actual nature of the violence. The answer is surprising: most violence was extremely petty.

The basis of the fining was the quality and quantity of the wounds inflicted; the intentions of the perpetrator were hardly considered. The law of Sweden prescribed a fine of three marks for one bruise. The fine was divided between the king, the court, and the plaintiff so that each received one mark. The fines for cases of more grievous assault were also determined according to this mechanical principle: an open wound brought a fine of six marks, two open wounds twelve marks, and so on. The fine for homicide was forty marks, if the culprit got off with a fine.[64]

Astonishingly, most cases involved a single bruise incurring fines of three marks. In the western parts of the province of Nyland (Uusimaa), the proportion of three-mark fines of all cases of assault ($N = 190$) in the 1540s was almost ex-

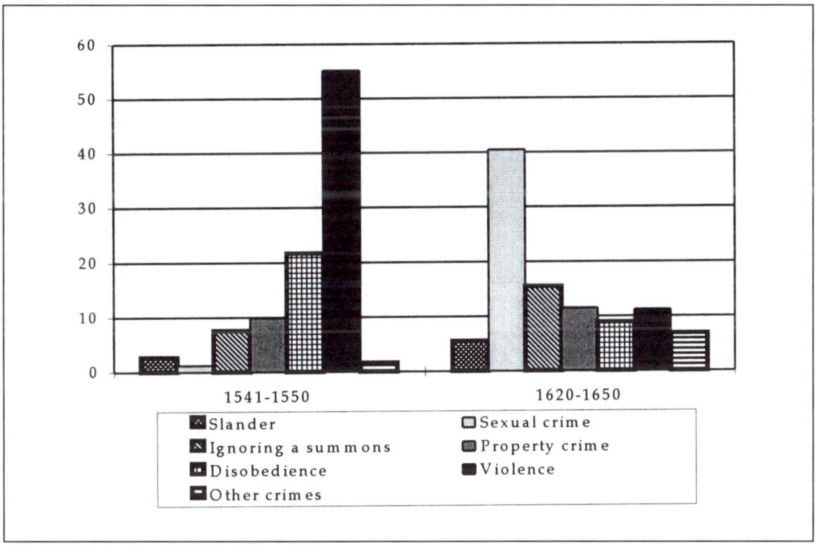

Fig. 1.3. Relative figures for fines in Lohja.

actly two-thirds.[65] For some reason, the people of the time were willing to undergo all the bother of bringing the matter to court. They had to obtain witnesses, summon the aggressor through the lay jurors, and make what was often a laborious journey of many leagues to get to the place where the district court sessions were held. There were originally three district court sessions a year, but these were later reduced to two as the number of cases decreased. Often the journey involved staying overnight. By the time the case was dealt with, several months might have elapsed. If the plaintiff won the case, he received not one mark, as the law prescribed, but half a mark, which represented the price of about half a sheep. For reasons that are not clear, it was the regular custom to halve the sum ordained by the law and to calculate the thirds for the king, the court, and the plaintiff from what was left.[66] The halving of the fine also seems strange in view of the fact that inflation had naturally weakened the value of the mark from what it had been when King Christopher's Law of the Land (*landslag*) was ratified in 1442.

Another important point to note is that these cases of petty assault disappear from the court records most rapidly. The average amount of the fine per case rose, and this seems to be somehow linked with the fact that the proportion of fights (in which both parties were fined for striking each other) in crimes of violence decreased, albeit only slightly, as figure 1.4 shows. What links these types

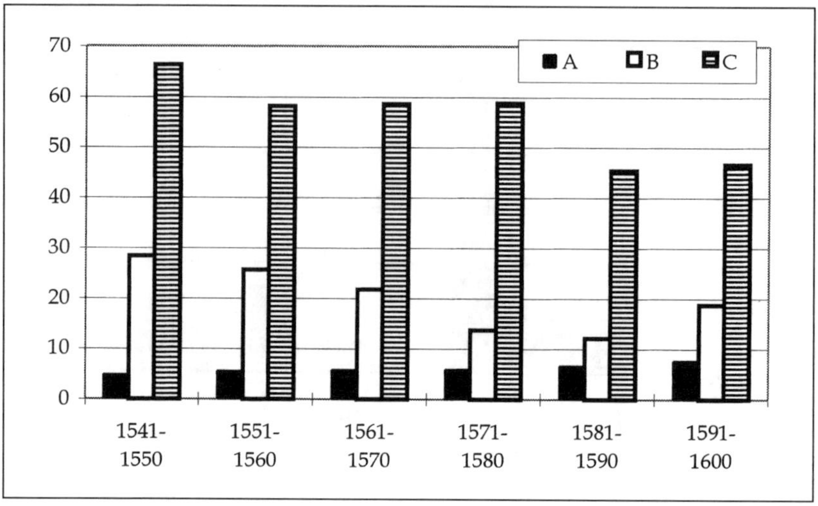

Fig. 1.4. The average fine in marks (A), the percentage of fights in crimes of violence (B), and the percentage of cases incurring fines of three marks (C) in all acts of violence dealt with by the district courts in the western part of the Province of Nyland (Uusimaa) in Finland, 1541–1600.

of cases—petty assault and cases in which both parties were guilty of acts of violence—is the ease with which they could be settled outside the court.

For some reason, some cases that had previously been publicly prosecuted began to be quietly settled out of court. However, the absence of lesser cases and fights is not alone sufficient to explain the decrease in officially reported crimes of violence, as the decrease in the number of fines for violence per district court was huge: over 200 percent, or almost fortyfold. This means that there must have been a decrease in more serious cases of violence as well, albeit a smaller one than in petty crimes.

There is further convincing evidence of this. In the Province of Finland Proper (Varsinais-Suomi) in southwestern Finland, on average three homicides a year were committed between 1540 and 1580, but the annual rate had fallen to one between 1580 and 1620. For the Province of Ostrobothnia in the west, the decrease was only slightly less.[67] In Savo in the east, too, there was a slight decline,[68] although the decrease is clearly smaller and slower in eastern Finland in general than in more westerly regions.[69] Similar data are available from the other Nordic countries, although in Norway and Sweden the decline in violence began later than in Finland.[70] The only possible conclusion is that there was generally less violence than before.

The Judicial Examination of Crimes of Homicide

An individual case. On the last day of July 1550, the district court of the parish of Loimaa in southwest Finland dealt with a case of homicide. The records describe the proceedings thus:[71]

"Olavi Paavonpoika of Oripää appeared before the court and made it known to the session that he had entered into an amicable agreement with Heikki Tuomaanpoika of Seppälä. In the agreement, Olavi Paavonpoika in the name of God gave and granted to Heikki Tuomaanpoika his life, although the latter had slain Antti Olavinpoika, the son of Olavi Paavonpoika, on condition that the said Heikki give the said Olavi forty marks in settlement. May they be thus properly and amicably reconciled. In accordance with the judgment of twelve jurors." The same panel of twelve jurors further declared that Heikki Tuomaanpoika of Seppälä was "a full manslayer because he killed Antti Olavinpoika of Oripää. However, his life was spared on account of the plaintiffs. For this, he undertook to pay fifty marks to the king, for he was caught in flagrante delicto. In accordance with the judgment of the panel of lay jurors. Fine reduced to 25 marks."[72]

Thus states the record of the case. The inquiry, or rather the record of it, raises a number of interesting questions. The father "granted" his son's killer his life; in other words, he obviously had the power to take it away as well. The condition for granting it was a considerable sum of money, the equivalent of the price of six cows in those days. What is interesting is that another judgment is immediately passed after this one: that of the actual panel of jurors, in which the guilty party is declared "a full manslayer." The record states that his life was spared "on account of" the plaintiffs, which apparently means on their behalf. The killer undertook to pay fifty marks to the king, and the justification for the sum is that he was caught red-handed. In the end, however, only half the sum, twenty-five marks, was paid to the king.

It seems then that in fact two agreements were made at the same time: one between the accused and the plaintiff, and the other between the convicted person and the king (or rather his representative, the bailiff). In both cases the life of the guilty party was spared, and in both cases it was apparently within the power of the other party to the agreement (the plaintiff and the king) to take his life.

The case seems so strange that one feels compelled to ask whether the judgment was in accordance with the law. We are in a position to give a full answer to this question. At that time, in Sweden, and thus in Finland, which belonged to it, the Law of the Land enacted by King Christopher in 1442 was in force. The law included provisions for homicide. It stated that a person who was convicted of homicide should be condemned to death if he had been caught in flagrante delicto or if he had been apprehended fleeing from the scene of the crime within a period of twenty-four hours. In these cases the killer could only get off with a fine if the deed had been committed in self-defense or by immediate heirs "in the first flush of anger" (*i första wrede*). The plaintiff could choose between the life of the killer and a fine if the culprit had not been caught red-handed but had been apprehended fleeing from the scene of the crime within a period of twenty-four hours and was found guilty by the panel of twelve sworn jurors. In all other cases, a fine of forty marks was stipulated, to be divided in three parts of thirteen marks eight örtugar (24 örtugar = 1 mark) and given to the plaintiff, the court, and the king. The only exception was murder, which was defined as concealed homicide. Whoever was convicted of murder in the district court was sentenced to death, in accordance with the law, even if the above-mentioned conditions were not fulfilled. In certain aggravated cases (the killing of a defenseless person, a relative, a minor, or a person who had authority over the guilty party), loss of property and deportation were prescribed in addition to fines. This wergild (*mansbot*) of forty marks was also imposed for cases of involuntary manslaughter.[73]

This information provides us with a good basis for deciding whether the judgments of the district court sessions in Loimaa in 1550 were in accordance with the law. They were not. This is clearly the case. Since the killer had been caught in flagrante delicto, he should have been sentenced to death. This fact is reflected in the judgment in that the share of the fine to be paid to the king had been raised considerably beyond that prescribed by the law, and the increase is justified by the fact that the culprit had been caught in the act. The idea behind this was that by raising the king's share far above the sum stipulated by the law, it was also possible to come to an agreement with the ruler and let the guilty party off with a fine.

But how was it at all possible for the district court of a small country parish to go against the Law of the Land in such a flagrant way? The answer may be simple: it is possible that it was a mere exception to the rule. What then was the normal judicial practice in cases of homicide?

Unlawful judicial practice. The prevailing practice was, however, exactly that which is revealed in the case described above. The Loimaa judgment thus represented not an aberration but the rule, and indeed a rule from which there were extremely few exceptions. In only very rare cases was a killer sentenced to death as the law prescribed, and even more rarely was he actually executed. Of 169 cases of homicide in the provinces of Ostrobothnia and Finland Proper between 1540 and 1620, the death penalty is known with certainty to have been carried out in only three or four instances.[74] In all other cases, fines were imposed.

Was it then that the judges and the lay jurors did not know the law? The Norwegian scholar Hans Eyvind Næss has come to this conclusion after finding that in Norway until the 1620s fines were invariably imposed for crimes of homicide, although according to the law they were punishable by death. Næss believes that the judges were ignorant of the law.[75] Is this interpretation valid?

It is not. In Finland, justice was dispensed in the town courts by magistrates and in the district courts in rural areas by a district judge who was a member of the nobility—or more often by a deputy with legal training appointed by him—together with a panel of twelve lay jurors elected to the position. These members of the courts were certainly familiar with the few simple provisions in both the Law of the Land and the city ordinances concerning crimes of violence. In the Lohja District Court on 8 February 1564, District Judge Nils Boije and the panel of jurors agreed to let a killer off with a fine because the plaintiffs had interceded for his life and he had not been caught in the act (*bleff intet fångin wed ffersk gerningh*).[76] The statement can be interpreted *ex contrario* as indicating that the sentence for a killer caught red-handed would have been different—execution. The same thing is even more apparent in a judgment given at the Lappi District Court in the province of Finland Proper on 1 November 1558; according to the court records, it was impossible to pronounce a sentence of death because the guilty party had not been caught in flagrante delicto (*och kvnde icke komma honom hals brott uppå, tij hann icke bleff fongenn widt ferska gerningh*).[77] There is so much evidence of similar cases from other places that it is pointless to analyze them in any further detail. To summarize, the courts understood the contents and intention of the law, but they were unwilling to apply them in practice.

Why were they unwilling to apply them? There were two legal grounds for not imposing the death penalty when the killer was caught in the act. One referred to a killing committed as an act of revenge "in the first flush of anger"; the other referred to self-defense. According to the Law of the Land (Intentional Homicide Code II), a killer should pay for a life with his own if it could be proved that he had committed the deed intentionally and not in self-defense (*så framt det kan visas, att han gjorde gärningen med lust och utan livsfara*). The court ordinances of 1560 express the intention of the law as follows: "If a person strikes another dead without being compelled to do so, the matter is aggravated; let him then give a life for a life."[78]

Then were the judgments we have claimed to be unlawful pronounced in cases of self-defense or in which the perpetrator had carried out the deed in a blood feud "in the first flush of anger"? I cannot find any mention at all of a killing taking place "in the first flush of anger," and appeals to self-defense were rare before the second half of the sixteenth century. It was not until the 1560s that they became more common, but then they increased so much that sometimes self-defense was mentioned as the justification for fining in almost half the cases.[79] One wonders whether assault and battery really increased so tremendously at the end of the sixteenth century.

There is at any rate no evidence to show that aggression in society in the form of civilian violence increased in the late sixteenth century. There is a slow decline in the homicide rate, and it should also be remembered that the proportion of fights (i.e., cases in which both parties were fined for violent behavior) appears to decrease at that time. Why then was appeal so frequently made to self-defense? Because it was a method generally used to circumvent the law by having fines rather than capital punishment imposed.

The pressure to evade the law grew when the authorities launched a mounting campaign to ensure that the law was enforced.[80] This tightening-up is most clearly apparent in a decree on grievous crime issued by King Eric XIV in 1563. (The decree was an almost word-for-word rendering of a decree issued in Denmark a year earlier.)[81] In the decree, crime was identified with sin, and appealing to the Mosaic law of blood guilt it stated that one single unexpiated deed had been the ruination of whole kingdoms. This was the consequence that God's vengeance brought upon a community that permitted innocent (= unexpiated) blood "to cry from the earth." The decree strictly forbade the imposition of fines when the law required the death penalty. The decree listed blasphemy, treason, murder, adultery, incest, rape, sodomy, and other such sins as crimes that deserved to be punished by death.[82]

The main burden of the decree was thus that an unlawful (i.e., lenient) sentence in cases of grievous crime brought the wrath of God upon the community. Blood had to be avenged with blood. In such circumstances, it became undesirable to impose a sentence of a fine without some kind of justification. The most legal way of avoiding the death penalty was sought, and self-defense filled the bill.

But it was only one of the justifications, albeit the most common. Appeal to other grounds for mitigation gradually became more common. At first, the courts gave no justification for using fines to punish cases of homicide. In Finland Proper and Ostrobothnia, almost half of the homicide cases (48.6 percent) that were tried before 1570 were settled with fines without any justification being mentioned. The fine was usually forty marks. This sum lent credence to the legality of the judgment, as the law stipulated a forty-mark wergild when the crime did not fit the conditions for a killing punishable by death. Between 1571 and 1620, the occurrence of such judgments fell to 27 percent; in other words, in just over a quarter of the cases no justification was given for imposing a fine rather than the death penalty.[83] At the same time, there spread a procedure in which the responsibility for unlawful fine sentences was shifted to the king by leaving the sentences to "His Royal Majesty's clement discretion" (*till Kungliga Majestetts nådiga behag*).[84] Originally the cases concerned Crown tenant farmers or "Crown servants,"[85] but later other cases were also handled in this way. According to the available sources, the method was first used in Finland when Duke John ruled the country as the Duchy of Finland (1556–63).[86] The presence in the country of the ruler was thus reflected in his authority. An example of the fact that fining was increasingly felt to be a dubious procedure in the late sixteenth century was the widespread practice of increasing the king's share of the fine beyond the amount prescribed by law. With increasing regularity the following rule was applied: the graver the crime, the higher the royal share of the fine.[87]

One can well ask just what leaving the sentence to the king's discretion meant. Were the sentences passed by the lower courts left to be ratified by the king? No, at least not usually. Probably the idea was that after taking due consideration of the case through an examination of the accounts (the fine rolls were submitted annually with the other Crown accounts for auditing by the treasury) the king would change the sentence by making it harsher or more lenient. Constitutionally, the king did not have the right to pass sentence, only to abrogate wrong judgments.[88] In any case, the responsibility was thus formally left to the king himself.

A very common ground for fining was the intercession of the plaintiff, usually the victim's family. According to the law of those days, it was only valid in a few cases, when the culprit was not caught in the act or escaping from the scene of the crime within a period of twenty-four hours but was nevertheless convicted of the crime in the district court.[89] In actual practice, this procedure was adopted in all kinds of cases. A typical example is provided by a homicide case in Finland Proper in 1569. The guilty party, Olavi Jaakonpoika, got off with fines, "because the plaintiffs interceded for him before the court and granted him his life" (*epter thett målseijare bodho för honom inför rätten och vnthe honom liif*).[90] No legally justified grounds are mentioned. The intercession for the condemned man's life was made by the plaintiffs, but sometimes the whole panel of jurors (*för hela nempdens bönn*), the "good men of the parish" (*godhe sokne bönder*), and the whole assembly present in the court (*och hele tings stempne*) endorsed it.[91] At the Muurla District Court in 1572, a killer's life was spared because the deed had been committed in self-defense and the plaintiffs did not demand his life (*efter målseigiendne icke stoodhe epther hans liiff*). The grounds for the sentence were that he had killed in self-defense, and clemency with a fine was ensured by leaving the matter formally to the king's discretion.[92] Sometimes, especially in the late sixteenth century, the reason given for sparing the guilty party's life was stated as being not only the intercession of the "good men" of the parish and the relatives but also Christian charity: "in the name of God."[93] Sometimes appeal was made to the lack of evidence (both parties were so drunk that the facts of the case were not clear), provocation by the victim, negligence in caring for the victim's wounds, and so on. A new ground for commuting the death penalty to fining appears in the last years of the sixteenth century. The killing is judged to have been committed in the heat of the moment (*hastigom modh*), on the basis of which the killer's life was spared. However, there was no basis in the law for such mitigating grounds in cases of homicide.[94]

In what kind of cases, then, was the killer not spared and actually went to the block? Such cases were for one reason or another exceptionally grave. On 20 July 1544, the Salo District Court sentenced Jöns Laurinpoika of Lumijoki to death for "full manslaughter." Laurinpoika had, with the complicity of his wife, killed his own child.[95] The Uusikirkko District Court sentenced Heikki Vidiola to death on 12 July 1557 for killing Jöns Kallela "in such an unchristian fashion."[96] In Laihia in 1576 a sentence of death was passed and, according to the sources, also carried out, but no grounds are given. Presumably, in this case, too, there was some aggravating circumstance.[97] These are the only death sentences actually carried out in connection with the 169 homicides committed in the Provinces of Ostrobothnia and Finland Proper between 1540 and 1620. The result fits extremely well with the evidence provided by the Homicide Collection, which contains references to 144 homicides in the period 1506–1600 and only 5 death sentences, although in some of the references no sentence is mentioned at all.[98]

Fining was thus almost the sole punishment meted out in cases of homicide at least up to the final years of the sixteenth century. It is, nevertheless, strange that when the killer was sentenced he was frequently declared "a full manslayer."[99] This procedure seems inconsistent. Why use this expression when only a fine was imposed and the law required the death penalty for a "full manslayer"?

There is another matter that seems odd. A frequently mentioned justification for fining is that the defendant and the plaintiff had made a settlement (*förlikning*).[100] Does this mean that a private settlement could bypass the law?

Reparations for homicide. That is exactly the case. The real reason why the plaintiffs were satisfied with having the culprit fined and did not demand his life was that in addition to their share of the fine, which was generally small, they received an indemnity, which was large.[101]

How big was it? In most cases, especially early on, no mention was made of the sum. Only the fact that the parties had reached a settlement was stated. This means that the indemnity had already been paid at the time of the court sessions.[102] Because the settlement had already been determined and the indemnity paid, it was no longer necessary for the district court to record the terms of the settlement in order to ensure the future payment. Sometimes the fact that the indemnity had been paid before the trial was explicitly mentioned or certified in the court records.[103] But there are also cases where the indemnity had not yet been paid and where the detailed contents of the settlement were made public in court. In this way the court attempted to ensure that the conditions of the settlement were properly fulfilled.

There is the following entry in the records of the Pöytyä District Court dated 23 July 1557: "Antti Laurinpoika of Korpi was sentenced to pay a fine of forty marks for a full homicide which Knuut Simonpoika had committed by striking the said Antti's father dead, after which Antti received from the aforementioned Knuut all his property, his house and his land, and the aforementioned Antti agreed willingly to be responsible for the fines of His Royal Majesty and of the court, amounting to thirteen marks, eight örtugar."[104]

The settlement with the plaintiff, the victim's father, thus cost the killer all his personal property and real estate. It is illustrative that it was the plaintiff who was sentenced to pay the fines to the king and the court and not the guilty party. Inevitably so, because the latter no longer had any property to pay the fines with. This points to the fact that the blood money involved sums that were considerable in those times.[105] On 13 May 1551, Niilo Huuhko of Lellainen in the parish of Eura promised to pay Mauri Tuomaanpoika, whose father he had killed, an amount of land that was undefined but that was evidently all that he owned, as well as thirteen marks, eight örtugar (the equivalent of the original share of the wergild payable to the plaintiff) in settlement.[106] At the autumn sessions of the Uusikirkko District Court on 9 October 1578, a settlement was recorded as four hundred marks (to be paid in *klippingar*).[107] The amount indicates that the settlement was the equivalent of the price of a farm. The sum was intended to ensure for the dependents of the victim the same security that they would have enjoyed if he had lived. This is clear in those cases in which the killing took place within the family. In 1565 in the parish of Halikko, a peasant named Ambrosius killed his own nephew Sigfried in self-defense. Ambrosius was sentenced to pay forty marks in fines and was required to provide for the wife and children of the deceased until the end of his life.[108]

Although no compensation was paid to the Crown and the court, the amount of the fine in their case, too, was in practice, if not according to the law, proportionate to the gravity of the crime. The forty marks provided for in the law (of which the king and the court each took a third) was not considered sufficient in the settlement negotiations.[109] The position of the Crown (the bailiff) was stronger than that of the court in the bargaining because the royal share of the fine went back to a concept called the King's Peace.[110]

The blood money still had to be paid even if the deed was found to have been committed in self-defense, although in such cases the sum was apparently smaller than in intentional cases of homicide. The forty-mark wergild also had to be paid.[111]

The same applied when the deed was found to have been carried out accidentally. The Pöytyä District Court sentenced Simo Matinpoika to pay a fine of forty marks for the unintentional manslaughter of Knuut Pitkäniitty. According to the court records: "The plaintiffs forgave him and sued him before the court for 110 marks as blood money, whence they shall be thus properly and amicably reconciled and not demand his life."[112]

The settlements rose to such proportions that in some cases one gets the impression that they tempted the relatives of the victims to indulge in a sort of cupidity. Valpuri Mikontytär of Nauvo struck Olof Eskelinpoika several times in a fit of anger because he drove her sheep off the village commons. She apparently struck him with the palm of her hand, because the record states that she also pushed him. The boy, who was weak and sickly, had been frequently ill before this, and a few days later he fell ill while working. This time, however, possibly at the instigation of his relatives, he sent a summons to Valpuri to come and agree to a settlement for assault and battery. For some reason or another, Valpuri failed to obey the summons before Olof died. Immediately after the boy's death, his brother, Erkki Eskelinpoika, in his capacity as plaintiff (it was at the plaintiff's discretion whether to prosecute for homicide in cases of assault leading to death),[113] had Valpuri arrested and imprisoned in Turku Castle. From there, she was taken to the Nauvo District Court, where the brother refused permission to have the body of the departed exhumed to determine the cause of death. Instead, he submitted the matter to the court's judgment, saying: "I know that my brother was sickly, but only God knows whether she is guilty of his death or not." On this basis, the plaintiffs did not require the death penalty but "contented themselves" with demanding the staggering sum of two hundred marks (in *klippingar*) as blood money. Valpuri agreed to the settlement. In addition, the king and the court got 75 marks each in fines.[114]

The family's support for the individual. On 22 March 1564 in the parish of Sääminki in Savo in eastern Finland, there was a case in which a certain Martti Kandarattinen and his relatives were the plaintiffs and Paavo Sipinpoika was the accused. Paavo Sipinpoika had been arraigned for killing Olavi, the son of

Martti Kandarattinen. The affair was settled at the very outset of the proceedings, for Martti Kandarattinen himself admitted that his son had died of a disease and not of the wounds he had received at the hands of Paavo Sipinpoika. "Four good yeomen" also testified to this, as did the local priest, to whom the boy had revealed the true state of affairs before his death. Thus, the innocence of Paavo Sipinpoika in the matter in question was fully and legally proven. Nevertheless, the parties came to a settlement in accordance with an ancient formula that emphasized the importance of the family. The settlement was made "on his [Martti Kandarattinen's] behalf and on behalf of his children as well as of all his relatives both born and unborn."[115] The blood money was also paid, for Paavo Sipinpoika "nevertheless gave" (*enn doch gaff*) Martti Kandarattinen "twenty marks in money, a half-barrel of rye and four pounds of copper, and Martti Kandarattinen before the whole court offered his hand to Paavo Sipinpoika and forgave him completely."[116]

Just what was involved here? Why was blood money paid and a reconciliation made if no crime had been committed? A possible explanation may be that relations between the families were thus repaired after being severed by the suspicion of manslaughter. The fact that it was a question of the family and a blood feud, or rather the prevention of a blood feud, is apparent from the expression "on behalf of his children as well as of all his relatives both born and unborn."[117]

The material compensation that was paid even though no crime had been committed, or which was paid in addition to the actual wergild, is called in the sources a *villgåva*, which can be understood to mean a voluntary gift. In the Joroinen District Court, a case of homicide was settled with a sum of fifty marks, in addition to which the perpetrator gave the victim's son a horse, his widow received a six-pound pot, and two other relatives received some strips of pasture as voluntary gifts (*och än tho tiill viill goffhuor*).[118] In Loimaa on 24 April 1551, the killer paid the father of the deceased "seventy marks as wergild and beyond the agreement a silver spoon weighing 3½ lod" (1 lod = ½ ounce) (*LXX marck ortiger mans båtth oc 1 silffsked öffuer förlikningen, som vågh 3½ lodh*).[119] Apparently, the voluntary gift, which was divided according to the closeness of the family relationship, though favoring the male rather than the female line, originated in an established order of inheritance from older times. That was why the items of property and the recipients were specified exactly.[120]

The autumn sessions of the Lappi District Court in the Province of Finland Proper on 1 November 1558 tried a case of homicide committed by one Yrjö Heikinpoika. The victim was a peasant named Eskil who had moved to the parish from Sweden that summer. The panel of jurors found that Yrjö Heikinpoika had carried out the deed "without any particular threat to his life or constraint" (*uthann synnerligh lifs trong och nödh*). For this reason he paid the plaintiffs a higher fine than normal: forty marks. The court record continues: "And thus the same deed has been agreed before the court now in session as a death which has been fully settled and concluded beyond further discussion for both the unborn and the born."[121] The final statement of the record goes thus: "Jacob [of the village] of Lahti, who is the nearest proxy of the children, stood here before the court and interceded on behalf of the killer, and it was not possible to pronounce a sentence of death upon the killer because he was not caught in flagrante delicto. In addition, the said killer shall give the wife of Eskil three marks for the rapine of her bed."[122]

The message of the records is clear. The kin of the victim made a settlement with the killer and promised that it would hold not only for the living but also for future generations of the family, thus nipping in the bud any possible spiral of blood vengeance. The wording of the agreement was certainly formulaic and no longer reflected the prevailing social situation. It is indicative that the affair was handled by the male blood relatives of the victim (the nearest proxy) and not his widow. The wife was passed over not because she was a woman but because she was a blood member of another family. Since it was thus impossible to pay the wife a compensation on the basis of blood relationship, another basis for doing so was adopted: "the rapine of her bed" (*för sängeråån*). It was considered that the wife should be compensated for the loss of her partner. The compensation was admittedly a small one—three marks—the same amount that the law stipulated as the fine for a bruise. Naturally the widow also benefited from the blood money through her children, although it did not legally belong to her.

This was not always the case. The male guardians of minors did not always hand over the money to their wards or provide it to be used for their benefit. In 1551 in the parish of Marttila, the court ordered Mikko Karhunoja to pay a woman named Margareta money belonging to some children that came from blood money paid for the killing of their father a decade earlier. Margareta was obviously the children's mother.[123] However, women were generally not totally ignored in the settlements. They were numbered among the plaintiffs, although usually only when the victim was a blood relative and when the plaintiffs included at least one man. There is, nevertheless, one case in 1556 in which two sisters, Marietta and Kaarina, of Viljakkala were the only two plaintiffs and members of the victim's party in making a settlement concerning the killing of their brother.[124] Usually the victim's side was represented in court by his father, his brother(s), and his son(s), and sometimes his mother, sister(s), or son(s)-in-law as well.[125] At the winter sessions of the Uusikirkko District Court in 1558, the mother, wife, and brother of the slain man sued for "both fines and peace [i.e., the life of]" (*bode wm boott och fridh*) for the accused. These were granted, and an agreement was made that emphasized the perpetual satisfaction of the relatives.[126] The wife of the dead man appeared among the plaintiffs less frequently than his female blood relatives, and then usually only together with one of his male relatives.[127] It was quite exceptional in the sixteenth century for the wife to appear as the sole plaintiff against the accused. It did happen in the case of Torsula Nielsdotter from the Swedish-speaking part of the parish of Vehmaa; in 1568 she appeared in court and made a settlement with Niels Thomasson, who had killed her husband.[128] With a couple of exceptions, more distant relatives such as grandparents and uncles do not appear as parties to the settlement either as plaintiffs or as beneficiaries.[129]

Thus the parties to the settlements were made up of extended nuclear families, in the case of the victim mainly the male members of his former and present nuclear families. The groups of beneficiaries thus constituted are designated in the sources by the word *släkt* (kin). The term explains why the wife of the victim was bypassed in the settlement. It was also used as a legal concept to indicate the collective group affected by the deed. Pietari Pietarinpoika from the parish of Lapua, who had committed homicide, was spared a sentence of death at the Pedersöre District Court in 1577 because "the kin gave him peace and had levied a wergild."[130] At the summer sessions of the same district court on 2 August 1582 a merchant, Oluff Jakobsson, was "reprieved" (*benåddes*) with a fine of forty marks for killing Erich Andersson in self-defense, "because the kin of the said Erich interceded for the life of Oluff and levied a Christian wergild."[131] At the Uuskirkko District Court in 1594, there was a laconic reference to the fact that Martti Antinpoika, who had committed homicide, "had settled with the kin" (*bleff förlichte med slechten*).[132]

Because an agreement involving fairly large amounts of property was involved, it was negotiated down to the smallest details. This is evident in those cases in which the agreement has been recorded for one reason or another. At the Loppi District Court on 15 January 1584, Tapani Mikonpoika Röysköla and his sister Riitta Mikontytär appeared before the court and made "a perpetual reconciliation and agreement" with Eskeli Pekanpoika, who "without valid cause or threat to his life" (*wtan någån skiälig orsack eller liiffznödh*) had slain Matti Mikonpoika, the brother of the plaintiffs. Tapani stated that he had received a horse worth two hundred rundstycker (1 rundstycke = 1 silver *öre*), an ox worth one hundred rundstycker, and a pound of grain, which was equal in value to five old marks. Riitta had been paid six marks in old money and five quarter-barrels of grain worth five marks. The wife of the victim had received a cow worth eighty rundstycker for "the rapine of her bed [*för sängeråån*]."[133]

In this case, too, the plaintiffs were the victim's blood relations, not the widow, who was compensated for "the rapine of her bed." Her compensation was, however, greater than in the previous case; there is also a report of the payment of a cow in compensation for the life of the marriage partner from Perniö in 1591.[134] This is an indication of a gradual decline in the importance of the blood relationship.

The detailed itemization of the articles of property shows just how tough was the bargaining that took place before the settlement.[135] There is also evidence pointing to this from the side of the guilty party. Because the reparations were so high, the culprit was not by any means always able to pay them without the help of his family. This feature of the family participating in the settlement of crimes of homicide was known throughout Europe.[136] Admittedly, some provincial laws in Sweden going back to the fourteenth century stipulated that nobody could oblige his relations to pay the "family fine" (*ätteböter*), but its payment was not forbidden either. It was therefore left to the kin.[137] At the Marttila District Court on 14 January 1601, the brothers of a farmhand who had killed a man and immediately fled the country paid the victim's mother and brother altogether 210 marks, in addition to which the employer of the killer promised 30 marks. (This is the first reference to a person outside the family helping to accumulate the blood money.)[138] The flight of the culprit overseas is an indication of the fact that sanctions had become harsher, a matter to which we shall return later.

Since it was in the power of the relatives either to accept a material settlement or to demand the life of the killer, and the Crown (the bailiff) and the court (the jurors, sometimes also the judge or his deputy)[139] had the same power, there sometimes arose a situation in which one party was willing to settle but another was not. Such a case was recorded in the fine rolls from the summer sessions of the Vörå District Court on 7 July 1546. The panel condemned Eskil Nilsson as a "full manslayer," and he offered a settlement with the relatives of his victim, Olof Bertilsson, but they declined the offer. The bailiff acting for the Crown was willing to accept the settlement, and thus a difficult situation of stalemate arose. Eskil appeared before five or six sessions with his offer of settlement, but the victim's relatives rejected his offer each time. Finally, the bailiff gave him "peace on behalf of His Royal Majesty" and accepted the share of the fine of thirteen marks eight örtugar stipulated by the law. There is no information as to how the affair ended, but evidently the victim's family eventually had to agree to a settlement once the king, through his bailiff, had done so.[140] Such situations of stalemate could hold up the final judgment for years. At the Uusikirkko District Court in 1578, the victim's widow agreed after two and a half years to be reconciled with the killer on condition that he leave the country.[141] In Vehmaa in 1571, a case was dealt with in which seven years had elapsed from the actual time of the crime.[142]

Sometimes the bailiff appears to have a decisive voice in determining the fate of the guilty party. The Tavinsalmi District Court in the eastern province of Savo on 1 January 1564 condemned Heikki Paavonpoika in the customary way as "a full manslayer." Then the description changes; the plaintiff appeared before the court and "interceded with the bailiff for his life," which he granted him (Heikki Paavonpoika) on behalf of His Royal Majesty, "because he has not been apprehended, but is hiding in the forest, and unless he were granted peace, he would flee to Russia."[143] The bailiff thus justified his stance by appealing to the national interest. In Mynämäki, the family reprieved a fratricide from death, and he paid the bailiff one hundred marks.[144] At the Vehmaa District Court on 15 November 1575, it was recorded that the plaintiff and the heirs of the victim had reached a settlement with the culprit and that "he therefore appeared here before the court and made a settlement with me concerning the merciful dispensation of H.R.M., and because the plaintiff has interceded on his behalf, I have imposed a royal fine of two hundred marks and the District Judge a fine of one hundred marks."[145] This formula was also used more generally.[146]

At the Uusikirkko District Court in 1558, the panel of jurors took a different stand from that of the plaintiffs. The wife and mother of Mikko Seppä and two male witnesses all testified that, on his deathbed, Mikko Seppä did not accuse Eskeli Erkinpoika of causing his death, although the latter had hit him in a fight six weeks earlier. In the opinion of the panel and many men in the parish, the connection between the two events was clear even though Mikko Seppä, who had apparently started the fight, was to blame for the wounds he had received in it. Thus the panel of jurors sentenced Eskeli to pay a wergild of forty marks. The mother, wife, and brother of the victim were reconciled with Eskeli, and they proclaimed an accord between the two parties on behalf of present and future generations.[147]

What kind of guarantees were there that the beneficiaries really got what had been agreed to in the settlement? If, as was generally the case, the compensation was paid before the trial, no guarantees were necessary. Prepayment meant that the plaintiffs agreed to intercede in the trial for the accused's life. It was a different situation when the settlement was made in court and the payment of the compensation was postponed. Even then, however, there was not much concern that it would not be paid, for it was secured by the strongest possible guarantee: the life of the guilty party. This applied in the first place to the fines. The Pellosniemi District Court noted laconically, "If the killer is unable to pay the fine of forty marks, then let him die" (*Oc om han förmo ecke vt draga bothen, så skall han gåå ifrom halsszen*).[148] The law was the same with respect to the settlements. At the Hattula, Lehijärvi, and Renko District Court sessions on 23 March 1583, the guilty party was ordered to pay the compensation he had promised by the next sessions "if he did not want to pay with his head" (*så framt han vill icke bittale medh huffudet*).[149] From early on, a procedure was employed whereby the killer was arrested and placed in a Crown prison, from which he was not released until his relations had paid the compensation and thus bailed him out.[150] This shows the reason why the guilty party was regularly first declared a "full manslayer" and only then sentenced—usually on the basis of some extenuating factor—to pay fines. Declaring him a "full manslayer" was a guarantee that the money would be duly paid. If it was not, the fact that the judgment permitted the death penalty to be enforced was invoked, and he was forced to pay at the risk of losing his life.

In such circumstances, it would have meant the loss of considerable material compensation for the family of the victim to demand the life of the killer. There is evidence from elsewhere in the Nordic countries that during the Middle Ages and the sixteenth century the same kind of system of punishing crimes of homicide with fines was used as in Finland. Dag Lindström has even found references to this from Stockholm, although in the big ports judicial practice in general began to take on some of the features of the harsher modern system of justice at an early stage.[151] Lindström reports a case in which the parties involved conducted tough negotiations in court about the amount of compensation and who should pay the king's and the court's share of the fine. In the end, the accused agreed to pay the family of the victim 150 marks in compensation, and they undertook to pay the fines.[152] There is research evidence of similar cases in Norway in which the importance and authority of the family is emphasized.[153]

The Birth of the Modern State and Its Influence on Judicial Procedure

A Revolution in the System of Justice

Judicial practice with regard to crimes of violence and homicide began to change at the end of the sixteenth century, but the real revolution in the courts came at the start of the seventeenth.[154] Among its characteristics was the gradual replacement of purgation by oath with modern judicial procedures. An oath of purgation witnessed by the jurors or relatives had been used to purge the accused of the charge of homicide, particularly when the charge was based on hearsay or when the victim survived the act of violence for a period of time.[155] This oath was no longer considered sufficient in principle, because the main purpose of the court inquiry became not to achieve a reconciliation between the parties but to find, judge, and sentence the guilty party according to the provisions of the law. For this, witnesses were needed, and unlike purgation by oath, the new juridical practice permitted the use of lawyers. This was naturally not possible when oaths of purgation were in use, because the oath had to be sworn in person—it was not possible for one person to swear an oath on behalf of another, although it was possible to swear one's belief in the other's innocence as a compurgator. The change in emphasis in the goal of the judicial process from settlement to truth also brought a fixed order of courts of instance into the justice system. It became possible to appeal a decision of the lower (district or town) court to the court of appeal and to take the appeal from the latter to the king (who was originally only empowered to abrogate wrong judgments). When the main goal of the judicial process was to achieve a settlement between the parties, there was no need for this hierarchy of courts of instance. The hierarchy required that the court proceedings be written down, because a purely verbal trial produced no documents on the basis of which appeal could be made to a forum of higher instance.[156]

In Sweden, these changes were finally made in the law in 1614–15, and in Finland the decisive change was brought about by the foundation of the Turku Court of Appeal in 1623. Because the court of appeal was given the task of supervising the lower courts, it meant that all court proceedings henceforth had to be recorded in writing. The series of records of judgments of the lower courts in Finland begin properly in 1623, though there are some earlier records, as it had been possible to appeal to the Svea Court of Appeal in Sweden ever since 1615.

What then were the essential factors that lay behind this judicial revolution? There was an increase in the power of the central authority (the king) and the birth of a premodern state with its foundations in an established army, a fixed taxation system, a civil service, and the regulation of society through the law. These changes got under way during the reign of Gustavus I Vasa and were completed under Gustavus II Adolf. In the present context, it is not possible to analyze in any greater detail the process that led to this result.[157] In any case, the fundamental point is that a strong state was able to include the direction and supervision of the system of justice within its sphere of influence.

On the other hand, it is appropriate here to consider the concrete consequences that the modern state entailed for judicial practice. What changed, why, and when, or did anything really change at all in the end?

The System of Justice Becomes Stricter

It has been shown that positive justice, that is, statutory law, was tightened up toward the end of the sixteenth century. An attempt was made to end the practice of giving unlawful lenient fines. We shall now consider just how successful this attempt was. Did sentences become harsher in the way intended or not?

The answer is partly affirmative. Sentences did become harsher. Of the forty cases of persons found guilty of homicide in southern Finland (mainly in Häme) between 1583 and 1600, eight were sentenced to death, and evidently most, and possibly all, were executed. These death penalties were incurred for the following crimes: killing the heir to the culprit's land, homicide in conjunction with a breach of the King's Peace (five cases), a vendetta killing (behind which lay a killing previously settled in court), the killing of a person while asleep, and two other cases of homicide. In three cases, the court rejected the intercessions of the plaintiffs and the court public for the lives of the accused and left the confirmation of the death sentence to Claes Fleming, the governor of Finland at that time.[158] Thus the state's grip tightened through the governor's office.

Some cases merit a closer investigation. On 21 January 1584, the Hattula and Lehijärvi District Court sessions dealt with a case of homicide for which a capital sentence was pronounced. The conflict that led to the killing had begun when the foot soldiers of the fortress quartered in the surrounding countryside set out to procure a sheep for their Christmas dinner from a farm, the denizens of which believed they had punctually paid all the tax that they owed. No requisition order had come for any extra sheep. A fight ensued and was settled, but then it broke out again and ended with the son of the peasant striking a soldier, who was attacking his father, with a piece of wood. The court considered that the boy had carried out the act intentionally, without duress, so the panel of judges was not able to spare his life, and "he had to suffer the punishment he deserved."[159] The Hauho District Court condemned three men from the village of Nurmoinen to death in 1594 because in a fight over the ownership of land they had killed a man from the village of Skinnarla on land belonging to Skinnarla. The deed was considered to be a breach of the King's Peace. The sentence was referred to Governor Fleming. The aggravating circumstance of breach of the King's Peace was also present in a Tuulos homicide case in 1595, which originated in a suspicion of theft. The suspect was whipped and beaten to death and his property was taken from his house, all without any legal sanction or any judgment being passed. The man who had apprehended and tortured the suspect and the bailiff's servant who had assisted him were sentenced to death according to Chapters 1 and 20 of the King's Peace Code (*Edsörebalken*). In 1596 in Asikkala, a man was condemned to death because he had avenged the killing of his son after the matter had been settled in court. The origin of the conflict had been an ownership dispute. In Sysmä in 1598, a fratricide was condemned to death, and in Masku in 1600, a man who had a previous conviction for homicide received a capital sentence. The relatives of the second victim demanded his death in the district court.[160] According to an old medieval principle of law, the relatives of the accused were only obliged to help a condemned killer in one case of homicide but not in further cases.[161]

Behind the severe penalties lay not only the tightening of official control but also a stricter legal code, as exemplified by Eric XIV's above-mentioned decree concerning grievous crimes. At the Kemiö District Court in 1572, a killing was described according to the decree as "a grievous crime" (*högmåla sach*), and the reprieve of the perpetrator with a fine was left to "the clement discretion of H.R.M." (*upå K.M gunstiigh behagh*).[162] Instead of the voice of the plaintiffs and the court public, the power of the panel of jurors to pass judgment was emphasized in the expression "and the twelve in the panel could not save his life, and he was sentenced to suffer the punishment he deserved."[163] Alongside the increasing severity of the sentences, the size of the royal share of the fine also began to rise. And more and more frequently the court's share began to be awarded to the judge or his deputy.[164] Both of these factors point to the tightening grip of authority looming behind the tougher sentences being passed.

In the late sixteenth century, judicial practice began to change fundamentally. At the winter sessions of the Kyrö District Court on 9–10 February 1582, Mikko Pentinpoika of Kauhajoki was fined forty marks for spreading an unfounded rumor because he had accused Pentti Heikinpoika of killing his wife. However, Pentti Heikinpoika took an oath of purgation together with eleven others who swore that he was telling the truth, and he was acquitted. According to the law, a person who spread a false rumor ought to have been charged with the crime of which he had accused the other party, as Mikko Pentinpoika indeed was, but since he could not afford to pay the fine, he was sentenced to pay four marks and "lose the skin off his back" through flogging (*men effter förenämnde Michill icke hade penningar att böthe med miste han rygghuden*).[165] There is no mention of the family. At the Parainen District Court in 1578, a man who had committed fornication with a woman who had been guilty of infanticide was made to pay a fine of twenty marks "as a warning to others" (*för androm till warnagel*), although he had had no part in the killing.[166]

The purpose of these sentences is definitely to punish, not to reach a settlement. In them the power of the family was broken. The authorities and the individual stood face to face. The point of view of the authorities rather than that of the kin is stressed in the use of punishment as a general warning to others. This view was to the individual's disadvantage, for if an admonitory example was needed, the individual could provide one. It was also the individual who was affected by corporal punishment, right up to its most extreme form in execution. The new attitude is also evident in the fact that the word *murder* is used to an increasing extent to describe a killing. According to the law, a murder was a homicide which the perpetrator attempted to conceal. The word was also used in the sixteenth century to refer to infanticide. The concept thus included the idea of premeditation. The punishment for murder was harsher than for homicide. The word *homicide* (*dråp*) began to be replaced by *murder* at the end of the 1580s.[167]

We can summarize judicial practice with regard to crimes of homicide during the late sixteenth century as follows: the amount of power is a constant. If it is increased in one place, it decreases elsewhere. The increase in the power of the central government and the state authorities was reflected in a crumbling of the power of the family among the peasants and other commons. In the research material, this is apparent not only in the increasing severity of the sentences but also in the growing number of references to the king and his regional functionaries, the bailiffs and governors. The growth in the power of the authorities also appears in another way. The relatives no longer necessarily came, or were not allowed to come, to the aid of a family member who had got himself into trouble. The weakening in the position of the family resulted from the increased power of the authorities, the impoverishment of the peasantry, or both.

Separate mention must be made of the fact that the situation in Finnish domestic politics, particularly in the 1590s, may have had the effect of making sentences harsher. The prolonged war being waged between Sweden and Russia (1570–99), the extremely high wages of the military, which they themselves levied directly from the peasants, and the gradually deepening dynastic conflict between the two branches of the Vasa family caused domestic tension and unrest, which in turn gave rise to harsh sanctions.[168] However, these contemporary political factors merely served to promote a development that was taking place anyway.

Despite the increased severity of punishments, it must be emphasized that fines and compensations remained the predominant means of atoning for crimes of homicide up until the 1620s. The above-mentioned domestic tension in the country and the nobility's growing aspirations for power caused the quality of the judicial sources for crime to decrease sharply around the turn of the sixteenth and seventeenth centuries. However, the few surviving fine rolls and judgment books of that time as well as some references in judgment books from later periods show that the old practice of fining continued. Thus, in Rymättylä in 1633, the relatives of a man convicted of homicide redeemed for the sum of forty marks an area of pasture that had been ceded to the victim's family as part of a settlement determined by a court in 1604.[169] In Halikko, Kerttu Paavontytär sued Mikko Tafwolla for the rest of the money he had been ordered to pay her in compensation for the death of her husband years earlier.[170]

The real change in judicial practice did not take place until the 1620s, when capital sentences began to be pronounced. This conclusion is strongly supported by data from the Homicide Collection.[171]

The Adoption of Harsh Punishments

The significance of the 1620s for changes in judicial practice becomes palpably evident in source material collected from the Masku judicial district in southwest Finland covering the years 1620–32 (the summer sessions for 1624 are missing). These sources provide information about fifteen trials for homicide and accidental manslaughter (see table 1.1).[172] The same sources also contain three cases of infanticide or concealing a fetus[173] and one case of suicide (Rymättylä 4 April 1628). Killings alleged to have been committed by sorcery (e.g., Rymättylä 24 February 1633, Mynämäki 30 June 1634) are not included, nor are cases of aggravated assault and battery, to which reference is made below in different contexts.

As control material for the analysis and interpretation of this data, sources for the district courts of Halikko and Piikkiö for the years 1623–26 have been used. They include references to twelve homicide cases.[174]

The results indicate that the level of homicidal crime continued to be high

Table 1.1. Crimes of Homicide in the Judgment Records of the Masku District Court, 1620–36

Year of Crime (trial)	*Place*	*Charge*	*Motive*	*Sex and Social Status of Accused*	*Sex and Social Status of Victim*	*Weapon*	*Sentence*
1618 (20)	Mynäm.	hom.	n.k.	m., f.s.	m., n.k.	knife	set.
1619 (31)	Mynäm.	hom.	slander	m., serv.	m., soldier	sword	death
1620 (21)	Lemu	hom.	s-d.	m., farmer	m., farmer	knife	set.
1620 (25)	Rymät.	a.m.	cattle	m., farmer	f., f.d.	ax	acq.
1621	Mynäm.	hom.	prop.	m., farmer	m., farmer	knife	death
1622 (25)	Rymät.	a.m.	prop.	m., farmer	m., f.s.	w.i.	oath
1623	Korp.	a.m.	n.k.	m., min.	m., n.k.	knife	acq.
1623 (24)	Mynäm.	hom.	cattle	m., farmer	m., farmer	ax	death
1625	Mynäm.	hom.	n.k.	m., n.k.	m., f.hand	ax	death
1628	Mynäm.	hom.	n.k.	m., n.k.	m., n.k.	n.k.	n.k.
1631	Maaria	a.m.	other	m., soldier	f., f.h.w.	n.k.	acq.
1631	Merim.	hom.	slander	m., n.k.	m., servant	knife	death
1631	Mynäm.	hom.	cattle	m., n.k.	m., servant	knife	death
1631 (32)	Maaria	hom.	slander	m., f.hand	m., f.h.s.	w.i.	death
1631 (32)	Maaria	hom.	slander	m., n.k.	m., soldier	ax	adj.

Note: Mynäm. = Mynämäki, Rymät. = Rymättylä, Korp. = Korppoo, Merim. = Merimasku, hom. = homicide, a.m. = accidental manslaughter, n.k. = not known, s-d. = self-defense, prop. = property, f.s. = farmer's son, f.d. = farmer's daughter, f.hand = farmhand, f.h.w. = farmhand's wife, min. = church minister, w.i. = wooden implement, set. = settlement, acq. = acquittal, adj. = adjournment.

or else that it had risen again: according to the Masku parish register there were 380 parishioners in 1634.[175] The total population can be estimated to be at least 10,000. This means an annual rate of 10 killings a year per 100,000 persons.

Table 1.1 raises some other questions. The first problems concern the sources. There are quite a lot of cases in the 1620s, but they end abruptly with homicides committed in 1631 and their trials the following year. Why are there no cases during the years 1633–36? Is it a mere coincidence, or is it perhaps because homicide cases that came before the lower courts were referred directly to the court of appeal, and since the archives of the Turku Court of Appeal were destroyed by fire in 1827, all records of the crimes have thus been lost?

There is solid evidence from the eastern parts of the Province of Nyland[176] of the practice of sending the revised records of the trial directly to the court of appeal without entering them into the judgment books of the lower court, and therefore the possibility that this was also the practice in Masku cannot be totally excluded. In the judgment books of the nearby judicial district of Piikkiö there are only very sketchy records of a number of homicide cases. The records of the Paimio District Court contain the following bare statement: "Matti Sipinpoika of Laitula versus Matti Ryttäri of Pöytyä for homicide."[177] Similar and even terser records were common in the Crown accounts and particularly in the fine rolls at the turn of the sixteenth and seventeenth centuries—the time when the control of the authorities in Finland was slackest and malfeasance among both the nobles and the Crown functionaries was most prevalent.[178] It was not until the court of appeal was established in 1623 that the situation began to change, because the court would no longer tolerate such sketchy records. It began to require more detailed information about the crimes and, for example, about the goods that the bailiffs and the sheriffs[179] had appropriated from the parents of a killer who had escaped.[180] Thus one can assume that after 1623 the recording of trials took place in greater detail and more strictly. In the case of Masku, it is hardly justified to assume that crimes of homicide went unrecorded in the revised records of the district courts, since the sources contain records of other cases which by law had to be submitted to the court of appeal after 1632 (the year when references to homicide cease). The sources contain three cases of infanticide or concealment of a fetus, two of them from the mid-1630s.[181] There are seven cases of adultery, the first from as late as 1634 (Pöytyä 27 February 1634), and the others from even later in the 1630s.[182] In these cases altogether twelve death sentences were passed, which means that they, too, were the kind of cases that had to be referred to the court of appeal for final ratification. Is it then to be concluded that the rate of homicidal crime began to decline in the area under investigation from the beginning of the 1630s? This is perfectly possible, although the validity of such a conclusion is weakened by the small population and the short period involved. However, there is evidence from the other Nordic countries to support it.[183] Samples from elsewhere in Finland point in the same direction. The judgment books of the judicial district of Ostrobothnia for the years 1683–85 contain only one real case of homicide and one case of accidental manslaughter, which ended in acquittal after an oath of purgation was sworn.[184] Since several cases of aggravated assault are to be found in the same source material, it cannot have been a question of cases submitted to the court of appeal being missing from the revised records of the lower court, at least not before this period.

The material raises another awkward question concerning the sources. They include cases of homicide that had taken place two, five, and even twelve years before the trial: a case of killing by sorcery was tried in Rymättylä on 24 February 1633, sixteen years after the victim died.[185] Thus crimes only came to trial after a considerable delay. Does this mean that a large number of cases may be missing from the source material? In other words, have some cases gone unprosecuted or otherwise escaped judicial control?

Apparently so, although the real number of crimes was probably not much different from that presented here. Furthermore, there was often a "natural" explanation for the omissions. The most important cause of the delay seems to have been the fact that the guilty party had fled. The authorities could not prosecute a case in the absence of the accused. After killing Klemetti Juhanpoika with a knife in 1618, Pekka Juhanpoika fled, and no one except his closest relatives knew of his whereabouts even in March 1620, when the matter finally came before the district court sessions at Mynämäki, where he was represented by his mother and his brother.[186] It was also at Mynämäki, in February 1631, that Herman Fleming's servant Sipi Jaakonpoika was sentenced to death for having killed a soldier with a sword while he was drunk twelve years previously. The victim, Matti Rokka, had knocked him off a bench on which he had been sleeping. After the killing, Sipi Jaakonpoika fled to Sweden, where he remained for eight years.[187] From the killer's point of view, flight was understandable. After all, his life was at stake. But for his family it was ruinous, especially in cases where the kin settled with the victim's relations. Various functionaries, from bailiffs and sheriffs to deputy district judges, then competed to remove property from the farmstead of the killer's father, or of the latter's close relatives, without informing them for what purpose the goods were being confiscated. Cattle, money, and chattels all went in this way.[188] The father was imprisoned in Turku Castle or put in stocks before the district court sessions, officially to make him divulge where his son was hiding. A truer reason may well have been to make him agree to pay large sums to the authorities.[189]

Another reason for the delays was mainly procedural. According to the law, homicide also included cases of manslaughter in which the connection between the assault and the cause of death was evident, at least in the opinion of the plaintiff, and where a period of no more than a year and a night had elapsed from the time of the assault. If the case was unclear, the court could order an oath of purgation (confirmed by the oaths of eleven compurgators), so it was in the interests of the authorities to let some time pass and raise the matter later, when it would be more likely to result in an order for an oath of purgation, which in turn would most easily lead to a conviction. The relatives and acquaintances of the accused were not always willing to support the accused with their own oaths (especially in cases of sorcery) if he or she had a bad reputation or was not liked.[190]

Moreover, the guilty parties themselves were wary of taking an oath of purgation. Hannu Stäckie, a farmer from Vuorenpää in Rymättylä, took advantage of this reluctance on two occasions. First, he brought an action to court in autumn 1624 against another farmer, Knuut Eskelinpoika Honka, whom he accused of striking his daughter, Malin Hannuntytär, on the shoulder with the back of an ax with the result that she died half a year later. The dispute had arisen because of some damage to crops caused by cattle. At the same sessions, Hannu Stäckie also accused Honka of a burglary, which the latter's farmhand had committed in his barn. That Stäckie's intention was either revenge or compensation is also apparent from the fact that he summoned a witness to see his dying daughter and tried to convince him that the girl's collarbone was loose and moving about under the skin in her neck. The witness, however, failed to see anything. The court acquitted the accused because immediately after the assault he had been fined twelve marks for it, and in the opinion of the panel of jurors it was not possible to sentence the same person twice for the same crime in the same parish.[191]

A couple of years later, on 30 September 1625, Hannu Stäckie took legal action again. This time he accused a farmer, Martti Olavinpoika of Alakylä, of assaulting his son Juha Hannunpoika in a field with the result that he died less than eight weeks later. The cause of the dispute had again been damage caused by cattle and ownership rights. Martti Olavinpoika had punched the boy twice and struck him twice with a sharp-edged stick. The court ordered the accused to take an oath of purgation together with eleven compurgators, judging that he himself would best know just how hard he had hit the boy. Three years later, on 27 October 1628, the brother of the dead boy demanded that the sentence be carried out; in other words, the oath had not yet been taken. The accused claimed that the deputy district judge, Gabriel Berendsson, had pronounced a wrong judgment out of anger and envy against him (the plaintiff had a recently acquired copy of the sentence with him). The court adjourned the case until the deputy district judge could be heard. At least by 13 March 1629, this had not happened, because the court of appeal issued a reminder about the matter. The final outcome of the case is not known.[192]

Apparently it also sometimes happened that the plaintiff or the authorities simply did not know whom to accuse of the crime, and thus the judicial handling of the affair was postponed. A reminder issued by the court of appeal on 13 March 1629 refers to the killing of one Simo Matinpoika of Mynämäki on a public thoroughfare in 1628. The court ordered the bailiff to arrest the killer, Matti Mikonpoika, bring him to trial, and sentence him to confinement in Turku Castle.[193] It is obvious that no charge had been made before this because the authorities had not known whom to accuse.

The ease with which a charge of homicide could be brought in cases of manslaughter had the effect of increasing the number of cases, while the flight of those who carried out the killings (which was connected to the increased severity of punishments) tended to decrease the number of actual trials. However, since in cases of unsolved homicide a fine was ultimately imposed on the parish, one can assume that most crimes of homicide came before the court in one way or another.

The judicial consequences. It is quite obvious that by the 1620s punishments were becoming harsher. In table 1.1, one can see that the normal punishment for homicide was death. Of the eleven cases that come under the heading of homicide, seven resulted in a capital sentence. Of the four remaining cases, two ended in settlements, one was adjourned in order to clarify a statement made by the victim on his deathbed, and the outcome of one is not known because the trial had not yet been held.

Since severity seemed to be the rule, from which there were hardly any exceptions, one must ask how it is possible that among the cases of homicide there are nevertheless two that ended in settlements. First, it should be noted that both are from the beginning of the period being studied, 1620 and 1621. Clearly, the process of making punishments more severe was not yet fully operative, and both cases still display strong characteristics of the practice of the sixteenth century. In the earlier case (Mynämäki, 13 March 1620), the guilty party, Pekka Hannunpoika, was caught in the act but he escaped and disappeared for a couple of years, and the settlement was made between the victim's wife and brother on behalf of his other relations, while the perpetrator was represented by his mother and brother. The value of the settlement was fifty marks, and it was taken from Pekka Hannunpoika's inheritance. The sum was called according to the earlier tradition a "Christian wergild" (*en christelig mansbot*), and the killer was released from any further charge or responsibility in the matter.[194]

The outcome of the second case bears even more the hallmarks of a settlement made between families. On 5 November 1621, Maisa Hannuntytär of Hunnikkala appeared in the Lemu and Masku District Court with her mother, Maisa, and her brother, Antti Hannunpoika, and accused Matti Ollinpoika of Hunnikkala of killing her husband, Simo Hannunpoika. One Matti Jaakonpoika from the parish of Raisio happened to be staying in Hunnikkala, and one evening in the parlor of a farmstead he got into an argument, which was possibly induced by drink, with Matti Ollinpoika. After saying his piece, he grabbed an ax and in the dimly lit room he struck Matti Ollinpoika three times with the back of it. Just as he was about to strike a fourth time, this time with the cutting edge, Matti Ollinpoika snatched his knife and wounded his assailant in the chest with it, or so he assumed in the dark. Incredible as it sounds in this account, the blow actually caught Simo Hannunpoika, who died three days later.[195] Matti Ollinpoika fled. Taking Holy Communion on his deathbed, Simo Hannunpoika told Pastor Josephus that he forgave his killer. There were several other persons present who testified to the events a year and a half later. The family of the deceased decided—with the court's approval—that the killer should depart and remain absent until such time as he was summoned to settle with the relatives of the victim. Matti Ollinpoika surrendered his real estate to the victim's son, who was still a minor, but he was allowed to keep his chattels, which he had acquired himself and not inherited. He also had to pay fines to the king and to the court (thirteen marks eight örtugar to each).[196]

The case displays a number of factors that go back to the clan-dominated society of the sixteenth century. One is the compensation of the dependents of the deceased with material goods. It is revealing that the family (i.e., inherited) land of the killer was used for this, not his acquired chattels, over which the individual traditionally enjoyed freedom of disposition. Thus the kin as a collective unit compensated for the death of the victim to his family, while the perpetrator as an individual paid the fines with his own assets. The record itself refers to the decisions of "the kin" (*släkten*).

Both cases happened before the establishment of the Turku Court of Appeal (1623). It is evident that the court looked askance at settlements from the very beginning. In October 1623, Heikki Knuutinpoika from the village of Torsböle in Kemiö killed Heikki Yrjönpoika with an ax in a fight that began over the ownership of a quarter-barrel of seal blubber. The deeper cause of the conflict is not known. The accused was sentenced to death on his own confession and the testimonies of two witnesses in accordance with Chapter 2 of the Intentional Homicide Code. After the sentence was passed, the wife of the victim was asked "if she would have been willing to agree to some settlement with the killer or with his family, or if she had previously taken any blood money."[197] The wife strongly denied that she had done anything of the sort and declared that from the very beginning she had wished to leave the matter "to the high authority" (*till höge öffuerheten*), meaning the court of appeal.

There were still some attempts to apply the practice of settlement. On the evening of Whit Sunday 1631, Klemetti Franssinpoika from Merimasku, after drunkenly ranting and threatening people, stabbed Tuomas Tuomaanpoika, a servant of the sheriff of Merimasku, who had asked the rioting Klemetti to show his travel pass. The stabbed man died four weeks later in Turku in the arms of a barber. Before he died, he told the local minister that he had been reconciled with Klemetti Franssinpoika. The minister, Clementis Koralis, informed the court of this by letter. The victim's wife also announced that she agreed to a settlement and renounced any claims that the killer be punished. Even so, the district court sentenced the accused to death, but decided with regard to the offered settlement "to submit it to the merciful judgment of the High Authority to decide to what extent it could be considered valid [*dett heemstelles till Högha Öfverhetens Nådiga betenckiande och om dett för giltt hållas skall*]."[198]

From elsewhere in the kingdom of Sweden we know that, despite the increasing opposition to settlements, they were nevertheless made and legally ratified at least in the early seventeenth century. According to Gösta Hasselberg, there still prevailed a custom even at that time of "family fines" (*ätteböter*), which were divided among the members of the accused's kin at special "fine meetings" (*bötestämmor*).[199] As far as Finland is concerned, it seems that fines and settlements were applied at least in cases where the guilty party had fled and only returned after a number of years. He was naturally hunted as a wanted criminal throughout the kingdom, but under the conditions that then prevailed, a runaway was difficult to catch. In his absence, the families of the parties concerned might come to a settlement. Another ground for settlements was a strong element of accidental manslaughter or self-defense.[200]

Naturally, the courts did not ratify all the attempts to reach a settlement, and these attempts decreased over the years, but there is still evidence of such attempts right into the beginning of the nineteenth century. By that time, however, they were secret in nature and involved bribery of the authorities.[201]

The judicial process. Let us return to the question of the revolution in the system of justice at the beginning of the seventeenth century. What changed, and what did not change?

The fact that the courts would now accept settlements only in exceptional cases and that they sought out the guilty party and imposed the punishment prescribed by law was a new feature. The process thus became oriented toward the courts and was inquisitorial, emphasizing the punitive power of the authorities. All of this points to change. On the other hand, there are no indisputable grounds for supposing that the courts followed the law of evidence, which had appeared in written instructions for judges for the first time in 1616, but which had been drawn up by Olavus Petri as early as the end of the 1530s.[202] It stipulated that a confession by the accused or the testimonies of two competent eyewitnesses were sufficient for a full proof. Nowhere, however, is any special mention made of this principle, nor is any reference made to matters of disqualification, which were central features of the theory. Even so, it is evident that the instructions for judges were known. One judgment mentions a principle according to which, if the case is unclear, it is better to acquit a guilty person than to punish an innocent one,[203] corresponding with Paragraph 40 of the instructions for judges. Again, the significance given to testimonies by the instructions would seem to be reflected in the fact that a statement made by the victim on his deathbed and conveyed to the court by a church minister did not necessarily have an effect on the trial's outcome because, naturally, the victim himself was not present in court to testify.[204] The reason for ignoring the victim's own statement was most probably because it was presumed to indicate that a settlement had been reached between the parties involved.

How, then, was guilt established? In the end, it was done above all through an inquiry by the panel of jurors. The question of the accused's guilt ultimately depended on how convinced the jurors were of it. In this sense, the process was a discretionary one that permitted a conviction to be made purely on the basis of circumstantial evidence. No confession on the part of the accused was required, let alone the evidence of eyewitnesses. Originally, the panel had been a body whose job was to further a settlement, and the interested parties had the right to choose the members (half were chosen by the plaintiff and half by the accused). From the mid-sixteenth century on, the same jurors served through the full sessions, often indeed through several, and the position of juror became permanent. Although sentences had previously been passed in the name of the panel, it was not until the end of the sixteenth century that a formulaic phrase came into use, which then became common in the seventeenth century: "The panel could not spare his [the accused's] life." Thus the panel changed from an institution whose purpose was to enable a settlement to be reached into an organ that exerted real judicial power.

Compurgation, which continued to be used in various cases, was likewise a remnant of older times. In crimes of homicide appearing in the sources from southwest Finland used in this study, it was only used once, but in cases of sorcery it was quite common and was apparently being used to an increasing extent; after all, it was not generally possible to obtain testimonies in such cases. For instance, in 1630 when a number of relatives of Lauri Pentinpoika presented to the court a written statement dated 1617, which claimed that Dirrik Hannunpoika and his wife had slain (*förgiort*) Lauri Pentinpoika, the accused was sentenced to take an oath of purgation. According to the statement, Lauri Pentinpoika had made this claim on his deathbed. Dirrik Hannunpoika offered to swear an oath to his innocence, and the court agreed to this, ordering the oath to be presented at the following sessions.[205] The widespread significance of the oath is shown by the fact that by no means all those who were accused of homicide by sorcery agreed to take an oath of purgation or at least could not find a sufficient number of compurgators to swear to their innocence. Evidently they were guilty of casting the alleged curse on their victims, and being superstitious themselves, they did not dare to take the oath. If they were guilty, they stood even less chance of finding compurgators to swear for them.[206] This created a procedural impasse. In Haanperä in Mynämäki, the widow and son of Simo Martinpoika year after year right up to 1634 vehemently accused their neighbor, Tuomas Eerikinpoika, of causing Simo's death in 1622. In their opinion, he had died as a result of curses Tuomas Eerikinpoika had cast on him when they had fallen into a dispute over a piece of grazing land in 1620. In court, Tuomas Eerikinpoika undertook at times to swear an oath of purgation and at others to make a settlement with the opposite party, but he never fulfilled either of his promises. In 1634, he was finally sentenced to death in accordance with Chapter 9 of the Judicial Code, and the sentence was referred to the court of appeal.[207]

There are other similar cases,[208] but in this connection it is sufficient to note that purgation by oath never became a very common procedure, because the suspects generally confessed to their crimes. The confession was backed up by evidence given by witnesses when it was available—and it generally was, which was why the accused confessed in the first place. On 10 May 1621, the Mynämäki District Court dealt with a case of stabbing caused by a dispute over a boundary mark. The plaintiff was the victim's widow, and she accused Lasse Torkkelinpoika of "full homicide" after the fashion of the sixteenth century. Lasse Torkkelinpoika confessed to the deed, but this was not considered sufficient proof, and the court justified its sentence by appealing to the testimonies of three eyewitnesses. The guilty party was sentenced to death according to Chapter 30 of the Intentional Homicide Code. The sentence was also pronounced with the formulaic expression "the panel could not save his life [*kunde*

Nemnpden icke wäria hans lijff."[209] After hearing the confession and the eyewitnesses' testimonies, the decision was at least formally left in the hands of the panel of jurors. In actual fact, it is obvious that the deputy district judge had a strong, indeed crucial, influence on the decision, but he considered it more expedient to allow the sentence to be pronounced by the panel, which represented the view that the source of justice lay with the people and not with the authorities.

Rarely—and in homicide cases never—was the opinion of the parties involved or the public attending the sessions sought. One exception is a judgment given in Nousiainen on 8 November 1620. Sipi Pentinpoika had slandered another as a murderer but had been unable to substantiate his accusations, for which he was sentenced to "forfeit his honor," meaning he was declared infamous. In reply to the earnest pleas and prayers of the jurors, the men of the village, and the accused himself, he was allowed to redeem his honor for the sum of forty marks.[210]

The tightening grip of the authorities over the courts is shown by the fact that the position of the panel of jurors was emphasized at the expense of the public attending the sessions and by the partial shift from a procedure in which the plaintiff played the major role to an accusatorial process, in which the authorities appointed a prosecutor to handle the case. On 15 November 1624 in Mynämäki, the trial of a case of patricide began with the presentation to the court of a letter of attorney in which Nils Bielke, governor of Finland and president of the Turku Court of Appeal, authorized the bailiff of the judicial district of Masku, Dijrick Hannunpoika, to act as prosecutor. The accused was one Yrjö Pertunpoika, who had got into an impassioned argument with his father, Perttu Jönsinpoika, because his pig had broken loose and begun eating the rye from the father's grain bin. The argument had ended in a fight in which the son had killed his own father with an ax. The boy fled to the vicarage of Pälkäne, where he was arrested many months later. Yrjö Pertunpoika was sentenced to the wheel and to death in accordance not only with the relevant sections of the law but also according to the Mosaic law, for he had raised his hand against his own father and thus broken the fourth and fifth commandments. The chattels of the condemned man were divided among the plaintiffs, the king, and the court.[211]

The reason the Crown bailiff appeared in this case as prosecutor was not just because the case was between members of the same family. In unclear homicide cases, the plaintiffs seem to have tried to strengthen their case by first contacting the authorities. On 4 April 1625, the Mynämäki District Court investigated the killing of a farmhand, Markus Laurinpoika, at a Candlemas market outside Mynämäki Church. The Crown bailiff thus acted as prosecutor, but the plaintiffs were also present in the persons of the victim's mother, uncle, aunt, and widow, "who are all relatives of the deceased." The deed had taken place on a dark road, and there were no witnesses. The accused, Paavo Pekanpoika, stated that the dead man had approached him on horseback and had asked him to exchange horses with him. Paavo had refused, saying: "Let the Devil change horses with you!" Then Markus had struck Paavo on the forehead with the back of an ax. Paavo claimed that there were others present who belonged to the same gang as Markus, but he was unable to substantiate his claim or to show any injuries on his person. According to his own story, he then wrenched the ax from Markus and struck him with it twice, first on the fingers and then in the side so that his innards were laid bare. The victim lived until the following morning. The panel of jurors considered that Paavo's wound "did not satisfy the law" (*är ogillat*), but that the killing did (*gilt*). Thus Paavo, without danger to himself or in self-defense, had "quenched the light that the Lord God has lit" (*wtsläckat det liuss som Herren Gudh optänt haffuer*). Since Paavo had been arrested within twenty-four hours of the crime, the panel was unable to save his life, and on this circumstantial evidence he was sentenced to death "unless he should enjoy the clemency of the High Authority" (*med mindre han särdeles niuter höghe öfferheetennes Nådher*). The case was thus left to the court of appeal to decide, and the relatives had no say in the matter.[212] Thus the source of justice was considered to be not only the people and the panel of jurors that represented it but also the "High Authority," which could alter the sentence.

A prosecutor was also appointed when crimes were tried that were in one way or another directed against the authorities. At the Nousiainen District Court sessions in October 1625, the bailiff, Dirich Hannunpoika, accused Simo Hannunpoika of stabbing Frans Sipinpoika in the hallway of the courthouse. The wounds were not serious, because both parties were immediately brought before the court. The court found that Simo had broken the peace that was strictly enjoined by the law for the period of the judicial sessions, and because he had been apprehended immediately after the deed, in accordance with Chapters 13 and 35 of the King's Peace Code, it sentenced him to the loss of his right hand and ordered that all his chattels be divided in three parts between the king, the relative, and the court.[213]

On the one hand, there was the jury process, in which the people were held to be the highest source of justice. On the other hand, there was the modern inquisitorial and accusatorial process in which justice emanated from the authorities, ultimately the king. However, there was no disruptive conflict between these two views of justice, because to an ever-increasing extent the scales were tipped in favor of the latter through the influence exerted by the courts of higher instance. Moreover, the panel of jurors of the seventeenth century was, strictly speaking, different from its sixteenth-century namesake. In the seventeenth century, the authorities began to accord the panel judicial power because it was becoming a more and more integral part of the official machinery. The jurors became involved in this role particularly through the function they exercised in collecting various overdue taxes. In September 1625, one Erkki Pertunpoika of Nousiainen attacked the bailiff and three jurors with a log when they came to collect overdue Crown taxes from him. Finally, he pulled out a knife and would have stabbed one of the jurors with it, had not a chaplain who happened to be present come between them. The bailiff tried to calm the man "with good words, the best he had learned," but in vain. The example of Erkki Pertunpoika inspired others to similar acts of recalcitrance. The situation became so serious that it was deemed necessary to read to the jurors the Manorial Law of King Gustavus I Vasa and on the basis of it to condemn Erkki Pertunpoika to death. The final decision naturally was left to the court of appeal.[214] In addition to collecting taxes, jurors were also present at occasions connected with debt collections and recovery, the conscription of men for military service, auctions, and the like. Resisting a juror in the performance of such duties was considered equal to resisting a public servant, and an augmented punishment was prescribed for any wounds or injuries a juror received in such circumstances.[215] All in all, the position of the jurors was totally different from what it had been in the sixteenth century.

The basis of the judgments. What was new compared with the sixteenth century was that grounds referring to the appropriate points of law were always cited for the judgments except in cases where a settlement was reached. This in itself indicates that the law was adhered to in a way that it had not been earlier. The most common source of law was King Christopher's Law of the Land of 1442. It was published in 1608 with a supplement that contained the main points of the Mosaic law. In addition to the Law of the Land, there were vague references to decrees, manorial laws, and the Bible. In any case, the laws which in the sixteenth century had been considered distant royal directives with at best a merely exhortatory force had now become the basis and guiding principle of judicial practice.

This stricter judicial practice was, however, not the result so much of any increase in the severity of the law itself but of a general adherence to it. The old Law of the Land contained sanctions for crimes of homicide, which, when they were administered, represented a harsh penal system. It was just that previously the law had not been applied, and now it was. Surprisingly enough, it was not only the authorities that were demanding "enforcement of the law"; the victims and their relatives also began to require it. The increase in severity would thus appear to have gone hand in hand with a change of outlook; more and more, people began to feel that settlement was too mild a form of punishment. This increase in severity, if that was what it was, can most easily be seen in cases of adultery, in which the aggrieved husband would ask in court for the parties to be treated according to the letter of the law.[216] The same procedure began to be applied in homicide cases as well. On the evening of Michaelmas Day 1631, Martti Tuomaanpoika of Mynämäki murdered his neighbor's son, Eskil Tuomaanpoika, who was at the time a foot soldier in the service of the sheriff. The victim's parents appeared in court and "stood on their rights, demanding that the matter should be dealt with according to their rights and the law of Sweden" (*stå på sin rätt, begärandes denn rätt effter Sveriges Lagh, wederfahres måtte*). Martti Tuomaanpoika had accused Eskil Tuomaanpoika of allowing his horses to graze on a clearing sown with rye. Eskil Tuomaanpoika interpreted this as an accusation of theft directed against his master and attacked Martti Tuomaanpoika, wrenching an ax out of his hands and poking him with it, at which point the two men fell apart. Then Martti Tuomaanpoika grabbed his knife, and Eskil Tuomaanpoika fled. Martti Tuomaanpoika gave chase and, catching up with him on the sheriff's land, stabbed him to death. The court held that if Martti Tuomaanpoika had used his knife when Eskil Tuomaanpoika was poking him with the ax, it would have been self-defense, but since he pursued his fleeing adversary, this circumstance was no longer valid. Moreover, Martti Tuomaanpoika ought to have put the matter in the hands of the law if he considered that Eskil Tuomaanpoika was acting against him in an illegal manner and not tried to exact revenge himself. As a result, he was condemned to death.[217]

What is crucial in the attitude of the panel of jurors is the question of legality and not a desire "for blood." When we speak of a change in outlook, this does not primarily imply a thirst for blood or a desire for revenge. The main incentive was the matter of legality, the requirement that the rule of law be observed. In less serious cases of violence, too, the importance of proceeding according to the law was emphasized. At the Korppoo District Court sessions, a man who had hit his neighbor's wife defended his action by saying that "if she hadn't ranted at him, he wouldn't have hit her" (*hadhe hon icke brukat mun på hånom, hadhe han icke slagit hänne*). The court considered the argument between the parties to be without significance, and emphasized that this did not give him the right to hit her, "for a blow is not [sanctioned by] the law." The man was fined.[218]

Thus the aim was that crimes should be punished by the law through the justice system and not by people taking the law into their own hands. The pressure to suppress and eradicate various kinds of self-help increased. One consequence of this was that the culprits began to feel such a burden of guilt over their deeds that they finally wanted to atone for them before the law. A young farmhand from Pöytyä, Simo Tuomaanpoika, had committed adultery with a soldier's wife, who had given birth to his child. Either she had murdered the child or it was stillborn, and she had hidden the body in a heap of manure. After this she had fled. The matter had come before the court a couple of times, but Simo Tuomaanpoika "had never been willing to make amends, nor was he now [25 October 1634], but had asked Mikko Sangar to answer for him; he recognized his guilt and surrendered to the law." He was sentenced to death.[219] A married woman, Margareta Matintytär of the village of Ristalho in Pöytyä, erred into a relationship with a widower and had the eighth of her eleven children by him. After a few years (during which she had three children), she was afflicted with a grave torment, "a dry pain" (*tårr Wärck*). In her distress, Margareta asked a wandering beggarwoman to help her, as beggars usually earned their bread by performing small services like weaving magic spells, offering quack remedies, helping unwed girls to hide a stillborn baby, and so on. The old woman said that the distress was a consequence of her adultery and that it would not get better before the matter had been brought into the open. Margareta confessed the deed to her husband, who took the matter to court in 1643, sternly demanding that both the guilty parties be given the death sentence—as indeed they were.[220]

This material allows us to answer the question of what actually changed in judicial practice in the 1620s. The procedure was changing, but the change had not yet been completed. The control of the authorities over the justice system tightened and led them to appoint a prosecutor in cases that they considered to be grave or where the injured party so desired. The main aim of the judicial inquiry became to establish the guilt of the accused. This was a crucial change. The truth was ascertained mainly through a confession by the accused and/or the testimonies of witnesses. If there were no witnesses and the accused denied his guilt, circumstantial evidence could be used. The presence of witnesses was crucial only in cases of infanticide. This was the salvation of many a woman, for if she claimed that the baby was born dead and there were no witnesses to the birth, she could not be convicted, and the case was referred to the court of appeal.[221] The opinion of the public attending the court was now sought only in rare cases and never in cases of homicide. More often the case was placed before the jurors. In sentences, it became common to state that no member of the panel wanted "to spare their lives," that is, to impose a more lenient sentence than the death penalty.[222] The importance of the panel of jurors explains why the law of evidence was not always followed: it was sufficient that the jurors were convinced of the guilt of the accused. The increased importance given to the panel is probably connected with the growing extent to which the jurors became identified with the local authorities. In such circumstances there was little danger that the panel would take a more lenient line than the authorities or the court of appeal. Alongside the panel of jurors, the role of the deputy district judge was also asserted. The emphasis in the judicial process thus shifted away from a lay forum to an institutional court and through this to the central government (the Crown).

Although the panel of jurors represented a doctrine according to which justice emanated from the people, the Crown began to be regarded as the supreme judicial authority. Capital sentences submitted to the court of appeal included such expressions as "if the High Authority wishes to pardon him." Back in the sixteenth century, it was different: judicial power lay with the people. That is why a locally constituted court of the estates was appointed in political trials, because the different estates were represented in it, and thus it could be considered as a way of channeling the judicial power of the people so as to influence the trial process.

Settlements between families of the parties concerned were no longer tolerated by a jurisprudence that kept to the letter of the law and was directed by the central authorities. Settlements represented a form of jurisprudence in which justice lay with the people. They were still accepted up to a few years before the establishment of the Turku Court of Appeal, but not after this event, apart from a few exceptional cases in which for one reason or another a long period had elapsed between the deed and the judicial inquiry.

The special position of the gentry. An important new factor had entered the judicial system: social position. A criminal could benefit from a high social position. The law was strict, but it was not necessarily the same for all. One could still not speak of a state in which the rule of law prevailed in all circumstances.

At the Korppoo District Court sessions in August 1623, Valpuri Heikintytär accused the preacher of Nauvo of killing her husband, Hampus. The court held that the preacher had acted in self-defense in order to ward off Hampus's attack. However, the preacher, who was said to have quarreled with the victim's son-in-law, slashed him many times in the face with his knife, and then, although Hampus had only dragged him to the floor by his hair and apparently punched him, when they got up from the floor, he retaliated by stabbing his unarmed assailant twice. The preacher's life had not been in any danger. It was claimed (by the preacher) that the deceased had expressed remorse for what he had done and had sought reconciliation with him. He had made no accusation against the preacher on his deathbed. Thus the preacher, who was of a higher social class, was acquitted of homicide, albeit with considerable misgivings on the part of the jurors. He received only a fine of twelve marks for wounding his assailant. The records indicate that the proceedings were conducted throughout in a way that was to the preacher's advantage.[223]

The special position of people of a higher social status became obvious in other types of crime, particularly sexual crimes, as Seppo Aalto has shown for the Province of Porvoo.[224] The same feature is revealed in the source material for the present study from Masku. Hannu Hannunpoika of Storgård Manor, an unmarried nobleman, took Agneta Matintytär, the wife of one of his tenant farmers, to live with him and fathered a child on her. On the initiative of the local minister, he was brought to justice. He immediately admitted his guilt. The district court decided to submit the case to the court of appeal, because the privileges of noble birth required that no nobleman could be compelled to appear in court to answer capital charges "before lesser men than his peers" (*för mindre män än deras wederlijkar*). Hannu Hannunpoika had other married women living with him, among them one Brita Matintytär, who had also borne him a child.[225] At the district court winter sessions in Nousiainen in 1636, Brita Matintytär was brought before the court and sentenced to death (as doubtless was Agneta Matintytär also) in accordance with Chapter 5 of the High Crimes Code (*Högmåla–balk*).[226] There is no information about what sentence Hannu Hannunpoika received. According to the minister he "had carried on numerous adulterous affairs"—which indicated not only a criminal way of life but also an extremely reckless one.[227]

The sheriffs, who in principle were responsible for law and order, were almost powerless in the face of the unruly and violent behavior of the truculent nobles. This was particularly true as long as the sheriffs came from peasant origins and could not read or write—at any rate in Swedish. The position of the sheriffs vis-à-vis the nobility improved only in the latter half of the seventeenth century, when most of them began to be recruited from the ranks of the gentry.[228] At the same time, the position of sheriffs of peasant stock grew worse, the rarer the appointment of peasants to the post became. In Rymättylä, the servants of the bailiff, Gabriel Berendsson, thrashed the sheriff on their master's orders because he had presumed to permit the use of a fishing seine in winter in front of the bailiff's Mäenpää Manor. The court's judgment on the matter was adjourned in order to see whether the sheriff would live. The final outcome of the case is not known.[229]

It is self-evident that the strong position of the gentry was sufficient to provide a cushion against the law for even the lowest of their underlings as well. If necessary, strict points of law were dug out from the nooks and crannies of history to endorse the judicial support of the upper classes. In Masku in 1627, when a couple of peasants drove two tenant farmers of the noblemen, Herman Fleming and Lars Carpelan, from a pasture, and even went as far as breaking their scythes and inflicting a few bruises on them, the court sentenced them to fines of forty marks, which it justified by reference to a decree of King Gustavus I Vasa on vandalism. The sum was the equivalent of a wergild fine for homicide. The disputed field had been taken under official consideration, but the question of ownership had not been decided.[230]

A position of authority could also protect the perpetrator of violence. In 1631, the Maaria District Court acquitted a noncommissioned officer who, together with seven other soldiers, had tried to arrest a farmhand whom he suspected of having some knowledge about an army deserter. The soldiers manhandled the farmhand so roughly that his wife had to intervene, as a result of which she gave birth to a stillborn baby and died herself a week and a half later. On her deathbed, she blamed the soldiers for her fate. The pastor conveyed the information to the authorities. However, because she had been unable to name her assailants, because the plaintiff in the case was only her sister and not her husband, and because, strange to say, there were no witnesses to the event, the soldiers were acquitted.[231] Apparently, the farmhand did not dare to take the matter to court himself out of fear of reprisals from the soldiers.

This hierarchical attitude based on social position and its influence on the system of justice were also apparent at the lower social levels, even among the servants of the manors. A servant working on the estate of the bailiff at Perno Manor asked another servant, Yrjö Martinpoika, to carry a pile of hides to the place where they were to be treated. The latter palmed off the job onto the son of one Klemetti Jaakonpoika, who was also in the employ of the manor. Klemetti Jaakonpoika took exception to this and struck Yrjö Martinpoika with the end of an ax. Yrjö Martinpoika retaliated by grabbing a wooden club and hitting Klemetti Jaakonpoika on the temple with it, killing him instantly. The widow of the victim "would not relent" and strictly held to her rights in demanding that the law be enforced and a penalty of death imposed. This the court did without taking into consideration the circumstance of self-defense involved.[232]

However, one should beware of exaggerating the inequality of people before the law. Compared, for example, with the last years of the sixteenth century, when Finnish society lapsed to a large extent into a state of lawlessness in which the strong exercised naked power over the weak and which ultimately led to civil war,[233] the justice system in the seventeenth century was stable, and it approached the condition of equality before the law at least to some degree, despite the privileges enjoyed by the upper social classes. The lower courts certainly sentenced numerous soldiers, servants of the nobility, and even public officials to pay the heavy fines prescribed by the law for breach of the peace or to lose their right hands and in extreme cases even their lives.[234] Although the system of justice was harsh and to some extent oppressive, it was indisputably more equitable than it had been at the end of the sixteenth century and the beginning of the seventeenth.

The advent of the power state. It has often been emphasized that the premodern state imposed a thoroughgoing discipline on society. This discipline included harsh new rules of criminal justice, a decrease in the autonomy of local government, and a corresponding increase in the powers of the state's local authorities, military conscription, and repressive sexual mores.[235] It is true that all of these had a disciplinary effect, especially military conscription, which particularly affected men whose behavior the community considered to be antisocial. Conscripts were permitted to pay another man to take their place in the army, and the *rote* (a unit comprising several farms that were obliged to provide and equip a soldier for the army) could come to the aid of a man whose turn had come. Alternatively, if the rote wanted to get rid of him, it could refuse him its help.[236]

A case that was recorded at the Nousiainen District Court sessions on 7 April 1625 is extremely illuminating in this respect: "Perttu Tuomaanpoika of Kaitarainen prosecuted his *rote* for being unwilling to come to his aid by paying for a soldier in his place in order that the holding on which he lived should be preserved and that the Crown should obtain its tax. Since he tills his holding alone and has just recently paid for a soldier, as the panel witnessed, the panel obliged the whole *rote* in its totality to pay for the soldier. In this way the king shall have both a soldier and his taxes. But if Perttu is conscripted into the ranks, his holding will be deserted, and the king will lose his tax."[237]

Perttu Tuomaanpoika would, therefore, have needed to be on good terms with his *rote* if he had wanted to keep his holding. Conscription and the desertion that it spawned were also the reason why a pass for internal travel was required and why those who employed persons who were not registered in the poll tax rolls received severe punishments. On the other hand, conscription also caused a chronic shortage of labor in rural areas. For example, it forced the farmers of Finland Proper to bring young children from the nearby town of Turku and elsewhere and take them into their employ.[238]

Increased sexual repression undoubtedly also had the effect of limiting people's behavioral freedom and tightening the grip of the authorities. One Pastor Johan appeared before the Raisio and Maaria District Court sessions on 4 December 1634 and reported that he knew of numerous cases of fornication that had gone unpunished. They included unmarried couples who had lived together for a long time. Nor were the gentry exempted from the zeal of the pastor. Everyone he named was prosecuted.[239] The disciplinary significance of trials for sexual crimes became palpably clear in cases where the aggrieved spouse interceded for the life of the guilty party. This happened at the Rymättylä District Court sessions on 3 March 1635, in a case concerning an adulterous relationship between a servant of the bailiff, Simo Matinpoika, and Filippa Heikintytär, both of whom were married. A child had been born of their liaison, and they confessed to their crime. At this point, Margareta, the wife of Simo Matinpoika, interceded for the life of her husband. The court considered the matter and came to the following conclusion: "Since this deed is in itself clear, and the said Simo Matinpoika, who has heinously broken the law of God and secular law, has stepped outside his marriage bed and yielded to relations with this Filippa Heikintytär, who herself has a husband, as Simo well knew, and in this way abused his wife, and injured her and their marriage, no one of the panel has therefore been able to spare his life. He is thus sentenced to death in accordance with Chapter 5 of the High Crimes Code [*högmålabalken*]."[240]

The increase in the severity of judicial practice was not primarily a result of new legislation, as has often been assumed. It was above all a consequence of the fact that the law—the old medieval Law of the Land—began to be enforced in a literal way—and not only in cases of criminal violence. It was also applied to property crimes, such as robbery.[241] The same observation holds true for all the Nordic countries.[242] Breaches of the King's Peace, particularly of the peace decreed for district court sessions and the public highway, were punished with particular severity.[243] Such breaches incurred the death penalty or at least the loss of one's right hand. The strict obedience to the law also explains why, unlike in the sixteenth century, it was no longer possible to fall back on the intercessions of relatives or fellow parishioners in order to obtain more lenient sentences. There was no point in intercession when the sentences were not mitigated anyway, and the law was strictly applied. In the sixteenth century, such intercessions had been recorded for the express purpose of obtaining grounds for deviating from the letter of the law. In this light, it was not so much the statutory law that became harsher in the seventeenth century but the practice of passing sentence. And what made this harsher was adherence to the law.

Why then did the courts begin to adhere strictly to the law? In the first place, we should note that it did not happen spontaneously, gradually from the bottom up. It was planned from above. The era is sometimes described, with good reason, as "the Age of Discipline." It meant increased control of sexual crimes through the branches of the church, and it meant strict surveillance particularly of people who were traveling, including the introduction of domestic travel passes. Gabriel Berendsson, a trusted bailiff, appeared at the Korppoo District Court in 1627 and announced that there were people who had defied the interdiction of the Crown by taking vagrants who had no travel passes into their service as farmhands at an unlawful time. This could not be tolerated. The situation had become quite apparent in the last tax assessment. There were seven such farmers who had received warnings from the district court and elsewhere against breaking this law, but they had simply ignored them. The guilty farmers were fined forty marks.

The governor had threatened to execute anyone who sheltered unknown persons or deserters from the army. The jurors and the sheriffs were urged to reveal names. One Tuomas Heikinpoika of the village of Sihvola was summoned to identify a farmhand whom he had employed. Tuomas Heikinpoika knew nothing of the man's background, but he pleaded that he was obliged to employ him at an unlawful time. The farmhand was called and asked where he had come from without a travel pass and certificate and why. He said that he had come to earn some money, and he claimed that he had not been conscripted for the army. Tuomas Heikinpoika was fined forty marks, and if it transpired that the farmhand was a deserter, he would lose his life under a recently published royal decree.[244]

Therefore, it seems quite clear that behind the increase in the severity of judicial practice lay the same factor that lay behind the increased harshness of the law: the state. The power state had come into being, and it imposed a strict order, the ultimate goal of which was to create a subject population ruled by the central administration. Local autonomy and the practice of justice by settlement conflicted with this aim, and thus they had to go. The law became the instrument by which the state was governed. It was for that reason that the courts of lowest instance were forced to adhere to the letter of the law. In this light, the legal standing of the plaintiffs and the jurors only reflected the will of the Crown.

Does advent of the power state then suffice to explain the widespread use of capital punishment? Obviously, it does not.

The parties involved in homicides and their motives. From table 1.1 we can infer that crimes of homicide in the judicial district of Masku in the 1620s and 1630s were dominated by two characteristics: they were connected with property, both real estate and chattels, and they were the result of conflicts among members of the farming community. It is, moreover, quite natural that these two features should coexist. Toward the end of the period dealt with by this study, other motives entered the scene, and at the same time the farmers tended to disappear from the ranks of those who were involved in acts of violence. They were replaced by vagrants, casual laborers, and, above all, soldiers. Thus violence became associated with the lower social orders, and at the same time it decreased. It is clear that as homicides were increasingly committed by persons who were not of the farming community, the significance of alcohol as an inflammatory or exacerbating factor in conflicts grew. In fights involving soldiers, heavy drinking of spirits or beer was nearly always a concomitant factor. Drinkers were prone to aggressive insults and abuse, and they were also more liable to react to such taunts with violence.[245]

The aggressive behavior of the farmers was clearly connected with the poor legal protection of real estate. Large areas of pasture and forest and even to some extent the most important arable fields of the villages were common land. Whosoever had a share in the commons had the right to clear land for himself by staking a proper claim—this was done by cutting marks in the trees bordering the area. However, the borders were always unclear, and there was no permanent land register. Enjoyment was generally held to be the criterion of ownership. Since the borders of a farmer's land were not always marked by a boundary ditch, and it was necessary to identify the area of land he owned from boundary marks, the ploughman or haymaker or reaper could easily end up trespassing on another's land.[246] Jaakko Simonpoika of the village of Kerävuori in the parish of Halikko wounded his neighbor's wife in the arm with a scythe in the course of a dispute that arose because she had trespassed by a distance of two plough shares over the boundary markers dividing their lands.[247] Thus the ownership of the land was always a matter of controversy and had to be decided on the spot if someone felt that he owned a "better right" to a bit of land than the one who had possession of it at the time. Disputes about boundaries and the ownership of grazing land were the most common ownership cases that appear in the judgment books of the lower courts of that period. Very commonly, conflicts became exacerbated when the land was to be partitioned, but the division had not yet taken place.[248]

But it was not only about the more distant pasture lands that disputes arose. The arable land around the village was also frequently under dispute because the prevailing method of partitioning the land, the open-field system, meant that the land possessed by each farm might be divided up into dozens or even hundreds of separate strips. The principle of the allocation of strips was that each farm should have equal amounts of good and bad common land. The huge number of strips made it impossible for the lands of the farms to be tilled separately, and this made it necessary for all the farmers to carry out their open-field tilling in the same way and at the same time. The village behaved as a single farm. The spring grain crop was planted by all in the same area, and it was harvested by all at the same time. The same applied to the autumn grain and other crops. Despite this, each farmer reaped his harvest only from his own strips, however small and narrow they might be.[249]

On Saturday, 14 August 1624, the villagers of Talvisilta in the parish of

Muurla were picking the pea crop. The work was done together, each on his own strip. One of the farmers, Sipi Eskelinpoika, ordered Jaakko Matinpoika to remove some sheep and calves that had strayed onto his strip and were damaging the crop. This caused an argument the following day between Jaakko Matinpoika and Sipi Eskelinpoika's son-in-law, Yrjö Krekonpoika. While they were quarreling, Sipi Eskelinpoika came along the road, and when he saw them, he ran across two strips of land and punched Matinpoika, causing him to fall onto a pile of peas. When the half brother of the felled man, Matti Sipinpoika, saw what had happened, he rushed to the scene and without uttering a word struck Sipi Eskelinpoika with a scythe. The blow caught him in the stomach, and he died within a few minutes. The body was taken to the church in a coffin the following day accompanied by a large group of mourners. Suddenly the killer ran up from behind, rushed past the mourners and the sleigh on which the coffin was resting, and disappeared. The district court declared him an outlaw (*fridhlöss*) and a proscribed person (*biltooger*) throughout the kingdom and sequestered his property against the security of six men.[250]

It is extremely difficult to find any crime of violence in the early years of the period covered by this material which was not connected in one way or another with ownership rights, damage caused by cattle, or boundary disputes.[251] The clearest of the few exceptions was a case of aggravated assault caused by a collision between sleighs on the highway that was tried in Pöytyä on 5 February 1621.[252] Ownership disputes over trifles could continue for years. On 25 April 1625, the Rymättylä District Court sessions dealt with the fateful consequences of a dispute that had begun three years earlier over a piece of pasture. The horses of the accused, Martti Olavinpoika, and of many others who held common land in Sorronpohja, had been put there to graze. When the men came to fetch them for carting the hay into the barns, they found that a son of one of the owners, named Juha Hannunpoika Stäckie, had driven them into the forest. Martti Olavinpoika could not find his animals for three days, during which time the hay had been spoiled by the rain. Angered by this, Martti Olavinpoika went up to the boy in the pasture and demanded: "Why did you drive my horses out of the field? Doesn't the pasture belong to me just as much as it does to your father?" He hit Juha Hannunpoika twice in the mouth and dealt him another two blows with a sharp-edged wooden club (*kantiska spiällka*), as he himself admitted. Two women saw him deliver the blows, but they were unable to say whether the blows from the club landed on the boy's back or chest. It turned out that the boy had not shown his wounds to anyone outside his family and that it was not he but his parents who had made a complaint. In any case, the boy died nine weeks later. The accused was sentenced to purgation by oath, but at the same time the court made it known that he would not be sentenced to death.[253]

Conflicts also arose because of the increasing disproportion between taxation and property. The old taxes based on intrinsic value gradually became fixed payments for each farm, and they decreased when the farms were divided among heirs. This bore no relationship to the size of the area under cultivation; there could be large farms with low taxes and vice versa. The situation caused a great deal of friction and even court cases.[254] The following case is typical: At the Nousiainen District Court sessions in October 1625, the bailiff, Dirich Hannunpoika, accused Simo Hannunpoika of stabbing Frans Sipinpoika in the hallway of the courthouse. The wounds he inflicted were not serious, because both parties were immediately brought before the court. The dispute had been about the pasturing of cattle and the ownership of the pastures.

Simo Hannunpoika said to Frans Sipinpoika: "I pay heavy taxes and dues on my land. I need it myself, so keep your cattle off it."

Frans answered: "It's our pasture. Where can we put our cattle to graze if not in our own fields?"

Simo replied: "Since you think I pay low taxes on a big farm, then exchange farms with me."

Frans agreed to the offer, saying, "Then I'll get a good cow to milk."

Simo, thinking that Frans was calling him a cattle thief, pulled out a knife and stabbed him in the shoulder. Simo was punished with the loss both of his right hand and of his land.[255]

Property disputes also resulted in nonviolent crimes. They were very commonly associated with sorcery cases, in which the origin of the dispute was the desire of one party to cause some evil to befall the other by means of a curse. Such a curse was laid in Mynämäki in 1620 as a result of a dispute about pasture, and it led to a long, drawn-out process, to which the last reference in the sources dates from 1636, sixteen years later.[256]

The situation began to alter by the 1630s at the latest. As far as the undeniably small amount of source material that is available allows us to draw any conclusions, it would seem that both the parties involved in homicidal crime and their motives changed. The number of soldiers not only among the perpetrators but also among the victims of violent crime began to increase rapidly. This picture corresponds exactly with data available from elsewhere in Finland. Certainly, soldiers began to instigate acts of violence and fights. In Nousiainen in 1636, a cavalryman assaulted the local sheriff with his sword and then turned on the victim's mother when she tried to come to her son's assistance.[257] "Boatmen," in today's parlance marines, were the cause of an increasing number of fights and breaches of domiciliary peace. In 1628, the Korppoo District Court investigated a case in which Marine Ensign Hannu Heikinpoika and his men stood accused of illegally collecting rations in several coastal parishes, assaulting peasants, and making unlawful arrests, of which there were several dozen instances, as well as other illegalities. Ensign Hannu Heikinpoika was sentenced to death for breach of the King's Peace.[258] On New Year's Eve 1631, a band of four marines ran riot in the house of the sheriff of Nousiainen: they stole beer for themselves from the cellar, breaking down doors and forcing locks, and they assaulted several people including the sheriff himself. This happened even though the frightened people in the sheriff's house did their best to fulfill the marines' every wish without delay. In order to demonstrate that they had the support of the Crown authorities behind them, the marines intimidated their victims by threatening to arrest them and drag them to prison in Turku Castle. The district court sentenced them to death for breach of domiciliary peace and the Christmas peace.[259]

As the social position of the criminals and their victims changed, so did the motives for the conflicts. It was now mainly drunken brawls with their concomitant insults and abuse that led directly to acts of violence. It was not possible for soldiers, farmhands, and their like to quarrel about the ownership of goods, because they owned very little to fight over.

Army deserters were another group associated with violent crime. They lived far from their home villages doing casual work. They lived irregular lives, drinking, fighting, constantly changing jobs, and so on. And they tended to lapse into crime and suicide.[260] At the Mynämäki District Court sessions on 4 April 1636, a general complaint was lodged about a deserter who had "behaved everywhere badly" (*hafuer allestädes illa handlatt*). The man was a wanted outlaw. Members of the public attending the sessions were warned against sheltering him, because if they did they would incur the same punishment as the deserter himself (when he was caught).[261]

Why the High Rate of Violent Crime Decreased

The Causes of the High Rate of Violence

It is now time to review and summarize our findings and thus return to the main subject of this research. We can start by asking what the explanation is for the high level of violence in the sixteenth century and its decrease in the seventeenth century.

As we noted above, in the seventeenth century the courts began to apply the harsh old laws. Compared with this factor, it was of minor significance that new regulations strictly controlling society and governing people's personal lives were enacted. Even the official widespread adoption of the Mosaic law in 1608 did not cause any fundamental change. What was crucial was the fact that judicial practice was tightened up, and this in turn entailed a strict adherence to the old Law of the Land.

But why was this not done before? Why was the law ignored in the sixteenth century? The immediate reason is that the state was too weak to enforce it. It simply did not have the resources to ensure that the law was respected. It took the so-called modern state to properly enforce its laws and regulations. But the modern state only finally came into being in the seventeenth century, for reasons which we are unable to go into in any greater detail in the present context. Previously, the law had been the law of the king, and its force was mainly that of providing guidelines for the courts. It might be adhered to, it might be cited as grounds for a judgment, but it was also possible to ignore it freely and to handle acts that were held to be offenses in other ways than those stipulated by the law. The king was accepted as a party to the settlement in a conflict, not as the agent that decided its outcome.

A fundamental question is, What kind of society was it that did not follow the law? In answering this question, it is appropriate to return to one of the cases referred to above. At the Mynämäki District Court sessions on 10 May 1621, Valpuri Juhantytär, a widow from Haloinen, together with her sons, Lasse and Matti Pertunpoika, her daughter, Kaarina Pertuntytär, and the daughter's stepbrother, Matti Pertunpoika, accused Lauri Torkkelinpoika of killing her husband, Perttu Tuomaanpoika. Lauri Torkkelinpoika had asked Matti Pertunpoika if he would be willing to swear (apparently in court) that there was no dispute between them concerning the boundary markers she wished to report. Matti Pertunpoika said that he would not swear, nor would his son, at which Lauri Torkkelinpoika snatched his knife and stabbed Matti Pertunpoika with it several times. He died eight days later, and Lauri Torkkelinpoika was sentenced to death in accordance with Chapter 30 of the Intentional Homicide Code.[262]

The fundamental point about this case is that right of ownership depended on whether the other party was willing to accept the boundary line proposed. There was no land register where the claim could have been checked, nor were there necessarily any old decisions surviving, at least none that were recorded in writing in sufficiently exact detail to make it possible to establish the boundary line on the land itself. It was also difficult in cases like this to turn to the jurors or any other disinterested party, for they would be unlikely to know with any exactitude where the boundary between two farms ran. In such circumstances, there was a strong temptation to resort to intimidation to make the other party give in. This was done by creating an atmosphere of terror that would force the other side to renounce his claim and submit to his opponent's will. The terror could be produced by the use of violence or by the threat of witchcraft.

This can be illustrated by a case in Mynämäki on 4 April 1636, in which a man called Eskil Salavainen accused his sister and her husband, Krister Antinpoika of Uusikaupunki, of causing his hernia by putting a curse on him and his wife some years earlier. Krister and his wife refused to swear an oath of purgation, but he undertook to release Eskil from his affliction if his sister-in-law would come and be reconciled with him. At this point, the court "would willingly have done something more," that is, continued the inquiry, but Krister fled, considering it to his advantage to maintain his reputation as a sorcerer.[263]

An even more persuasive example is provided by the origin of a sorcery case in Mynämäki in 1620. It was proven in court that Tuomas Erkinpoika, a farmer from Haanperä, who was losing his dispute over pasture with his neighbor, Simo Martinpoika, "had put a curse on him, to ever requite his opposition" (*hafuer han unsagtt denna Simon låffwatt honom alltijd löna för omakett*).[264] Paavo Martinpoika Riihilä of Nousiainen also resorted to violence when he felt that he had been excluded from the ownership of a strip of land that was being partitioned. He grievously assaulted one of the co-owners of the land and his son. The purpose of his violence and intimidation was to ensure his own rights to ownership.[265]

In the light of these examples, the violence of the sixteenth century was merely an expression of a society that was unable to guarantee order by means of the law. In a "lawless" society it was necessary to defend one's position and interests by force and violence. Individuals turned to their nearest relatives, the members of their former and present nuclear families, in an attempt to create for their kin such an intimidating reputation that it would protect them from other ambitious individuals and families. The society of the Middle Ages and the sixteenth century was certainly no haven of peace and harmony, amicably controlled by the local district courts and the panels of jurors. It was a society corrupted with fear and violence, dictated by the laws of subjection and submission.

There is one fact which does not seem to fit this picture: the large number of cases of minor assaults in the district court records. If we assume that the law was only a set of guidelines, that the role of the panel of jurors was mainly that of a broker between the parties involved in a crime, and that the real power lay in the hands of the immediate relatives, then how is it possible that people took one another to court by the hundreds for the sake of a single bruise? One possible interpretation would be to see these petty assaults as arising from economic conflicts; another would be to regard them as attempts to defend one's honor. Both of these interpretations can be supported by reference to individual cases in which the act of violence can be shown to have been preceded by an attempt to deprive another person of his property or by an affront to a person's character. There is also a high correlation between these two types of cases and crimes of violence generally.[266] In other words, statistically, the rates for slanders and property crimes follow the development of the violent crime rate. Although the high correlation is not sufficient in itself to prove a causal relation between the two, it does nevertheless oblige us to give careful consideration to the possible validity of these alternative explanations.

Let us first consider the assumption that there was a mutual connection between crimes of violence and property crimes. Since the main sources consist of the fine rolls, it may have happened that a case was brought before the district court but not recorded because it was a matter of civil law. Only the assault was recorded in the fine rolls because it incurred a fine, one-third of which went to the king. This assumption is strongly supported by the fact that the rare court records that survive from this period are full of disputes over ownership and property. It is, therefore, not difficult to suppose that some of them led to physical assaults.

The other possibility is to regard the bruises that were inflicted as insults, that is, material injuries as opposed to verbal injuries. This interpretation is supported by the fact that, according to the Swedish Law of the Land, falsely accusing another person of a criminal act in itself was a punishable offense. If, for example, one person accused another in their everyday dealings of being a thief, he could be taken to court, where he would be punished unless he could prove his allegation. If he could not, in principle he received the same punishment that would have been imposed on the object of his defamation if he had been able to prove it. It was for this reason that by far the most common cases of slander were those in which the other party was accused of being a sorcerer or witch, a thief, or a whore. After these came "murderer" in fourth place and in fifth "executioner," which was tantamount to accusing someone of being a criminal, because a criminal could be forced into becoming an executioner as a result of having his sentence commuted by the court. The slanders were thus more in the nature of defamations (allegations of criminal acts) than insults (mere affronts).[267]

The range of affronts which came within the legal sphere of slander does not increase until the seventeenth century, when insults were punished to a wider extent than in the sixteenth century. For example, the word *kelmi* (rogue) is a fairly common term of abuse in the seventeenth century.[268] The increase in the number of slander cases in the seventeenth century is partly a result of the fact that the provisions of the Law of the Land began to be interpreted in such a way that they permitted slanders to be punished by law. Chapter 43 of the Judicial Code (*tingmålabalken*) of the Law of the Land had made slander committed before the court a criminal offense. This provision in the law speaks of insults uttered in the heat of the moment (*okvädinsord*). Six men who were present in the court were required to investigate whether it was a question of an insult and, if so, whether it was the result of a rush of anger or of a long-standing enmity.

Another reason, or rather a precondition, for the increase in the number of slanders was the laws of privilege. The situation can be illustrated by a case in Lohja in 1665. A drunken man who was following the bishop's tour of inspection remarked to the man next to him that the bishop had perhaps bought the sable skin from which his fine fur hat was made from "whores" in Tallinn in Estonia, and he suspected that the chaplain of Lohja had done the same thing. The man was prosecuted for slander and required to take an oath of purgation. Not managing to get the necessary compurgators, he was sentenced to death under Paragraph 22 of the Privileges of the Clergy and Chapter 31 of the Royal Code (*konungsbalken*). His words were considered to have insulted "the respect and dignity of the office of the Lord Bishop" (*H. Biskopens Embets Respekt och Wyrdighet*).[269]

A similar case, also from Lohja, is equally descriptive of the situation. During the Candlemas market in 1687, the cantor of Lohja, Erkki Juhanpoika, entered the tavern of Lt. Johan Laellius and, raising his mug of beer, said to Christer Gerdtz, a merchant from Turku, "Drink to my good fortune!"

Gerdtz took offense at the suggestion and the familiar tone of the cantor and answered coldly, "We have not made any covenant with you.[270] Go away." At the same time, he underlined his point by raising his glass to Laellius.

Infuriated, the village cantor began to shout, "Why won't you drink to me? Aren't I as good a man as you?"

With biting scorn, Gerdtz answered, "My dear cantor, I have nothing to do with you. Go back to the rectory and look after the Dean, as your duties require!"

The cantor ran out, shouting from the door, "Come out, you rogue, you tramp, you skin and bones from Turku!"—three terms of abuse that were common at the time. The merchant, however, did not budge. The cantor disappeared out of the door, but after a short while a threatening group of people approached the tavern. It was led by the cantor and included his mother, his brother-in-law, and his sister, all with staves in their hands. They were not allowed to enter the tavern, but from under the window the cantor repeated his abuse, demanding that the merchant come out and fight with him. This, naturally, did not happen. The high and mighty merchant from Turku did not relish the idea of fighting with the lowly cantor, his mother, and his sister. Later Gerdtz brought an action against the cantor and sent a legal representative to the Lohja District Court, and the humiliated cantor was fined forty marks for slander.[271]

It was the cantor's misfortune that he had not yet comprehended the rules of the game inherent in the new hierarchical order of society. He considered himself to be as worthy as a Turku burgher, a mistake for which he was to pay dearly.

Cases of slander mostly concerned the gentry and the upper stratum of the farming classes, the cavalry estate owners (*rusthållare*). The ordinary peasant farmers were excluded as not being owed any particular respect. In 1687, a cavalry ensign entered a tavern in Lohja. The peasants inside immediately took off their caps in humble fashion, at which a drunken farmer named Mikko Erkinpoika demanded of his neighbors: "Hey, you whoresons, why are you doffing your caps?" The peasants nodded in the direction of the ensign and pointed out that there was gentry present. Mikko Erkinpoika urged them with oaths not to pay any attention to such toffs: they paid for their own drinks, so they didn't need to take their caps off to anybody. The ensign prosecuted Mikko Erkinpoika, but the final outcome of the case has not survived for posterity.[272]

Let us return to the main theme of this research: whether we can show that cases of slander or property crimes can explain the huge number of cases of petty assault that came before the district courts in the sixteenth century. Possible explanations are vitiated by certain weaknesses. If violence was a lesser concomitant of a dispute over property, could it not have been easily settled out of court, thus avoiding a public inquiry into the case? Again, if a bruise was felt to be an insult, might one not expect the aggrieved party to have avenged himself without going to court? Why should he take some petty legal action for an injury for which the fine prescribed by the law was halved even after its value had been eaten away by inflation over the centuries? If, on the other hand, we assume that violence was a part of the intimidation of others in order to strengthen and protect one's own position as far as possible, then how can we explain the courage of the offended party in daring to take the matter to court?

It would appear that all of these paths lead to dead ends. Perhaps, however, we can arrive at the correct answer from two basic facts. The law—the exhortatory royal law discussed above—nevertheless provided some form of security for the weaker party, in actual fact the only form. The offense was also, and perhaps, primarily, against the family rather than against the individual. Family pressure both motivated and encouraged an individual to seek legal redress in order that the stronger party should be punished in some way for his behavior.

The weaker party had no other recourse than to turn to the law. In conditions where people did not enjoy the security afforded by a strong administration, the families, nuclear and extended, protected their honor in the same way that sovereign states do in this day and age. An insult had to be answered; otherwise, the offender would go completely unpunished and might more easily repeat his offense.

However, it is possible that this apparently reasonable explanation is not completely correct. Cases of homicide are characterized by a feature in which there is a regularly repeated formula that says the case has been completely settled and "fully discussed" (*övertalad*) forever with the payment of the agreed fines and compensations, and that the settlement was valid for members of the family both born and unborn. In addition, the accused or his family gave presents to the victim's family beyond what had been agreed in the settlement as well as in cases where the cause of death was found to have been something other than the assault. This can only mean that the intention was to put relations between the families on a proper footing, to reestablish them as they had been before the crime.

If we examine the question of prosecuting minor assaults against this background, we begin to suspect that we are dealing with the same phenomenon that existed in homicide cases. Even though the deed was a petty one, it had nevertheless upset relations between families, nuclear or extended. Therefore, there had to be a public settlement and reconciliation, in order that no further damage to the relations between the clans might ensue. If we accept this interpretation, we must nevertheless remember that we are dealing with a state with a weak administration and public authorities who were unable to guarantee law and order. This situation placed families in approximately the same position as sovereign states in the present age. They, too, are extremely quick to react to the least insults to which they are subjected, and further they require that the matter be settled before a large forum. They, too, strive to maintain good relations with their neighbors in order to maximize their own security. This comparison helps us to understand people's sensitive reaction to petty crimes and why there were so many of them—after all, the number of independent extended and nuclear families was huge.

The society of the Middle Ages and the sixteenth century was in any case not one that was blessed with peace and harmony. It was characterized by a constant power struggle between families. One sign of this was the nicknames that were given to people. In the Finnish countryside in the mid-sixteenth century they were mainly names of animals like Härk (Ox), Karhu (Bear), Kettu (Fox), Pässi (Ram), Kana (Chicken), Sika (Pig), Rotta (Rat), Mulli (Bullock), and so on. Apparently they were given with the qualities of the animal in mind. However, there are some that are purely offensive and refer to human physical attributes or behavior. They include such names as Sianluomi (Hog's Wart), Pahka (Mole), Neuvo (Counsel), Laviapää (Bighead), Mulkku (Prick), Juoppo (Sot), Peluri (Gambler), Mustapää (Black Head), Möykkä (Lout), Verkatakki (Woolcoat), Suupaltti (Windbag—for a priest), and so on. Correspondingly there were burghers in the town of Turku in the sixteenth century with nicknames like Karvatasku (Hair Pocket), Hirvi (Stag), Ketara (Shank), and Palttu (Blood Pudding). Of course, in the Middle Ages, agnomina were commonly given to kings: Edward the Confessor, John Lackland, William the Conqueror, Edward Longshanks, Ethelred the Unready, Richard the Lionheart, and so on. At all levels, however, disparaging and malevolent nicknames outnumber those indicating respect. It is indicative that in the fine rolls for Lohja in western Nyland (Uusimaa) in the sixteenth century there are slightly more persons with nicknames among those convicted of assault (64) than among the victims (52). From this we can deduce that altercations started off with insults and name calling, followed by fisticuffs. This assumption is supported by a record of the Lohja District Court in 1636. It states that the composition of scabrous ditties was a common "Finnish folk custom."[273] However, since the law did not recognize any such crime as the use of nicknames, the fine rolls only contain a reference to assault, for, as the instructions for judges put it, it was always he who delivered the blow that broke the law. In any case, in the light of this source data, there is no doubt that the people of medieval times and in the sixteenth century did slander one another, and they did so at least as much as people do today, but there were no convictions for slanderous behavior in the courts. Either cases of slander were not prosecuted, or they were not punished by the courts.[274]

Thus we conclude that the high rate of criminal violence was a consequence of the fact that in a state where the law did not afford them protection, individuals turned to their families, and the families tried to strengthen their position by intimidating and terrorizing those around them. The weaker party tried appealing to the law for whatever small protection it could afford in the circumstances. If he had not done so, he would have weakened his position even further by swallowing the insult. The situation among the common people was much the same as that which obtained among the nobility in the seventeenth century and to some extent even later, when the nobles were forever engaging in litigation over questions of insult and precedence or defending their honor in duels.[275] As far as jealously protecting their reputations was concerned, the aristocracy behaved in the same way as the sixteenth-century peasantry. A noble family reacted immediately if it felt that its honor had been called into question. It did so in order not to place itself under the law. It was not until the latter half of the seventeenth century that the Age of Autocracy brought it to heel. It also brought an end to duels between members of the nobility with strict decrees in 1662 and 1682.[276]

The Pacification of Society

When we consider the reasons and explanations for the pacification of society and the defeat of violence, it is easy to suggest that it was the harsh punishments that had these effects. By no longer accepting settlements, ensuring that the law was strictly adhered to, and making the criminal code harsher, the authorities created a deterrent that brought the flourishing wave of crime to an end.

However, in criminology, one cannot generally assume that it is possible to affect the crime rate in any fundamental way by means of harsh punishments. The reasons for crimes, whatever they may be, together with the criminal's belief that he will not get caught, always seem to overcome the fear of punishment. Sanctions have been made more and less severe quite independently of trends in criminality. Changes to criminal law have been mainly connected with the democratic or undemocratic nature of the way in which power was wielded, or—and it amounts to practically the same thing—with social equality and inequality. In unequal societies where power lies in the hands of a central authority, it has been necessary to resort to a harsh penal code in order to maintain the system, whereas in equitable, democratic societies punishments have been made more lenient because the threat of revolution is felt to be less than in societies characterized by great differences in social status and power.[277]

In this case, however, the process would seem to have been different: the harsh criminal code and the strict adherence to it had the effect of wiping out violent crime until it was no more than one small sector of the whole criminal spectrum. This, one would assume, happened because the centralized administrative machinery of the modern state together with a powerful army ensured that the will of those with whom decision-making power lay, the king and the Council of the Realm, was carried out even in areas where they themselves could not be physically present. It is here that the regimes of the sixteenth and seventeenth centuries differ so much from each other. In the sixteenth century, the will of the ruler was only effectively enforced where he himself could be physically present with the backing of a sufficient military force. It is for this reason that for a long time there was no capital city, and the ruler made frequent tours of his realm holding royal courts of redress as he did so.[278] The exploitation of the system of justice for political ends could only be accomplished in places where the king himself or a mighty lord was present with sufficient backing. Christian II, the king of the Scandinavian Union, bloodily crushed the opposition in Sweden in 1520 by appointing a court that sentenced his political opponents to death and saw to it that the sentences were carried out immediately. Gustavus I Vasa, Eric XIV, and Charles IX all personally appeared as prosecutors at political trials in courts which they themselves had set up for the purpose and saw to it that the sentences of execution were carried out—indeed, Eric XIV himself acted as executioner.[279]

Must we then take it that it was the modern state with its harsh laws and cruel punishments that put an end to violence? Perhaps not quite. According to one view that has been strongly advanced by scholars, the society of the premodern state was reasonably balanced and harmonious. Conflicts were solved by settlement in a way that was satisfactory to all the parties concerned. Punishment aimed not at retribution but at repairing breaches in society.[280] Is this then the true picture? Hardly. The huge number of those who died as a result of violence is alone enough to prove it false, indicating as it does not so much harmony as the lack of it. This is only what one might expect. As the old saying has it, the law is the refuge of the weak. Societies where there has been no law, or where it has not been enforced, have not usually been paradises where all is peace and harmony. Rather, in them have reigned the law of the stronger, intimidation, oppression, and despotism, "such a war as is of every man against every man," to quote Thomas Hobbes, who described the society that preceded the modern state in his book *Leviathan* (1650).

In the nineteenth century, there was a wave of violence afflicting one county of Finland, Southern Ostrobothnia, which became known as the Age of the Knife Fighters, and it provides a good example of such a society. With the system of justice crippled by terrorization, violent gangs carried out crimes against property and person. Their leaders rose to positions of influence at the same time as the number of victims increased to staggering proportions.[281] It is extremely significant that during the Age of the Knife Fighters the people of Southern Ostrobothnia warmly welcomed law officers who were firm and even prepared to go beyond the bounds of the law. They approached the status of folk heroes.[282] The people desired law and order above everything else, and in return they were prepared to accept unlawful procedures in court as well as the unlawful methods used by the authorities.

Let us return to the 1620s and from that perspective cast a glance back into Finnish history. What do we see? We see confusion, lawlessness, and disorder. One might almost say chaos. The situation came to a head in the so-called Club War, a peasant uprising that lasted from 1595 to 1597. In it the Finnish peasantry of the north took up arms against the despotism of the Swedish army and the rapaciousness of the nobility. The peasants attempted to break through the chain of fortresses stretching from Turku through Hämeenlinna to Olavinlinna and Vyborg in the east and invade the estates of southern Finland. The attempt was doomed from the outset. Its only purpose was probably to try and make the rulers of the state realize just how desperate the position of the majority of the population had become. The uprising was bloodily suppressed by the army led by the nobles.[283] However, it did bring about one change desired by the peasants in that it helped Duke Charles to power in Sweden when the king of Sweden, Sigismund, who was residing in Poland, was deposed. The change also brought a slight improvement in the situation of the peasants insofar as the new regime introduced numerous new measures to reduce lawlessness.

Seen in a broader perspective, the suppression of the revolt spelled the end of the peasants' local autonomy and the rule of the clans over society, as well as the advent of a society and state based on the power of the central authorities, the domination of the nobility, and a hierarchical administration based on written law. The determined installation of a provincial administration working under Finland's central government began in 1616, and a royal court of appeal was established in Turku in 1623. One of the first tasks of both was to restore order, legality, and peace to society. In carrying out these reforms, King Gustavus II Adolf spoke of Finland as an outback where disorder had been rife, and Nils Bielke, the first president of the Turku Court of Appeal, described the Finns as "an evil and barbaric people," by which he meant that both the officials and the common people had lived outside the bounds of the state's control.[284]

Against this background, it is no wonder that the people of those times, and particularly the common people, did not react adversely to the introduction of harsh punishments for crimes. Although there were some attempts to continue the old system of settlements, in most cases the plaintiffs required the literal enforcement of the law, which in the worst crimes entailed the death penalty. This had been extremely rare in the sixteenth century, when almost without exception the plaintiffs had been willing to settle for fines and indemnities. It must be emphasized that the outlook did not change because people had become more bloodthirsty. Rather, it was felt that if the law was to be upheld in one respect, then it had to be upheld in others as well. There were widespread references to the necessity of adhering to the law in order to prevent and decrease violent crime. The reason behind the desire for legality was not so much an attempt to stamp out physical violence as an opposition to the oppression that the ordinary people were suffering at the hands of the gentry, a rising social class between the peasants and the nobility. The advent of the modern state gave the local gentry and local authorities a degree of power and authority that could easily be misused to oppress the commons. Acts of violence and persecution, including unwarranted arrests, on the part of the officials—the bailiffs and sheriffs and their assistants—were extremely common. The judgment books of those days are full of such cases. Nevertheless, the law was needed not only to ensure physical safety but also, and perhaps primarily, to guarantee the safety of property and economic security. What is important here is not the severity of the law but the fact that it was enforced efficiently and, if at all possible, equitably. It was necessary that it could be relied upon. To put it briefly, in demanding a strict law, people were above all expressing a desire for legality. In this respect, at least, the interests of the supreme power and the lowest ranks of the people coincided.

The coming of the centralized modern state removed the sway of the clan at the level of the common people, but among the nobility the power of the family continued and grew in some respects. The aristocracy was registered by family in the rolls of the nobility, it was represented by family in the Diet, and it defended the position of the family with strict rules of intermarriage. It should be noted that when the power of the families disappeared, it was not primarily a question of a change in people's way of thinking. It is generally wrong to think that a society ruled by clans was some kind of primitive stage in the development of mankind in relation to the modern state and that it disappeared of its own accord as society developed. The reasons for its appearance and disappearance were historical—in other words, they were caused by definite factors. They were not anthropological developments automatically following laws of their own.

There was a change of this kind in the seventeenth century. A centralized administration with its ministries, provincial government, official regulations, standing army, and so on, ensured that the decisions of the government were enforced, that suspected criminals were hunted the length and breadth of the kingdom, and that sentences were carried out even in areas that were distant from the seat of the ruler and the nation's capital. The protection afforded by the law to physical security was soon extended to property and economic life. Although the harsh and brutal system of justice created a kind of state terrorization, as scholars have often emphasized,[285] it also ultimately created a state of law and order in which crimes of violence decreased. An efficient state justice system with its machinery of coercion offered the individual a kind of external way of defending himself against injuries.

The development we have described here is by no means typical of Sweden alone. It is definitely not just a case of some isolated "Swedish model." Judicial practice in Norway was tightened up in the 1620s, almost exactly when the sources used in this research indicate that the process happened in southwest

Finland.[286] In England the period when the law was strictest was probably in the latter half of the sixteenth century. In any case, harsher punishments were doled out there in the seventeenth century than in the eighteenth.[287] One is thus justified in assuming that the development throughout western and northern Europe was the same. Probably the reasons for the high rate of violent crime before the end of the sixteenth century and in the seventeenth and for its subsequent decline were also much the same everywhere in these areas. Such differences as there were are to be found in the cities, because they developed to a great extent independently of the state and were protected by a high degree of autonomy. But in the Nordic countries there were no large cities.

Abbreviations

D	Dråpmålabalken (The Homicide Code)
HAik	Historiallinen Aikakauskirja
HArk	Historiallinen Arkisto
KA	Kansallisarkisto (National Archives of Finland)
KrL	Kristofers landslag (King Christopher's Law of the Land)
MEL	Magnus Erikssons landslag (King Magnus Eriksson's Law of the Land)
SVT I and *II*	*Suomen vanhimmat tuomiokirjat* (for full information, see Sources: Published Sources)
S	Sårmålabalken (Injury Code)

Notes

1. Gurr 1981, 313; Stone 1983, 25; Beattie 1986, 108.
2. *WHO Annual Health Statistics* 1986–95.
3. For a summary of various studies see, for example, Spierenburg 1994, 702.
4. Rousseaux 1992, 142–43; Rousseaux 1996, 14. See also Johnson 1995, esp. 109–43, 229–38; Castan 1989, 51, 58–59; Eisner 1998.
5. Sandnes 1990, 74.
6. Österberg 1991a, 73; Österberg and Lindström 1988, 43–48, 54, 88.
7. Stevnsborg 1984, 217.
8. Karonen 1996.
9. Gurr (1992, 463) tentatively suggests that violence was more common in the countryside than in the towns before industrialization and urbanization. This is evidently not the case; in the Middle Ages, and certainly in the sixteenth century, the towns were attracting criminal elements in large numbers.
10. Österberg 1991a, 73.
11. Sandnes 1990, 71f.
12. Ylikangas 1976a, 123–30.
13. Ylikangas 1976a, 123ff.
14. Pirinen 1982, 511.
15. Ylikangas, 1976a, 126.

16. Matikainen 1996, 33; Pirinen 1982, 510; Ylikangas 1971, 1976.
17. Österberg 1983, 25; Larsson 1982, 47–56; Sandnes 1990.
18. Sandnes 1990, 70–71.
19. Cf. Næss 1982, 86–87; Söderberg 1990; Österberg 1991a, 72–73.
20. Renvall, 1949b, 224–25; Blomsted 1960, 193–94; Ylikangas 1971, 114–15; Pirinen 1982, 506–7.
21. Ylikangas 1976a, 123; Koskelainen 1995, 99.
22. Söderberg 1993, 10–12.
23. Verkko 1949. Admittedly Verkko's principal sources—the population tables, which were based on information given by the local church ministers—only indicate the minimum number of homicides. Exact regional comparisons have shown that the number of cases dealt with as homicides in courts of law was considerably higher. Ylikangas 1987, 651–52.
24. Næss 1994, 68–69.
25. Pirinen 1982, 508–9; Matikainen 1996, 33.
26. Koskivirta 1996, 47–48.
27. Stone 1983, 32.
28. Cf. Lindström 1988, 67–68; Österberg 1994, 21.
29. Renvall 1949a.
30. Elias 1994.
31. Gurr 1992, 462–63.
32. Elias 1994, 156–68, 441–524.
33. Renvall 1949a, 180–99.
34. Elias 1994; cf. Jarrick and Söderberg 1994, 11; cf. Rakkolainen 1996, 18–19; Matikainen 1996, 30–31.
35. Elias 1994; cf. Österberg 1991b, 115; cf. Matikainen 1996, 30.
36. Gurr 1992, 462. Cf. also Cohen and Johnson 1982, 477–501.
37. Cf. Anderson 1974.
38. Cf. Garland 1991, 96–115.
39. Behind this process of mitigation lies the slow but continuing progress toward social equality, or democracy in the broader sense. The threat of revolution is less in a democracy than in a dictatorship, and thus it is not necessary to protect the power system with harsh penal laws. Kekkonen and Ylikangas 1983, 159–78.
40. Cf. Gurr 1992, 563.
41. Ylikangas 1976a, 99.
42. For further discussion, see von Hentig 1962; Lindström 1988, 92; Stevnsborg 1984; Lenman and Parker 1980, 12–13.
43. There are references in Finland dating from the Middle Ages to wanted criminals who fled to Tallinn. Among those who escaped to Tallinn were the leaders of the popular "Uprising of David" in the 1430s. Cf. Voionmaa 1916, 385–86; Blomstedt 1937, 32.
44. Cf. WHO statistics.
45. See, e.g., Franke 1994, 77 and elsewhere.
46. Lehti 1997.
47. It should be remembered that figures before the twentieth century are taken from the population tables and are somewhat lower than the real numbers. Cf. Ylikangas 1987, 651.
48. Sundin 1992, 47–49, 230, 241–46; Österberg 1991a, 79.
49. Verkko 1949, appendix.
50. Ylikangas 1985.

51. See Petrovitch 1971 (for France), 67–91; Sharpe 1977, 98–99 (Britain); Mechler 1970, 63–64 (Germany); Taussi Sjöberg 1981, 153–54 (Sweden); Ylikangas 1985, 136, 235; Koskivirta 1996, 70 (Finland).

52. The Homicide Collection (Henkirikoskokoelma) in the Department of History, Helsinki University. The material has been collected from published local histories. In them crimes are often recorded in tables with no mention of the social position of the criminal or the victim and without distinguishing between, for instance, infanticide and other forms of homicide. Often the texts include only cases selected at random to illustrate this aspect of life. However, since the material comprises hundreds of cases, it has probative force in several respects as a result of the law of large numbers.

53. Sandnes 1990, 69–70.

54. Lindström 1988, 88–89.

55. Ylikangas 1971, 132–33.

56. Sharpe 1984, 94–95.

57. Lindström 1988; Schüssler 188, 253.

58. Petrovitch 1971, 213, 232, 245; Sharpe 1977, 98–99; Ylikangas 1976a, 14; Perrot 1975, 67–91; Marja Taussi Sjöberg 1981, 153–54.

59. Cf. Österberg 1991b, 8–24.

60. For further discussion, see Ylikangas 1971, 118–19.

61. Cf. Rousseaux 1996, 3–4.

62. See "Savon tuomiokirjat 1559 ja 1561–1565," in *SVT I.*

63. Ylikangas 1971, 121 n. 71.

64. MEL S I, D I-II; KrL S I, D I-II.

65. Ylikangas 1971, 151.

66. Österberg and Lindström 1988, 63; Pirinen 1957, 526.

67. Ylikangas 1976a, 128.

68. Pirinen 1982, 510.

69. Matikainen 1996, 32–34.

70. Söderberg 1990, 240–43; Österberg 1994, 17–19; Ylikangas 1971; Sundin 1992, 110–11; Næss 1994, 71; Sandnes 1990, 84.

71. Translator's note: Direct quotations from the records have been translated as literally as possible, even to the extent of violating English usage.

72. *SVT II,* 20.

73. MEL and KrL D I-II, S I.

74. Ylikangas 1976a, 107–8.

75. Næss 1990.

76. KA 3256:12v; Ylikangas 1976a, 104.

77. KA 757:4; Ylikangas 1976a, 104.

78. In Swedish the ordinance reads: "Then ther någon ihielslår [en annan] utan nödtwingat ther till, så är saken mycket större, och gifwe Lijf för Lijf." Schmedeman 1706, 46.

79. Ylikangas 1976a, 109.

80. For further discussion, see Ylikangas 1971, 118–21.

81. Stevnsborg 1984, 211–12.

82. It is indicative that the decree does not limit itself to crime. Toward the end, it exhorts Swedes to adopt the barn-drying method for grain that was used in Finland. Finally it emphasizes that the subjects of the king must obey all orders given by the authorities, from

the cultivation of the fields and land clearance to the maintenance of hop gardens or the felling of oak trees or fruit trees. The intention was thus to emphasize the power of authority generally. It would be difficult to find a clearer example of the fact that the drive to enforce the criminal law more strictly was prompted more by an effort on the part of the Crown to reassert its power than by an attempt to combat crime. Schmedeman 1706, 47–48.

83. For further discussion, see Ylikangas 1976a, 107–12.

84. See, e.g., KA 1242:98v.

85. KA 4727:66 and 1127:82v.

86. See KA 692:7v.

87. The principle of "higher fines" for gross cases is mentioned *expressis verbis* in a judgment in 1558 (KA 757:4). This is illustrated very clearly by the following case: in 1571 the Kaarlela District Court had sentenced a woman called Marita to death for intentionally killing her daughter-in-law's daughter. She was given a fine of 120 marks, on the basis of which her life was spared. KA 4727:64v.

88. Inger 1980, 14–20; Letto-Vanamo 1995, 133–51.

89. Ylikangas 1976a, 98.

90. KA 1133:6.

91. KA 880:8v; 1039:8v, 21.

92. KA 1205:123.

93. "So att han vntte honom liiff för Gudtz skuld och för gode mens bön skuld på alle sine frenders vegne." *SVT II*, 67. Cf. KA 1328:61a.

94. Ylikangas 1976a, 112.

95. KA 4532:26v.

96. KA 703:20.

97. KA 4746:102v.

98. Homicide Collection, Department of History, Helsinki University.

99. For example, KA 4532:18v, 25, 26v. The term appears fairly regularly in sentences.

100. For example, KA 4532:25 (Ii District Court 13 July 1544); KA 4534:22 (Kyrö District Court 1546).

101. Earlier on, and sometimes later as well, this indemnity was included in the plaintiff's share of the fine and not paid separately.

102. "Är förlickt med moolsegende . . . hade han tillförene förlickt sigh medh målsägande." See also KA 618:3v (Uusikirkko 9 May 1556, three homicides); KA 1062:6 (Parainen 11 August 1556); KA 1143:27v (Piikkiö 10 December 1569); KA 1143:35v (Parainen 6 July 1576); KA 4727:66 (Pietarsaari 21.8. 1571); KA 1306:10v (Marttila 3 January 1576).

103. KA 4688:5v (Oulunsuu District Court 29 July 1566).

104. The actual text in Swedish reads: "Anders Larsson i Korvis till 40 mk för ett fult mandråp som Knut Simonsson bedreff therför han ihiell slagit förenämnde Anders fader, och Anders anamadhe effter sijn faders död aff offtabenemndh Knut all hans lösöre, huus och jord, och haffer förenämnde Anders welwiliegelig loffvat svare för K.M. sacköre och härads, dt-18 mk 8 ortiger." KA 698:39v.

105. *SVT II*, p.67.

106. *SVT II*, 73.

107. KA 1364:71v.

108. "Förenämnde Ambrosius skall hysse Sigfrieds hustru och barn så lenghe han lefwer." KA 1039:21v.

109. At the summer sessions of the Salo District Court on 5 August 1566, the guilty party paid each of the three beneficiaries—the king, the court, and the plaintiff—a total of 150 marks in settlement, i.e., fifty marks to each.

110. The King's Peace was first declared for certain places—markets, churches, homes, district court sessions, etc.—or certain times like Christmas and Easter. The declaration of the King's Peace meant that every crime that was committed in the area covered by it was also committed against the king. Finally the practice of declaring the King's Peace nationwide at coronations was adopted, which meant that the new sovereign took responsibility for peace and order throughout his kingdom for the duration of his reign. In 1495 an "Eternal Peace" was declared for the first time throughout the territory of the Habsburg Empire by Maximilian I. Whosoever committed a crime broke the King's Peace (Ylikangas 1983, 22–23). At the beginning of the sixteenth century in Finland, payment of the royal share of the fine was reported as restoring the King's Peace to the culprit.

111. On 20 February 1567, the winter sessions of the Jakobstad (Pietarsaari) Town Court found that Olaf Matsson had killed Marcus Andersson apparently in self-defense. Even so, he was sentenced to pay a fine of forty marks, and he also settled to pay the plaintiffs, Jöns, Anders and Erich Persson, "a suitably sized boat" (*en höffuisk both*) to the value of thirty marks, and the widow of the victim a quarter of frieze cloth. Thus "peace and friendship" (*fridh och wenskap*) were brought about between the parties and any further discussion on the matter was closed. KA 4696:10.

112. The words in Swedish in the record read: "Och målseijande gåffvo honom till, och upbar aff honom manzboot 110 mk för rätten, och wåre thermed wäll och wänligen förlijckte och icke begierede hans liiff." KA 1133:36–36v.

113. Cf. the Kemi District Court, 30 June 1546, KA 4534:26v.

114. KA 3 October 1579.

115. "Opå sine vegne och sine barnes vegne och opå alles slettinx vegne, både födde och ofödde." See following footnote.

116. *SVT I*, 172–73.

117. In the seventeenth century, testimonies given by the victim on his deathbed as well as by third parties to the effect that battery by the accused was not the cause of his death may be an indication that a settlement had been made on the quiet. The purpose of the testimonies was to avoid the pronouncement of the death sentence in court. This conclusion does not work for the sixteenth century because in practice the death penalty was not applied then.

118. *SVT I*, 99.

119. *SVT II*, 73.

120. *SVT I*, 112; Ylikangas 1976a, 118.

121. The original Swedish record reads: "Och ther medt bleff samma gerning nu herföre sittiande rett förlickt uthi enn platt dödt och öffvertalat saack, så för ofödda som födda."

122. The court records: "Och Jacob i Lacden som näst barna molsman är stodh her för retta och bad för dråparen, och kunde icke komma honom hals brott uppå, tij hann icke bleff fongenn widt ferska gerningh. Ther till skall och förenämna dropare giffua Eskils hustru 3 mk för senga rånid." KA 757:4.

123. KA 533:2v.

124. KA 618:3v.

125. The son-in-law is mentioned, for instance, in KA 1184:21 (Vehmaa 20 August 1571).

126. KA 757:6v. Cf. KA 618:3v.

127. E.g. KA 1364:83v.

128. KA 1116:12.

129. The following exceptions may be mentioned: In connection with a homicide in Pöytyä in 1577, the plaintiffs and victim's party to the settlement were his brothers and grandmother; at the Mynämäki District Court on 18 March 1584, the plaintiffs and party to the settlement were the mother and her two sons and one daughter (KA 1439a:2v–3); in Perniö on 4 February 1591, the plaintiffs were Marita Mikontytär, her two sons, and her son-in-law.

130. "Men efter slächten gaff sig till friids och hade mansboot opburitt." KA 4749:91v.

131. "Effther thet förenämnde Erichs slächtinger bådhe för Oloffs liiff och toghe christeligh mandsboott." KA 4764:106. Cf. KA 4773:162.

132. KA 1548:109v.

133. KA 217:46.

134. KA 1520:66.

135. Cf. KA 1116:12 (Vehmaa 16 August 1568).

136. *Handwörterbuch zur deutschen Rechtsgeschichte I* (Holzbauer), 1466–74; Schüssler 1988, 249–50.

137. Hasselberg 1957, 520.

138. KA 1609:60v.

139. See KA 880:8v, 1242:96.

140. KA 4534:34v.

141. KA 1364:72.

142. KA 1184:7–8.

143. "Och tigde honom lijff aff slåttz fougtenn, thet han och honom effterlett på K. Ma:ttz wägne, effter han bleff inthet begripin, wtan höltt skogen, och om han hade icke fåtth fred, så hade han giffuit sigh till Rijdzlandh." *SVT I,* 142.

144. "Gick i förlichning medh K.M. fougte, och utgaff K.M. 100 mk." KA 1214:15v.

145. "Dherföre kom han och her för rätta, och giorde en förlickningh medh migh på K.M. nodige behagh och effther målsijenden sielff haffva beditt för honom så haffver jagh upburitt oppo K.M. wegna 200 mk i konungens sack, och häradshöffdingen 100 mk." KA 1290:92v.

146. KA 1290:89v.

147. KA 757:6v.

148. *SVT I,* 54.

149. Ylikangas 1976a, 122.

150. Cf. KA 1290:49; *SVT II,* 60; Ylikangas 1976a, 114.

151. Cf. von Hentig 1962.

152. Lindström 1988, 103.

153. Sandnes 1990, 70–71.

154. Furuhagen 1996, 22–25; Sundin 1992, 447–52; Lenman-Parker 1980.

155. For example, KA 1364:61v and 4764:101v. The suspect swore an oath of purgation, and eleven compurgators swore to its veracity.

156. Inger 1980, 112–19; for a longer and more detailed treatment, see Pihlajamäki 1997, Appeal, 15; see also Letto-Vanamo 1995.

157. Anderson 1974; Nilsson 1990; Ylikangas 1991.

158. Ylikangas 1976a, 112–15.

159. "Kunde the tolft i Nempden icke frije hans liiff wtan bleff fällt att stå then rät som han förtientt haffer." Ylikangas 1976a, 113. The severity of the sentence may have been

influenced by the fact that relations were bad between the farmers and the soldiers, who levied large amounts in taxation (the so-called quartering tax) directly from them. The deputy district judges usually took the side of the soldiers because they themselves were obliged to furnish cavalry soldiers for the army, and they levied the same taxes on the populace for them. For a further discussion, see Ylikangas 1997, 39f.

160. Ylikangas 1976a, 113–15.

161. Hasselberg 1957, 524.

162. KA 1205:119v.

163. "Kunde the tålft i Nemnden icke frije hans liiff wtan bleff fällt att stå then rät som han förtientt hafer." KA 217:55v–57v.

164. Cf. KA 1920:89v, 92v.

165. KA 4764:101v.

166. KA 1475:48v.

167. Cf. KA 4786:65, 67.

168. For a further discussion, see Ylikangas 1997.

169. KA, Masku I KO a 2, 86v.

170. KA, Piikkiö I KO a 1, Halikko 16 October 1623, 58v.

171. The Homicide Collection, Department of History, Helsinki University.

172. The cases are contained in two books of judgments in the Finnish National Archives (formerly the Finnish State Archives, abbr. KA), sign. Masku I KO a 1 (1620–29) and Masku I KO a 2 (1630–36).

173. KA, Masku I KO a 1, District Court sessions of parishes in the judicial district of Masku: Rymättylä 15 February 1628; Masku I KO a 2, Maaria 31 January 1634; Mynämäki 10 September 1636 (folio numbers are missing).

174. The district court records can be found in the series Piikkiö I KO a 1 in the National Archives.

175. KA, the Masku parish register for 1634 (mf ES 637).

176. Aalto 1996, 44.

177. "Madz Sigfredsson i Laitula till Madz Ryttare wthi Pöyttis s. om dråp." Since similar brief statements in the document have been later underlined, they were probably only intended to be reference notes. KA, Piikkiö I, KO a 1, Paimio 29 March 1625, 47.

178. Ylikangas 1996, 41–53.

179. Translator's note: The office of "nimismies" was approximately that of the American sheriff.

180. See KA, Piikiö I KO a 1, reminders of the court of appeal 1627, Province of Muurla 3 June 1626, 3v.

181. KA, Masku I KO a 1, Masku District Court sessions: Rymättylä 15 February 1628; KO a 2, Maaria 31 January 1634; Mynämäki 10 September 1636 (folio numbers are missing).

182. KA, Masku I KO a 2, Masku District Court sessions: Maaria 31 January 1634, Rymättylä 21 March 1635, Nousiainen 10 June 1635 (three cases), Mynämäki 10 September 1636 (folio numbers are missing).

183. Österberg 1991a, 73.

184. Henkirikokset KA, Etelä-Pohjanmaa KO a 1, Lapua 12–15 March 1683 and Isokyrö 15 May 1684, 138–39, 279–86.

185. KA, Masku I KO a 2, 86.

186. KA, Masku I KO a 1, 4v.

187. KA, Masku I KO a 2, Mynämäki 9 February 1631, 33.

188. See KA, Piikkiö I KO a 1, reminders of the court of appeal 1627, 1–2, 3v.
189. KA, Piikkiö I KO a 1, Muurlan lääni 6 February 1626, 11v–12v.
190. See, e.g., KA, Masku I KO a 2, Mynämäki 30 June 1634, 142v–143v.
191. KA, Masku I KO a 1, Rymättylä 25 April 1625, 136–37.
192. KA, Masku I KO a 1, 154–55, 255, 278v.
193. KA, Masku I KO a 1, 254v–55.
194. KA, Masku I KO a 1, 4v.
195. It remains extremely unclear just why Matti Jaakonpoika did not deliver the fourth blow with the ax if nobody prevented him from doing so. It seems that the description of the incident is to a great extent fictional, its purpose being only to persuade the court to accept the settlement.
196. The original record reads, "Wardt således aff slechten bewilljadt och samtychtt, att offtabe:the Madz Ollssonn skall fhara sin koos ifrån dens osijnn, dett och han dömdis effterkomma epther 12 cap: dråpmåla mz wilia, in till des han kan biudha vara för sigh, och komma epther förlikning med dem." KA, Masku I KO a 1, 47–47v.
197. "Derhoss blef och den s: mans hustro Karin aluarligen tilfrågatt, att om hon skulle hafua welatt gifua sigh vdi någon förlijkningh med droparen eller hans slechtt eller tagett der någre böther före." KA, Piikkiö I KO a 1, Kemiö 1624, 10v–11v.
198. KA, Masku I KO a 2, Merimasku and Naantali 19 July 1631, 41–41v.
199. Hasselberg 1957, 520.
200. The Homicide Collection, Department of History, Helsinki University.
201. In 1821, a farmer from Vörå, Mårten Svens, offered money to the parents of a farmhand whom he had killed so that they would not prosecute him. The parents refused, and proceedings were initiated. Sometimes a settlement was reached even in cases of clear homicide; the actual deed and the settlement were both kept secret from the authorities, or they were silenced with bribes (Ylikangas 1976b, 209–10). In 1810 in Kauhava, a casual laborer of ill repute named Tuomas Flink was killed in a public gathering, but the judicial inquiry into the deed only began three and a half years later. It turned out that the local people—the sheriff, the minister, and even the provincial medical officer—all conspired to hush the matter up. They were successful until the victim's brother reported the deed. He said that he had not taken the matter to court earlier for "lack of evidence." In actual fact, it seems that the sum agreed in the settlement had not been paid in full. Ylikangas 1976b, 245–47.
202. Ylikangas 1988, 15ff.
203. KA, Masku I KO a 1, Korppoo 11 etc. August 1623, 58v.
204. Cf. KA, Masku I KO a 2, Maaria 7 June 1631, 36v–37.
205. KA, Masku I KO a 2, Rymättylä 24 February 1633, 86.
206. KA, Masku I KO a 2, Mynämäki 4 April 1636, 220v.
207. KA, Masku I a 2, Mynämäki 30 June 1634, 142v–43v.
208. Cf. KA, Masku I KO a 2, Mynämäki 4 April 1636, 220v.
209. KA, Masku I KO a 1, 36.
210. KA, Masku I KO a 1, 18v.
211. KA, Masku I KO a 1, 76–76v.
212. KA, Masku I KO a 1, 115–115v.
213. KA, Masku I KO a 1, 172–172v.
214. KA, Masku I KO a 1, 173–173v.
215. KA, Masku I KO a 2, Maaria 7 June 1631, 41.
216. KA, Masku I KO a 2, Pöytyä 27–28 February 1634, 109v.

217. KA, Masku I KO a 2, Mynämäki 11 October 1631, 42–42v.

218. KA, Masku I KO a 2, Korppoo 14 February 1632, 48v.

219. The relevant part of the record reads as follows: "Men denne aldrig welat comparera eij heller nu vthan begeret af Michell Sangar i Mäckers att swara för honom, kenner sig skyldig och gifuer sig vnder lagen." KA, Masku I KO a 2, Pöytyä 25 October 1634, 147v.

220. KA, Masku I KO a 2, Pöytyä 27–28 February 1634, 109–109v.

221. Cf. KA, Masku I KO a 1, Rymättylä 15 February 1628, 257–58.

222. KA, Masku I KO a 2, Maaria 31 January 1634, 114–114v. This was a case of "single adultery" (only one of the fornicators was married) and infanticide. A death sentence could be given even when the man was unmarried and the deed did not lead to infanticide. The original record describing the stand of the panel reads: "And therefore none of the twelve in the panel was for such a grievous deed able to save their lives" (*och fördenskull nu ingen af dhe 12 i nemnpden war för sådan grof gerningh deras liijff frija kunde*). Cf. KA, Masku I KO a 2, Pöytyä 27–28 February 1634, 109v.

223. To judge from the large number of sections in Latin, the cleric seems to have practically written the records himself. The following expressions also point in the same direction: "Judgment belongs with God" who "will not let himself be blasphemed against." Several parts of the text, apparently written by the deputy district judge, have been struck out. Masku I KO a 1, 57v–58v.

224. Aalto 1996, 162–63.

225. KA, Masku I KO a 2, Nousiainen 10 June 1635, 171.

226. KA, Masku I KO a 2, Nousiainen 2 April 1636, 215.

227. KA, Masku I KO a 2, Raisio ja Maaria 4 December 1634, 160.

228. Ylikangas 1996, 80ff.

229. KA, Masku I KO a 2, Rymättylä 28 March 1636, 210v–211.

230. KA, Masku I KO a 1, Masku 6 February 1627, 218v–219; Nousiainen 22 September 1628, 27v–273.

231. KA, Masku I KO a 2, Maaria 7 June 1631, 36v–37.

232. The entry in the court records reads as follows: "Hustrun be: the Elin sthår på sijn rätt, och begärer hännes rätt wederfaras måtte och will inga lunda effter gifuett." KA, Masku I KO a 2, Maaria 9 February 1632, 44v–45.

233. Cf. Ylikangas 1997.

234. Cf. KA, Masku I KO a 2, Nousiainen 16 June 1636 and 14 September 1636, 224, 241v–242.

235. Österberg 1991c, 152; Larsson 1982, 20, 55; Kekkonen and Ylikangas 1983, 159–78.

236. Huhtamies 1997, 3ff.

237. The original record reads as follows: "Bärtill Tomasson i Kaijrtarwijs kierde till sijn Rottelagh att de icke wella wara honom behieleligh, att leija knechtet. Och han doch lijkwäll nyss tillförendhe och leigdhe knechtet: Opå dett att hemmanet som Bärttill på boor, måå bliffua behållit, och Cronan få sijn wttlaghur. Effter Bärttill är ellena manhiälp, och nyss tillförende leijgdt haffuer, så de 12 i nämpden wijttnadhe och affsagdhe, att heella Rottalaghitt skolla samptelighen leija en knichtet, så fåår konunghen bådhe knechthen och wttlaghurenn aff Bärttill. Men taghes Bärttill wtt, så bliffer hans hemman ödhe och konunghen mister wttlaghurerne." KA, Masku I KO a 1, 118.

238. Cf. KA, Masku I KO a 1, Korppoo 1 August 1627, 231ff.

239. KA, Masku I KO a 2, 160.

240. The original reads: "Be: the Margreta hans egen hustro beder för honom. Emedan nu denne gerningh, är i sigh uppenbar, och be:the Simon Madzon befinnes sigh emott Gudz och wärdzligh lagh grofweligen föreseedt hafua, trädt ifrån sin ächta sängh och inlåtit sigh mz denne Philippa Hinrichzdåtter den och sin ächta man hade, dett han wäll wiste, och i så måtto misshandlatt och illa emott sigh och sitt ächtenskap giordt hafuer, och fördenskuldh nu ingen af dhe 12 i nempden hans lijff frija kunde. Ty nu han efter-5 kap:tt i högmåla dömdt ifrån lijffuedt." KA, Masku I KO a 2, 165.

241. Cf. KA, Masku I KO a 2, 19 February 1635, 162. Three Crown trappers were condemned to death for assaulting and stealing the gun and hat of a man who was tracking them.

242. Stevnsborg 1984, 211–12.

243. Cf. KA, Masku I KO a 1, Nousiainen 3 February 1621, Pöytyä 5 February 1621, 31–31v, 32–32v.

244. KA, Masku I KO a 1, Korppoo 1 August 1627, 231–32.

245. Cf. statements by soldiers and servants: Uusikirkko District Court summer sessions 10 July 1561, KA 921:8v–9; Ostrobothnia, Pietarsaari District Court winter sessions 20 February 1567, KA 4696:10; KA, Masku I KO a 1, Nousiainen 3 February 1621, 31–31v; Rymättylä 4 April 1628, 265v–266; Masku I KO a 2, Mynämäki 9 February 1631, 33; Nousiainen 16 June 1636, 224; Piikkiö I KO a 1, Muurla Province 9 June 1626, 19–20v.

246. For early landownership, see Korpijaakko 1986, 28ff.

247. KA, Piikkiö I KO a 1, Halikko 16 October 1623, fol. 57v.

248. KA, Masku I KO a 1, 218v–219, 272v–273.

249. Jutikkala 1963, 19ff.; Soininen 1974.

250. KA, Piikkiö I KO a 1, Muurlan lääni 1624 (no date), 8v–8.

251. See, e.g., KA, Masku I KO a 1, Raisio ja Maaria 13 November 1620, 23v; Pöytyä 2 May 1625, 141v.

252. KA, Masku I KO a 1, 32–32v.

253. KA, Masku I KO a 1, 136–137.

254. See, e.g., KA, Masku I KO a 1, Pöytyä 9 December 1624, 106v–107. See further, Jutikkala 1963, 110–30.

255. KA, Masku I KO a 1, 172–172v.

256. KA, Masku I KO a 2, Mynämäki 30 June 1634 and 4 April 1636, 142v–143v, 221.

257. KA, Masku I KO a 2, Nousiainen 16 June 1636, 224.

258. KA, Masku I KO a 1, 267v ff.

259. KA, Masku I KO a 2, Nousiainen 7 February 1631, 29v–30.

260. Cf. KA, Masku I KO a 1, Rymättylä 4 April 1628, 265–66.

261. KA, Masku I KO a 2, 220v.

262. KA, Masku I KO a 1, 36.

263. KA, Masku I KO a 2, Mynämäki 4 April 1636, 220v.

264. KA, Masku I KO a 2, Mynämäki 30 June 1634, 142v–143v.

265. KA, Masku I KO a 2, Mynämäki 30 June 1634, 142v–143v.

266. See Ylikangas 1971, 155.

267. For a further discussion, see Ylikangas 1971, 161–88. The lawmaker had attempted to reduce the range of punishable verbal insults from the provincial law upwards.

268. E.g., KA, Masku I KO a 2, Maaria 5 November 1632, 72.

269. Ylikangas 1971, 167.

270. Translator's note: This refers to an agreement to address each other in a familiar way using the second person singular form, which the cantor had used when speaking to the burgher.

271. Ylikangas 1973, 221.

272. Ylikangas 1973, 218.

273. Ylikangas 1973, 134.

274. Ylikangas 1971, 182–83.

275. Cf. Alifrosti 1990, 302.

276. Schmedeman 1706, 325ff., 764ff.

277. For a further discussion, see Kekkonen and Ylikangas 1982; Kekkonen and Ylikangas 1983, 159–78. Cf. Aho 1981, 235–37; Petrovitch 1971, 232; Rusche and Kirscheimer 1939, 197ff.

278. Tamm 1989, 83.

279. Ylikangas 1993.

280. Cf. Lindström and Simonsson 1993, 101–6; Furuhagen 1996, 21–22; Österberg and Lindström 1988, 55, 63–64; Sundin 1992, 448.

281. Ylikangas 1985.

282. Ylikangas 1974, 261–64.

283. Ylikangas 1997.

284. Pohjolan-Pirhonen 1960, 546–52; Luukko 1967, 45, 47ff.; Ylikangas 1973, 190.

285. For example, Schmidt 1951, 63ff.

286. Næss 1990, 23ff.

287. Hair 1971, 17; Radzinowicz 1948, 142, 152, 155; Kekkonen and Ylikangas 1982, 19.

Sources

Archive Sources

Kansallisarkisto (KA) (Finnish National Archives)
  Tuomiokuntien arkisto (Judicial District Archives)
    Court records
  Bailiffs' accounts
  Account books
  Court records

Published Sources

Court records of Ala-Satakunta, 1550–52. Edited by John E. Roos. *Suomen vanhimmat tuomiokirjat II* (*SVT II*). Helsinki, 1964.

Court records of Savo 1559 and 1561–65. *Suomen vanhimmat tuomiokirjat I* (*SVT I*). Edited by Kauko Pirinen. Helsinki, 1954.

Court records of Southwest Tavastland, 1506–10. *Bidrag till Finlands historia I.* Edited by Reinhold Hausen. 1881–83.

Kuningas Kristoferin maanlaki 1442. Muinaisruotsista suomentanut Martti Ulkuniemi. Suomalaisen Kirjallisuuden Seuran toimituksia 340. Vaasa, 1978.

Magnus Erikssons lanslag (I nusvensk tolkning av Åke Holmbäck och Elias Wessen). Skrifter utgivna av Institutet för rättshistorisk forskning. Serien I. Rättshistoriskt bibliotek. Vol. 6. Lund, 1962.

Schlyter, D. C. J., ed. 1862–69. Samling Af Sweriges Gamla Lagar (Konung Magnus Erikssons Landslag, Konung Magnus Erikssons Stadslag, Konung Christoffers Landslag). Vols. 10–12. Lund.

Schmedeman, Joh. 1706. Justitie Werket. *Kongl. Stadgar, Resolutioner och Förordningar angående Justitien ifrån åhr 1528.* Stockholm.

Svenska landkapslagar tolkade och förklarade för nutidens svenskar. Edited by Åke Holmbäck and Elias Wessén. I–V. Uppsala, 1933.

WHO Annual Health Statistics. 1986–95. Geneva.

References

Unpublished Works

Koskelainen, Liisa. 1995. "Vankeus oikeusjärjestelmän osana: Hämeen linnan vangit 1726–1776." Master's thesis in Finnish and Scandinavian history, Department of History, Helsinki University.

Koskivirta, Anu. 1996. "Omankädenoikeutta itärajalla. Kymenkartanon ja Savon läänin henkirikollisuus 1748–1774." Master's thesis in Finnish and Scandinavian history, Department of History, Helsinki University.

Published Works

Aalto, Seppo. 1996. *Kirkko ja Kruunu siveellisyyden vartijoina. Seksuaalirikollisuus, esivalta ja yhteisö Porvoon kihlakunnassa 1621–1700.* Biblioteca Historica XXII. Helsinki. With English summary.

Aho, Timo. 1981. "Vankiluvun kehitykseen vuosina 1881–1978 vaikuttaneista tekijöistä." In *Suomen vankeinhoidon historia I.* Helsinki.

Alifrosti, Kari. 1990. *Sauvon historia I.* Salo.

Anderson, Perry. 1974. *Lineages of the Absolutist State.* London.

Beattie, J. M. 1986. *Crime and the Courts in England, 1660–1800.* New York.

Blomstedt, Kaarlo. 1937. *Davidin kapina v. 1438.* HArk. Helsinki.

Blomstedt, Yrjö. 1960. *Hallinto ja oikeuslaitos, osallistuminen valtiopäiviin.* Hämeen historia II:2. Hämeenlinna.

Castan, Yves. 1989. "Politics and Private Life." In *History of Private Life,* pt. 3: *Passions of the Renaissance,* ed. Roder Chartier. Cambridge, Mass.

Cockburn, J. C., ed. 1977. *Crime in England, 1550–1800.* London and Cambridge.

Cohen, David, and Eric A. Johnson. 1982. "French Criminality: Urban-Rural Differences in the Nineteenth Century." *Journal of Interdisciplinary History* 12 (Winter).

Eisner, Manuel. 1998. "Modernization, Self-Control and Violence: The Long-Term Dynamics of European Homicide Rates in Theoretical Perspective." Paper presented at the Second European Social Science History Conference, Amsterdam, 5–7 March.

Elias, Norbert. 1994. *The Civilizing Process.* Vol. 1: *The History of Manners;* vol. 2: *State Formation and Civilization.* 1939. Oxford.

Foucault, Michel. 1980. *Tarkkailla ja rangaista.* Keuruu. Translation of *Surveiller et punir: Naissance de la prison.* Paris, 1975.

Franke, Herman. 1994. "Violent Crime in the Netherlands: A Historical-Sociological Analysis." *Crime, Law, and Social Change* 21.

Furuhagen, Björn. 1996. *Berusade bönder och bråkiga båtsmän. Social kontroll vid sockenstämmor och ting under 1700-talet.* Stockholm/Stenhagen.

Garland, David. 1991. "The Rationalization of Punishment." In *Theaters of Power: Social Control and Criminality in Historical Perspective,* ed. Heikki Pihlajamäki. Publications of the Matthias Calonius Society 1. Jyväskylä.

Gurr, Ted Robert. 1981/1992. "Historical Trends in Violent Crime: A Critical Review of the Evidence." *Crime and Justice: An Annual Review of Research* 3. Reprinted in *Violence and Theft,* ed. Eric H. Monkkonen. Crime and Justice in American History 9, part 2. Munich and New York.

Hair, P. E. H. 1971. "Deaths from Violence in Britain: A Tentative Secular Survey." *Population Studies: A Journal of Demography* 1.

Handwörterbuch zur deutschen Rechtsgeschichte I. 1971. Edited by Adalbert Erler und Ekkehart Kauffmann, with Ruth Schmidt-Wiegard. Berlin.

Hasselberg, Gösta. 1957. "Böter." In *Kulturhistoriskt lexikon för nordisk medeltid II.* Helsingfors.

Huhtamies, Mikko. 1997. "Ersättare och ödesmål. Utskrivningar i Eura och Kumo under trettioåriga kriget." *Historisk tidskrift för Finland* 1.

Inger, Göran. 1980. *Svensk rättshistoria.* Lund.

Jarrick, Arne, and Johan Söderberg, eds. 1994. *Människovärdet och makten. Om civiliseringsprocessen i Stockholm 1600–1850.* Uppsala.

Johnson, Eric A. 1995. *Urbanization and Crime: Germany, 1871–1914.* London.

Jutikkala, Eino. 1963. *Bonden i Finland genom tiderna.* Helsingfors.

Karonen, Petri. 1996. "Pohjolan vaarallisimmat asuinpaikat. Rikollisuus, pelko ja turvattomuus Suomen uuden ajan alun kaupungeissa (noin 1540–1660)." In *Laittomuuden laitatiellä. Rikos Suomessa 1500-luvulta nykypäiviin,* ed. Sari Forsström. Helsingin yliopiston historian laitoksen julkaisuja 1/1996. Helsinki.

Kekkonen, Jukka, and Heikki Ylikangas. 1982. *Vapausrangaistuksen valtakausi. Nykyisen seuraamusjärjestelmän historiallinen tausta.* Helsinki University, Department of Criminal Law, Judicial Procedure and General Jurisprudential Studies.

———. 1983. "Frihetsstraffets genombrott samt regionala och tidsmässiga variationer i bruket av frihetsstraff." *Nordisk tidskrift for kriminal-videnskab.*

Korpijaakko, Kaisa. 1986. "Maanomistuksen kehityksestä ruotsalaissuomalaisen oikeusjärjestyksen mukaan." In *Oikeudellisen sääntelyn kehityslinjoja,* ed. Jukka Kekkonen, Kaisa Korpijaakko, and Heikki Ylikangas. Juva.

Larsson, L.-O. 1982. *Småländsk historia: Stormaktstiden.* Malmö.

Lehti, Martti. 1997. "Homicide Trends in Estonia between 1971 and 1996." In the present work.

Lenman, Bruce, and Geoffrey Parker. 1980. "The State, the Community, and the Criminal Law in Early Modern Europe." In *Crime and the Law: The Social History of Crime in Western Europe since 1500,* ed. V. A. C. Gatrell, Bruce Lenman, and Geoffrey Parker. London.

Letto-Vanamo, Pia. 1995. *Käräjäyhteisön oikeus. Oikeudenkäyttö Ruotsi-Suomessa ennen valtiollisen riidanratkaisun vakiintumista.* Oikeushistorian julkaisuja 2. Helsinki University, Department of Criminal Law, Judicial Procedure and General Jurisprudential Studies.

Lindström, Dag. 1988. *Våld, förtal och förlikningar i Stockholm 1475–1625.* Rättshistoriska studier. Vol. 14. Skrifter utgivna av Institutet för rättshistorisk forskning, grundat av Gustav och Carin Olin. Serien II. Lund.

Lindström, Dag, and Örjan Simonsson. 1993. "Fru Justitia i statlig tjänst?" In *Makt och vardag. Hur man styrde, levde och tänkte under stormaktstiden 15,* ed. Stellan Dahlgren, Anders Florin, and Åsa Carlsson. Stockholm.

Luukko, Armas. 1967. *Suomen historia 1617–1721*. Porvoo.

Matikainen, Olli. 1996. "Miksi näkisimme vaivaa vanhan miehen veren takia? Näkökulmia arkipäivän väkivaltaan 1600-luvun Karjalassa." In *Laittomuuden laitatiellä. Rikos Suomessa 1500-luvulta nykypäiviin*, ed. Sari Forsström. Helsingin yliopiston historian laitoksen julkaisuja 1/1996. Helsinki.

Mechler, Achim. 1970. *Studien zur Geschichte der Kriminal-Soziologie*. Kriminologische Studien 5/1970. Göttingen.

Næss, Hans Eyvind. 1982. *Trolldomsprosessene i Norge på 1500–1600-tallet*. Oslo.

———. 1990. "Forbrytelse og straff." In *Tingboka som kilde*, ed. Liv Marthinsen. Oslo.

———. 1994. "Vold." In *Normer og sosial kontroll i Norden ca. 1550–1850. Domstolene i samspill med lokalsamfunnet*. Det 22. nordiske historikermöte. Oslo 13.–18. Rapport II.

Nilsson, Sven A. 1990. *De stora krigens tid. Om Sverige som militärstat och bondesamhälle*. Acta Universitatis Upsaliensis. Studia Historica Uppsaliensia 161. Uppsala.

Österberg, Eva. 1983. "Våld och våldsmentalitet bland bönderna. Jämförande perspektiv på 1500–och 1600-talets Sverige." *Scandia* 49.

———. 1991a. "Kontroll och kriminalitet i Sverige från medeltid till nutid. Tenderser och tolkningar." *Scandia* 57.

———. 1991b. "Social Arena or Theater of Power: The Courts, Crime, and Early Modern State in Sweden." In *Theaters of Power: Social Control and Criminality in Historical Perspective*, ed. Heikki Pihlajamäki. Jyväskylä.

———. 1991c. "Brott och social kontroll i Sverige från medeltid till stormaktstid. Godtycke och grymhet eller sunt förnuft och statskontroll?" *Historisk tidsskrift* (Norway) 2.

———. 1994. "Normbrott och rättspraxis i Norden under förindustriell tid. Problem och positioner." In *Normer og sosial kontroll i Norden ca. 1550–1850. Domstolene i samspill med lokalsamfunnet*. Det 22. nordiske historikermöte. Oslo 13.–18. Rapport II.

Österberg, Eva, and Dag Lindström. 1988. *Crime and Social Control in Medieval and Early Modern Swedish Towns*. Acta Universitatis Upsaliensis. Studica Historia Upsaliensia 152. Lund.

Perrot, Michelle. 1975. "Déliquance et système pénitentiaire en France en XIXe siècle." *Annales ESC* 1.

Petrovitch, Porphyre. 1971. "Recherches sur la criminalité à Paris dans la seconde moitié du XVIIIe siècle." *Cahiers des Annales* 33.

Pihlajamäki, Heikki. 1997. *Evidence, Crime, and the Legal Profession*. Rättshistoriskt bibliotek. Vol. 54. Lund.

Pirinen, Kauko. 1957. "Böter." In *Kulturhistoriskt lexikon för nordisk medeltid II*. Helsingfors.

———. 1982. "Rajamaakunta asutusliikkeen aikakautena." In *Savon historia* 2:1. Pieksämäki.

Pohjolan-Pirhonen, Helge. 1960. *Suomen historia 1523–1617*. Suomen historia 7. Porvoo.

Radzinowicz, Leon. 1948. *A History of English Criminal Law and Its Administration from 1750*, vol. 1: *The Movement for Reform*. London.

Rakkolainen, Mari. 1996. "Agraariajan rikollisuus ja rikollisuuden selitysmallit Euroopassa." In *Laittomuuden laitatiellä. Rikos Suomessa 1500-luvulta nykypäiviin*, ed. Sari Forsström. Helsingin yliopiston historian laitoksen julkaisuja 1/1996. Helsinki.

Renvall, Pentti. 1949a. *Suomalainen 1500-luvun ihminen oikeuskatsomustensa valossa*. Turun yliopiston julkaisuja, sarja B, osa 33. Turku.

———. 1949b. *Varsinais-Suomen historia*, 5:1. Turku.

Rousseaux, Xavier. 1992. "Existe-t-il une criminalité d'Ancien Régime? Réflexions sur l'histoire de la criminalité en Europe (XIVe–XVIIIe siècles)." In *Histoire et criminalité de l'Antiquité au XXe siècle: Nouvelles approches*, ed. Benoit Garnot. Publications de l'Université de Bourgogne 71, Série du Centre d'études historiques 1. Dijon.

———. 1996. "From Medieval Cities to National States, 1350–1850: The Historiography of Crime and Criminal Justice in Europe." In *Crime History and Histories of Crime: Studies in the Historiography of Crime and Criminal Justice in Modern History*, ed. Clive Emsley and Louis A. Knafla. Contributions in Criminology and Penology, no. 48. Westport, Conn.

Rusche, Georg, and Otto Kirscheimer. 1939. *Punishment and Social Structure*. New York.

Sandnes, Jörn. 1990. *Kniven, ølet og æren. Kriminalitet og samfunn i Norge på 1500- og 1600-tallet*. Oslo.

Schmidt, Eberhard. 1951. *Einfürhrung in die deutsche Strafrechtspflege*. Stuttgart.

Schüssler, Martin. 1988. "Vergleich von Theorien der historischen Kriminologie zum Verbrechensanstig un zum hohen Niveau der Verbrechensrate im England des 13. und 14. Jahrhunderts." *Monatsschrift für Kriminologie und Strafrechtsreform* 4.

Sharpe, J. A. 1977. "Crime and Delinquency in an Essex Parish, 1600–1640." In *Crime in England, 1550–1800*, ed. J. C. Cockburn. London.

———. 1984. *Crime in Early Modern England, 1550–1750*. Singapore.

Soininen, Arvo M. 1974. *Vanhamaataloutemme*. Historiallisia tutkimuksia 96, pub. Suomen Historiallinen Seura. Helsinki.

Spierenburg, Pieter. 1994. "Faces of Violence: Homicide Trends and Cultural Meanings: Amsterdam, 1431–1816." *Journal of Social History* (Summer).

Stevnsborg, Henrik. 1984. "'Tak Gud min Sön, at du ikke kom för Riberett.' Retspleje i Ribe, 1590–1594." In *Tradition og kritik. Festskrift till Svend Ellehøj den 8. September*. Copenhagen.

Stone, Lawrence. 1983. "Interpersonal Violence in English Society 1300–1980." *Past & Present* 101.

Sundin, Jan. 1992. *För Gud, staten och folket. Brott och rättskipning i Sverige 1600–1840*. Rättshistoriskt bibliotek. Vol. 47. Lund.

Söderberg, Johan. 1990. "En fråga om civilisering. Brottmål och tvister i svenska häradsrätten 1540–1660." *Historisk tidskrift* (Sweden) 2.

———. 1993. *Civilisering, Marknad och våld i Sverige 1750–1870. En regional analys*. Stockholm.

Tamm, Ditlev. 1989. *Laerebog i Dansk retshistorie. Forelobig udgave*. Denmark.

Taussi Sjöberg, Marja. 1981. *Brott och straff i Västernorrland 1861–1890*. Kungälv.

Verkko, Veli. 1931. *Henki -ja pahoinpitelyrikollisuuden kehityssuunnan ja tason määrittämisestä*. Tilastollis-metodologinen tutkimus. II. Muut maat. Helsinki.

———. 1949. *Lähimmäisen ja oma henki. Sosiaalipatologisia tutkimuksia Suomen kansasta*. Suomalaisen lakimiesyhdistyksen julkaisuja, B-sarja nro 33. Jyväskylä.

Voionmaa, Väinö. 1916. *Keskiajan kansankapinat Suomessa*. HAik. Helsinki.

von Hentig, Hans. 1962. "Kriminalstatistische Daten aus früheren Jahrhunderten." *Schweitzerische Zeitschrift für Strafrecht 1957*.

Ylikangas, Heikki. 1971. *Väkivaltarikosten motivaatiopohja 1500-luvulla Suomessa*. HArk 65. Helsinki.

———. 1973. "Lohjalaisten historia Ruotsin vallan vuosisatoina." In Heikki Ylikangas and Ari Siiriäinen, *Lohjalaisten historia I*. Helsinki.

———. 1974. *Härmän häjyt ja Kauhavan herra. Kuvaus puukkojunkkareitten ja virkavallan välisestä yhteenotosta 1860-luvulla*. Keuruu.

———. 1976a. "Henkirikos keskiajan lopun ja uuden ajan alun Suomessa." *Jurisprudentia.*
———. 1976b. *Puukkojunkkareiden esiinmarssi. Väkivaltarikollisuus Etelä-Pohjanmaalla 1790–1825.* Keuruu.
———. 1976c. "Major Fluctuations in Crimes of Violence in Finland: A Historical Analysis." *Scandinavian Journal of History.*
———. 1983. *Varför förändras rätten. Lag och rätt såsom en del av den historiska utvecklingen.* Juva.
———. 1984. *Murtuva säätyvalta.* Porvoo.
———. 1985. *Knivjunkarna. Våldskriminaliteten i Sydösterbotten 1790–1825.* Borgå. Published in English as *The Knife Fighters: Violent Crime in Southern Ostrobothnia, 1790–1825.* Academia Scientiarum Fennica. Jyväskylä, 1998.
———. 1987. "Rikollisuus Etelä-Pohjanmaalla autonomian aikana." In *Etelä-Pohjanmaan historia VI.* Vaasa.
———. 1988. *Valta ja väkivalta keski- ja uuden ajan taitteen Suomessa.* Juva.
———. 1991. "The Historical Connections of European Peasant Revolts." *Scandinavian Journal of History* 16.
———. 1993. "Ylimmän tuomiovallan kehitys." (Juhlaesitelmä Korkeimman oikeuden 5-vuotisjuhlissa, 1 October 1993). *Lakimies.*
———. 1996. *Wallesmanni. Kuusi vuosisataa kansan ja esivallan.* Jyväskylä.
———. 1997. *Nuijasota.* 4th ed. Keuruu.

Other literature

The Homicide Collection. Department of History, Helsinki University. Copies of excerpts relating to historical criminology from local annals and other comparable sources.

CHAPTER 2

A Life for a Life versus Christian Reconciliation

Violence and the Process of Civilization in the Kingdom of Sweden, 1540–1700

PETRI KARONEN

Translated by Gerard McAlester

Violence as a Research Problem

THE STATE PROSECUTOR, HANS FÄLLERMAN, ARRIVED AT the Stockholm Town Court in October 1584 with a sad duty to perform: he was to accuse one Anders Bengtsson of grievous crimes. According to the charges, Anders had perpetrated violence against "the law and justice and the subjects of His Royal Majesty."[1] In addition to other acts of wickedness and violence, he had killed his own son. The city recorder noted that Anders was "an unchristian man and a tyrant" who had "murderously beaten his son to death." A witness in the case testified to having seen him carry out this savage assault and stated that he had called on Anders a score of times to stop beating his child. After the father's mishandling, the boy was said to be "so weak and battered that both his head and his body sagged limply." The town court stated in its grounds that the normal penalty prescribed by the law of Sweden under the Accidental Manslaughter Code for parents who chastised their children too harshly was a fine.[2] However, in this case, it was not a question of an accident. Anders's action is described as "tyrannical and inhuman." He had not chastised his son for his betterment; rather, he had acted "like an executioner, in an unchristian way that was contrary to natural love." The town court found that the deed could not be atoned for with a fine, and so it sentenced Anders Bengtsson to execution by the wheel.[3]

In all its gruesomeness, the case is nevertheless an interesting one, and it exemplifies numerous important aspects of violent crime in the Kingdom of Sweden at the beginning of the modern age. First, the rhetoric employed in the case expresses the deep repugnance of the court and the court public for the father's cruel act. Second, the state's role in handling the case is clearly revealed: the criminal action was brought by the state prosecutor, because in this case the plaintiffs, that is, the family of the deceased, were also the family of the accused. The Crown, too, made its voice heard in the proceedings: Anders's deed was a crime against the whole state, not just against this particular community or the child in question and his kin. Religion and arguments based on it were also very much to the fore. The condemnation of the city community in general and its individual members (the witnesses) for the seemingly irrational deed of Anders leaves no room for doubt. Finally, the harsh sentence to a painful death demonstrates the attitude of the community: this man deserved to die.

In the sixteenth and seventeenth centuries, Sweden represented an exceptional state in Europe, for unlike many other countries, the Crown maintained a strong hold over all parts of the realm. The modern state came into existence at a very early stage in Sweden. It was, indeed, one of the very first of the "great" powers of Europe in this respect. Sweden was also exceptional in terms of the social structure of its population: at the time, over 90 percent of the people lived in the countryside, and by international standards the position of the peasantry was excellent. Correspondingly, the significance of the towns was fairly low, and they did not constitute the same kind of counterbalance to the state that they did in many other countries in Europe. Sweden was also extremely homogeneous in terms of religion, being totally Lutheran.[4] This strong grip of the state authority and the homogeneity of religion make the study of violence, especially homicide, a particularly interesting subject for research.

Nearly all studies of violence at the beginning of the modern age point out that registered violence decreased considerably with the passage from the Middle Ages into the modern era. The rapid and steady decline in homicidal crime that began in the Nordic countries in the latter half of the seventeenth century has especially been noted.[5] However, there has been little research into any but the most serious violence. In the opinion of many scholars, "ordinary", "everyday," and "petty" violence is almost impossible to trace, at least in quantitative terms. Nor has it excited much interest in other respects. In discussing the hidden figures for this type of crime, it is usually pointed out that the majority of petty cases may not have come to the cognizance of the courts or may have been settled out of court.[6] Apart from homicide, the quantification of violence has been eschewed. Another area that has received little attention has been the *nature* of crimes of homicide: Were they spontaneous or planned?[7]

Even so, studies of the "perilous" Middle Ages have found that by no means all acts of violence were directly intended to take the life of a fellow man. Most violence was petty and fairly innocuous. All over Europe one comes across cases in which the violence seems to be spontaneous and brutal, but the view that the Middle Ages were exceptionally violent is probably wrong and is partly a consequence of the laconic records that constitute the sources. The same problem is familiar later as well: usually only facts directly relevant to the inquiry were entered into the judgment books and other lists of crimes. Undoubtedly, the recorders abridged those sections of the witnesses' statements that they judged to be irrelevant, which has the effect of making the killers' deeds seem more callous and spontaneous than they really were. One must also take into consideration the fact that people in those days had a different concept of time. For example, Swedish people in the seventeenth century had great difficulty in distinguishing and estimating short periods. This is something that scholars may have failed to appreciate when the source material contains a great deal of "trivial information."[8]

Historical criminology has been particularly criticized in recent years because its concentration purely on the records of crime distorts the findings. Research has concentrated primarily on studying "deviance," although crime is only one area of human activity. The quantitative approach has also come in for a considerable amount of criticism, even though the major focus of the scholars' interest has been on the *decrease* in homicidal crime. One alternative is the new perspective offered by microhistory, which has been partly influenced by anthropology. The study of systems of norms and values broadens the perspective and makes it more comprehensive.[9]

Several explanations for the decrease in violence have been put forward. Perhaps the best known, or at least the most frequently quoted, is Norbert Elias's theory of the civilizing process. The actual process of the decline in violence does not play a particularly significant role in the theory. According to Elias, some time between the Middle Ages and the eighteenth century a process of civilization began in the royal courts and the upper classes and then spread as the common people gradually adopted the refined manners of the elite.[10] Somewhat similar views have been advanced in the acculturation theory. Robert Muchembled proposes a combination of the Counter Reformation and the attempts of a strong monarchy to acculturate the common people, which involved the rise to positions of power of clergymen and jurists who "worked steadily towards the acculturation of the masses, by spreading fear." The "pedagogy of fear" practiced by the clergy and the judges had a central role in the process. Muchembled's view, like the original theory of Elias, has been the object of strong criticism.[11] Nevertheless, both theories are interesting and offer considerable food for thought; the background significance of the state, the church, and religion for the decline in violence can certainly not be ignored.[12] It may be that research has not yet sufficiently taken account of the practical importance of religion as a way of molding the ideas of the common people. On the other hand, its significance at the level of ethical norms (e.g., the Mosaic law) has long been recognized.[13]

Johan Söderberg and Arne Jarrick have proposed a new theory of what they describe as the spontaneous civilizing process in Sweden.[14] By spontaneity they specifically mean that the process took place without any actual intervention on the part of the state authority. People's self-control and communicative abilities improved. One essential feature—albeit certainly not the only one—of this process was a significant decrease in violence, which according to their findings began in Stockholm in the 1630s.[15] If, previously, the significance of "the will of the community" in the abatement of violence has been underestimated, in the interpretation of Söderberg and Jarrick it is the role of the state that has been ignored.

In what follows, we shall examine the role and attitudes of the state executive, the church, and religion in preventing and judging violence. The subject of the analysis is the nature of violence and how it may have changed over time.[16] Attention will be paid above all to interaction and possible conflicts between communities and the state and the church (which at the onset of the modern age in Sweden were to a great extent two sides of the same coin). At the same time, we shall take issue with the debate on the causes of the decrease in violence: Did the Swedish bourgeoisie become civilized? If so, from which direction ("above" or "below") did the process take place? We shall approach the subject by following the *longue durée* of violence in four cities, which have been selected from different parts of the Kingdom of Sweden: Stockholm, the capital; Arboga in the province of Svealand; Vadstena in Götaland; and Turku (Åbo)[17] in southwest Finland, which then belonged to Sweden.[18]

Around the year 1540, the position of the king of Sweden, Gustavus I Vasa (reigned 1523–60), as head of state was clear, and this provides a good starting point for this research. The endpoint of our study of the four cities under consideration is the year 1660, when a long series of wars in which Sweden had been engaged came to an end. The examination of the subject will be extended through source material offered by the records of the courts of appeal up to ap-

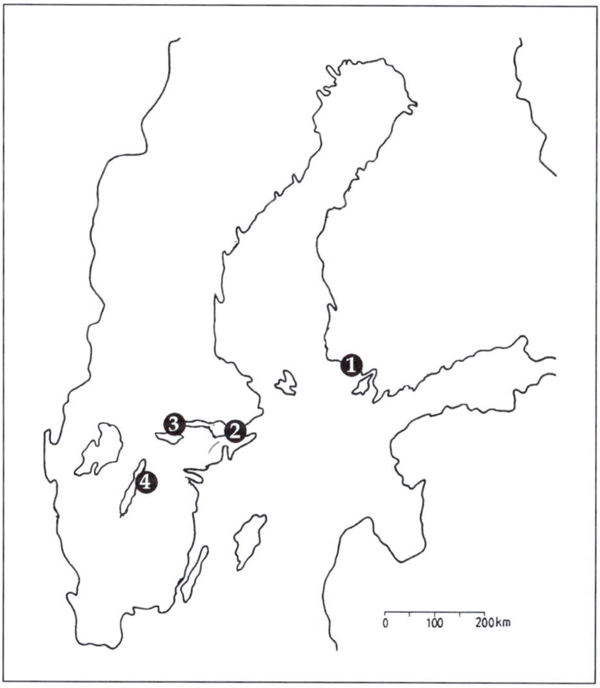

Map 2.1. Towns studied: 1. Turku (Åbo), 2. Stockholm, 3. Arboga, 4. Vadstena.

proximately 1700, when Sweden became embroiled in the prolonged Great Northern War, which ultimately led to its demise as a great power. The length of the period makes it possible to scrutinize the *longue durée* of violence, to investigate attitudes toward it, and to analyze any changes that may have taken place in the way it was perpetrated.

In a study of Swedish and Finnish cities, it is possible to avoid many common problems connected with sources and their comparison that emerge elsewhere.[19] The Town Law of King Magnus Eriksson was enforced throughout the kingdom, and this in itself led to a highly uniform system of justice. Furthermore, it should be remembered that the centralization of power in Sweden ensured a strict control of the courts of law. The court system was also an extremely simple one. The town court (*rådhusrätt*) took the most important cases, and the lower treasurer's court (*kämnersrätt*) handled petty crimes and settled disputes.[20]

The source materials for the cities are homogeneous. For Stockholm, Arboga, and Vadstena, court records called "notebooks" (*tänkeböcker*) from the sixteenth century contain exact records of crimes, disputes, and administrative matters.[21] The notebooks are almost as comprehensive as the most important revised judgment books of the period, which were kept according to approximately the same principles in all the cities. As far as the sixteenth century is concerned, the fine rolls are another important source. As their name implies, they contain information about cases that were punished by fines. Thus cases for which the death penalty or corporal punishment was imposed are not always to be found in this material. In the case of Turku in the sixteenth century, the only extant sources are the fine roles, and they are rather meager.[22]

The coverage of the source material improves even further from the second decade of the seventeenth century on, when courts of appeal were established in Sweden to supervise the lower courts. One of the most important functions of the Svea, Turku, and Göta Courts of Appeal was to scrutinize the records sent to them by the lower courts and to ensure that justice was properly administered in them. Another important function of the courts of appeal was to pass judgment in all the most serious cases, including homicides.[23]

In our examination of the general level of homicidal crime that follows, we shall use almost all the information surviving from the seventeenth century concerning judgments passed by the Svea and Göta Courts of Appeal. The sources for the Göta Court of Appeal contain not only the court's own judgments but also material collected during the judicial inquiry in the lower courts.[24] For the judgments of the Svea Court of Appeal, on the other hand, the information has been obtained from the copies of the judgments sent to the provincial administration, and it is thus less comprehensive. Even so, the material that is available indicates the kinds of homicidal crimes that were committed and the ways in which they were punished.[25]

Of the towns under investigation here, Stockholm was by far the largest. In the 1560s it boasted seven to eight thousand inhabitants, but a century later the number had increased to thirty-six thousand. Stockholm enjoyed the particular protection of the Crown, and considerable efforts were made to ensure its development. The other towns were ostensibly smaller. In the sixteenth century, Turku had a population of twenty-five to thirty-five hundred, and at its highest, at the end of the 1650s, it had over six thousand inhabitants. In the 1570s there were about a thousand inhabitants in Arboga, rising to a maximum of two thousand between 1610 and 1630. In 1660 the city boasted a population of about sixteen hundred. The slowest population growth is to be found in Vadstena.[26] The town had flourished in the Middle Ages and even in the early seventeenth century, for in the period 1523–1611 Vadstena had had a population of over one thousand, but by 1660 the number had fallen to about four hundred.[27]

The towns thus differ from each other. Stockholm was the most important from the economic and political point of view. Turku was the second largest city in the realm in terms of population, and in the seventeenth century it was an important "staple city" (one with foreign trading rights), and during the period under investigation it enjoyed a position of considerable economic stability. Arboga was a flourishing country town, which the central government strove to promote by strongly developing its administration. It had the advantage of being well placed as an intermediate stage between Stockholm and the world markets for the export of iron. Economically, the town was thriving halfway through the seventeenth century. Vadstena, on the other hand, is an example of a town in decline.[28]

The Norms and Practices of the State, the Church, and the Communities

At the beginning of the modern era, the Town Law of King Magnus Eriksson, dating from the mid-fourteenth century, was in force in the towns. It prescribed the punishments for the illegal employment of violence according to how grave and reprehensible it was. The most petty cases—involving the infliction of a bruise, for which the fine was three marks—had already been rendered irrelevant by inflation at the end of the sixteenth century. The more serious, grievous, and reprehensible crimes were dealt with under the High Crimes Code, the King's Peace Code (*edsörebalken*), and the Intentional Homicide Code (*Dråpamålsbalken*). Most of the crimes that came under these codes were also punishable by fines.

The Intentional Homicide Code distinguished three major categories of killing: (1) the perpetrator committed the crime without duress and was caught in the act; (2) the crime was committed in self-defense; and (3) the perpetrator escaped. Of these, only the first was punishable by death, and even then the courts tended to commute the sentence to a fine at the intercession of the relatives.[29]

However, the situation began to change in the sixteenth century. Olavus Petri was one of the most influential figures of the Swedish Reformation. He also played a highly significant role in the legal sphere, because in the 1540s he published his celebrated "Instructions for Judges," a work which is particularly of interest with regard to the present study because it contains rules for judges on how to carry out their duties. One of the instructions declares that if God should find a judge guilty of misconduct (i.e., passing a false judgment), then His wrath will be aroused, and wars and other banes will ensue.[30] In the religion-saturated atmosphere of the times, this was a very serious matter. The "Instructions for Judges" were disseminated throughout the kingdom, so this rule was also familiar to all members of the courts. What is interesting here is that God's wrath was later associated with unexpiated sin. But it was not only the clergy who were aware of the problems that could accrue from malfeasance; the judges of the lay courts and most citizens were also cognizant of the consequences that it would incur.[31]

The strict commandments of the Old Testament began to be applied more widely in Sweden in the latter half of the sixteenth century. For example, it was deemed necessary to punish homicide severely, for an unexpiated sin could arouse the wrath of God against the community and indeed against the whole state. However, it was not until the 1590s, during a domestic political crisis, that Duke Charles, later known as Charles IX, actually equated unexpiated sin and God's wrath. As a result, serious crimes, which according to the laws of Moses included killing and assaulting one's parents, were made punishable by death. Behind this lay the ruler's attempt to enforce a strict Lutheran three-estate doctrine that emphasized the king's almost limitless power over his subjects. Although the laws of Moses and God were not fully implemented during the age when Sweden was a great power, criminal justice in the seventeenth century was still based on deterrence and retribution. The lawyers tended to refer less to the Bible than to sin, intimidation, and admonition and to the mercy that it was in the power of "the higher authority" (i.e., the court of appeal and the Crown) to bestow.[32]

The concept of honor is central to the study of violence, for it was considered justified to use violence to defend one's honor. In many respects, violence and honor are closely enmeshed all over Europe. In continental Europe there were ritual forms of violence in which gangs of young men engaged in fights more to shame their adversaries than to kill them.[33] However, it is difficult to distinguish the many aspects of honor and reputation that may have been involved in crimes of violence committed in the towns of Sweden, for there existed differing conceptions of honor and of its importance for the individual and the community. People were living in an age in which values were changing.

Honor was not normally the property of any single individual; rather, it was collective, defined according to social hierarchies and group affiliation.[34] It has been suggested that honor had already become an individual attribute in the sixteenth century. According to a royal decree of Gustavus I Vasa in 1538, those who had committed certain grievous crimes were disqualified from becoming judges, jurors, or witnesses and they could not swear an oath. Prominent among these crimes were acts of violence. According to the stipulations of the decree, a person was not juridically "honorable" and legally competent until his crime had been atoned for with both the court and the church. In Stockholm, from the 1660s on, cases of petty violence and slander in particular began to be mutually settled in court, a development that, according to Hans Andersson, indicates a decline in the prevailing "honor-centered" culture during the seventeenth century.[35]

The situation was thus a complex one. In the sixteenth and seventeenth centuries, matters of honor and reputation were affected by mutually conflicting factors. The interests and attitudes of the state, the church, and the local communities did not always coincide, but they were all intimately bound up with the general process of civilization—irrespective of whether it took place from above or below—and particularly with any decrease in violence that there may have been. In the towns, concepts of honor were molded by the following partly conflicting and partly overlapping views, which lie along two axes: individual/collective and harmony/hierarchy:

1. The collective "folk" concept of honor: honor is not the property of the individual. Each group has its own norms and concepts of honor. In the towns the collective concept of honor was particularly emphasized among the artisans. On the other hand, among the merchants and other non-manual workers, the traditional concept of honor became irrelevant in the early seventeenth century.[36]
2. The more individual concept of honor propagated by the state: each person is responsible for his or her own deeds.
3. A strong religious orthodoxy propagated by the church and supported by the state, which partly conflicted with the previous concept. In it collective responsibility and sin played central roles. An unexpiated sin, such as a killing that went unpunished, aroused the wrath of God.
4. A further attempt on the part of the church and the state to establish harmony and unity.[37] Internal disputes had to be resolved, including cases of violence and slander that disrupted the functioning of the community.
5. An attempt on the part of the municipal courts to settle many petty cases unofficially. This was connected with the previous view, and it also partly represented an attempt on the part of the courts to lessen their burden of work by hiving off cases of petty crime to be settled out of court.

Partly because of these conflicting views, it is difficult to point to many homicides that were directly linked to the concept of honor. Nor did the town courts, for example, make any mention of defense of one's honor as a reason for clemency in their statements of extenuating circumstances or motives. In fact, the sentences contain no references whatsoever to honor or to the need to defend it. In practice, it only emerges in connection with its opposite: infamy.

Later there are numerous examples of cases involving infamy in connection with serious cases of homicide. Moreover, even in other cases of violent crime the condemnatory attitude of the community and the town court is clearly perceptible. For example, a farmhand from Vadstena was chastised because he was "a big farmhand and he had assaulted a small boy."[38] A similar contemptuous attitude can be discerned in a criticism leveled at a burgher who had drunkenly beaten a child: "The court admonished him severely and remarked [asked] what kind of man it was that proved his manhood on a small child."[39]

A sensitivity about honor is clearly to be seen in cases which one could describe as "duels of the common people." Characteristic of such cases was a challenge to fight by appealing to the adversary's sense of honor. An example of such an incident, which eventually ended in the death of one of those involved, took place in Stockholm in 1556. According to numerous witnesses, a barber named Jacob had gone to a house in which there was a large group of soldiers. As soon as he entered the parlor, he drew his dagger and brandished it at everyone there, challenging three of the soldiers to come out and fight with him. They were less than enthusiastic about the barber's proposal and offered to fight him the following day when there would be some "honest country foot soldiers" present. Finally the barber began to quarrel with one Jakob Skåning, who had tried to pacify him. He declared, "Because no one else wants to fight me, then you'll have to." Since the soldiers scorned to fight with the man, he had to provoke a fight forcibly in order to maintain his honor.[40]

The attitudes of the state and the local town communities with regard to behavioral norms differed considerably, but the multiplicity of concepts of honor in itself lessened the conflict. How is this reflected in attitudes toward violence?

The "Strict Law": United Attitudes toward Cases of Premeditated Murder, "Irrational Killing," and Rape

Violence in the towns of Sweden and Finland was mainly trivial: a squabble between two men (women were not usually involved) resulting in a small fine.[41] More serious cases were rare, although particularly in the late sixteenth century the number of homicides was high compared with later times. Even so, the number of killings out of all the cases that came before the courts as well as out of all crimes of violence continued to be small. Table 2.1 shows the relative proportion of killings in Stockholm, Turku, Arboga, and Vadstena among all registered crimes and among all crimes of violence.

Violence generally, and homicide in particular, decreased in the seventeenth century. The decline was greatest in Stockholm, which nevertheless re-

Table 2.1. Relative Proportion of Homicides among All Registered Crimes and among All Crimes of Violence, 1540–1660

	Stockholm		*Turku*		*Arboga*		*Vadstena*	
	A	*B*	*A*	*B*	*A*	*B*	*A*	*B*
1540–1599	5	20	**	**	1	4	3	6
1600–1660	3	10	1	4	1	5	2	5

Sources: See figs. 2.1–2.4.

Notes: Column headings are as follows: A = the percentage of homicides among all registered crimes, and B = the percentage of homicides among all crimes of violence.

The missing years have not been estimated in calculating the relative figures. Thus the figure for Stockholm in particular is somewhat too high for the sixteenth century, because some of the earlier cases of violence were only entered in the fine rolls, which have not been preserved for all years.

mained the most violent of the towns. Even in the seventeenth century, 10 percent of violent crimes were murders or manslaughter, whereas for the other towns the percentage was only 5 percent. It seems, therefore, that the towns of Sweden and Finland underwent a process of major pacification between 1540 and 1660, as earlier research has indicated.

We shall investigate attitudes toward violence by dividing our analysis into two broad sections: (1) cases in which the attitudes of the state and the local communities were the same, and (2) cases in which they conflicted. The division is naturally somewhat arbitrary, as it is difficult to draw a precise line between the two categories.

In certain cases, there was no disagreement between the policies of the state, the church, and the local communities with respect to violence. Such cases were without exception extremely grave and reprehensible. They included murders, irrational homicides, and rapes.

Studies of the society of the Middle Ages and the early modern age often emphasize the fact that the most killings were spontaneous, impulsive, and seemingly irrational acts. There rarely seems to have been any premeditation. Calculation and planning are usually associated with later ages. Pieter Spierenburg has put forward a hypothesis according to which homicides gradually became more "rational" and were directed ever more frequently against the perpetrator's immediate family.[42]

Murders, which in the sixteenth and seventeenth centuries meant premeditated homicides that the perpetrator attempted to conceal,[43] were extremely rare in Sweden. Such as there were took place in Stockholm. Six murders were committed in the capital in the early part (1523–1611) of the Vasa dynasty, of which four were carried out within a period of two years in the

1540s. The victims were a husband, an employer, a girl, and a woman killed on the highway. The killings were planned; for example, the girl's killer had lain in wait for her for days beforehand. She said that her motive for killing the girl was to steal some valuables that she was wearing.[44]

According to Aarne Jansson, altogether twenty-seven murders were committed in Stockholm in the seventeenth century. However, when one considers that at the same time the population of the city increased six- or sevenfold, one cannot claim that the murder rate increased. On the other hand, this figure also indicates there was little in the way of a civilizing process, at least when measured according to this somewhat macabre variable. Nor was there any increase in the rationality of homicidal crimes. Jansson has drawn attention to the fact that nineteen out of the twenty-seven murders in Stockholm were "suicidal murders" (*suicidalmord*), in which it was the aim of the perpetrator to get himself executed for murdering another person. Behind this lay the idea that a person who committed suicide was doomed to eternal damnation; therefore, it was better to kill somebody else and thus go to the block. Many of these murders were the deeds of desperate but determined and cold-blooded persons.[45]

There are no suicidal murders in the other cities of Sweden and Finland in the seventeenth century. This is almost as true of "ordinary" murders as well: there is no evidence of murders occurring in Arboga, Vadstena, or Turku in the early Vasa period. All in all, there are very few cases outside Stockholm in the seventeenth century.[46] The most shocking of these occurred in 1650 in Västervik, when one Sven Svensson murdered a burgher called Clas Engelske ("the Englishman") and his wife, stabbing the man twenty-three times and the woman fourteen times with a knife. His motive was straitened financial circumstances, which according to his own confession he tried to rectify by killing the couple and robbing them.[47]

When studying the spontaneity or "rationality" of crimes of homicide, it is important to understand what the people of that age meant by a phrase which is frequently found in the grounds for the judgments when they state that the deed was carried out "without cause" (*ingen orsaak*). During the period under investigation, this really meant "without any reason for hostility (or conflict)." In other words, there was no obvious long-standing grievance behind the killing. Therefore, the Stockholm Town Court cited as grounds for the capital sentence it passed on Gregers Eriksson in 1547 the fact that the victim had never previously uttered a single word to his killer. The meaning of the phrase emerges even more clearly in connection with a case tried in court forty years later, when the perpetrator confessed that he had never quarreled with or even known his victim.[48]

Even so, this certainly does not mean that a killing could not be "rationally" justified in some way or another by the criteria of the age. Completely "irrational" homicides were rare in the sixteenth and seventeenth centuries. If cases contained horrific or reprehensible features, the reactions of the public were damning, and the sentences were severe. Most homicides of this kind were committed during the earlier Vasa period and mainly in the capital.

Assaulting a person who was unable to defend himself was considered to be a particularly incriminating factor, and there is very little difference between the attitudes of the state and the local communities toward the judging of such cases—as was discovered by one Per Månsson, who had killed his fellow servant, although he was able to prove that he had first been assaulted by his victim. However, the enraged Per had subsequently sought his revenge by stabbing his adversary in the back with a sword while he was on his knees lighting a fire.[49] Per Nilsson, a soldier who had broken into the home of a merchant called Clemet Clemetsson, assaulted the master of the house, and when Clemetsson's pregnant wife ran naked out of the sauna to help her husband, entreating the soldier to spare his life, he stabbed her to death in the abdomen with his sword, thus causing the death of the unborn child as well.[50]

In these cases, the courts passed unconditional capital sentences. This was not in itself a demonstration of the "brutality" or exceptional harshness of the justice system but a consequence of the grievous nature of the crimes, which called for tough measures. Thus, the court ordered that the killer of Clemet Clemetsson's wife should have his right hand amputated first "as a warning and example to others" before he was executed.

The situation changed somewhat during the seventeenth century, when Sweden became a great power. Despite the strict norms, the courts passed more lenient sentences than the letter of the law required, although grievous crimes of the kind described above still received harsh punishments. However, there were fewer such cases. Gross cases of homicide still incurred severe penalties, as a killing in Falköping in 1645 demonstrates. The bailiff of the marshal of state stabbed a burgher in the back with his sword for no sensible reason. Although the plaintiffs would gladly have settled for a fine in compensation for the death of their relation, the court of appeal passed a sentence of death, appealing to the gravity of the crime and not heeding the intercessions of the plaintiffs or even a plea in a letter from the marshal of state himself. Although a profitable financial settlement would have suited the plaintiffs, it is probable that in this case the community as a whole—not just the members of the town court—were unanimous in endorsing the court's decision.[51]

Rapes were extremely rare in Swedish towns.[52] In the towns dealt with in this study, there were fewer than twenty cases of rape between 1540 and 1700, and half of these were cases where there was not sufficient evidence to justify a condemnatory sentence.[53] According to Paragraph 11 of the King's Peace Code of the Town Law, "breach of female peace" incurred a severe punishment. The burden of proof was considerable, but if the man was caught in flagrante delicto, the crime was punishable by death. The strictness of the law is reflected in the fact that, according to the Trial Ordinance of 1614, rape was one of the few crimes that did not need to be ratified by the court of appeal, and in a proven case a capital sentence could be put into effect immediately.[54]

While the threshold to prove guilt in a case of rape was undoubtedly high, there is no evidence to suggest that rape cases were not prosecuted or that the victims were bribed or intimidated into keeping quiet. The severity of the law was probably the most important factor that made rape such a rare crime. A person convicted of rape received no sympathy, and the courts of appeal, which often commuted the sentences passed by the town courts in other cases, saw no reason for clemency when it came to rape. The wages of sin were death.[55]

Rapists were themselves well aware of the risk they were running. In 1625 in Arboga, one Anna, the wife of a burgher, accused a vagrant of rape. The man confessed to the deed, saying, "Honored and good men, since I see that I am going to die because of bodily injury [i.e., rape], I most humbly entreat you that I need not spend more time in prison."[56] That the guilty party was aware of the gravity of his crime and its religious implications is evident in a case of the rape and murder of a serving maid that caused a scandal in Stockholm in 1627. The perpetrator finally confessed to the deed and begged to be executed by the sword and to be buried in consecrated ground.[57]

The rarity of rapes and the consequent general horror and contempt that they excited is confirmed by a case in Stockholm in 1656 of a rape committed by one Hindrich Ewertsson. This married man had sexually assaulted a nine-year-old girl. The court pronounced the death sentence upon him in words of utter contempt. Even the judges and the people of Stockholm, inured as they were to the seamier side of life, considered the case an exceptionally grave one.[58]

All these cases are characterized by the harshness of the punishments they incurred. These harsh sentences were demanded by the norms created by the Crown in the stricter forms (divine law) that they assumed at the end of the sixteenth century and indeed by the local town communities themselves. The "tougher" death sentences associated with these cases were part of the systems of intimidation, warning, and expiation of crime that the state, the church, and the towns required. However, the views of these three actors did not correspond so well in all cases of violence.[59]

From Private Agreements to Settlements Guaranteed by the State: "Ordinary" Homicides and Everyday Violence

According to Eva Österberg, at the beginning of the modern age the courts settled various kinds of conflicts. They also redeemed those who broke the norms of society as socially acceptable citizens and removed from it the truly criminal elements. In the early modern era, the courts constituted the means whereby the state was able to exercise increased control over the towns.[60]

Österberg is right, but her theory is too uniform and general with regard to the cities. The hierarchical Weltanschauung created by the doctrine of the three estates on the one hand and the attempt to achieve harmony and unanimity on the other became badly confused, and there were considerable fluctuations in the degree of state interference in the operations of the local authorities and the judicial system. The local court systems and their methods of operation could vary considerably.

In the sixteenth century, "ordinary" crimes were dealt with almost everywhere on the basis of settlement, which often entailed circumvention of the law. When punishments were meted out, the amount of fines was frequently much lower than that stipulated by the law. This was possible because the grip of the central executive was still weak. In the seventeenth century, religious orthodoxy, with its strict injunctions regarding grave crimes, was enlisted as an important tool in the legal system. The tighter grip of the Crown was clearly to be seen in the towns.

These conflicting norms and the independent traditions of the individual towns explain the disparities in the punishments that were meted out for crimes. Although the law was everywhere the same, the ways in which it was implemented could differ. In the sixteenth century, the judges of the town courts and the members of the community were still socially closely associated with each other. In the seventeenth century, when Sweden became a great power, the central control of the local communities and particularly of the courts tightened up considerably, which may have had an effect on the difference in views between the courts and the local communities with regard to the punishment of violence, for example. Even so, we can take it that the "bureaucratized" town courts of the seventeenth century were in full agreement with the community they represented in matters concerning violence.[61]

The towns can be divided into two broad categories with regard to their procedural principles: those that strove to achieve harmony and reconciliation, and those where the exercise of justice was based on strict punishments and the use of various deterrents. The emphasis in the latter was on the social hierarchy and the "strict law."

Naturally, there were modes of operation which were situated between these two main types, sharing features of both. Although the main types are formally very different, in the opinion of both the secular and the ecclesiastical authorities, both kinds of community nevertheless acted "correctly"; both the "strict law" and the settlement of crimes served the purpose of atoning for sin and thus avoiding the wrath of God. In the seventeenth century, the courts of appeal, which strictly controlled the work of the town courts, did not interfere in matters of procedural policy, even though different towns adopted totally different approaches.

The differences in the legal culture of the four towns studied here are clearly discernible. In Stockholm, the courts followed the "strict law" line even in cases that did not offend the communities' notions of morality. On the other hand, Vadstena and Turku favored the policy of "harmony" for almost the whole period, while the policy of the Arboga Town Court changed from that of harmony to the "strict law" approach.

In Stockholm, both homicide and other crimes of violence received severe sentences, and there were fewer settlements than in other towns. Already in the sixteenth century, the sentences for homicide in Stockholm followed the letter of the law, whereas a more lenient stance was adopted elsewhere. Cases in which the family of the victim demanded a life for a life were more common there than in other towns. Settlements and informal agreements were not usual in cases of violent crime.

In the sixteenth century, many cases came before the court in Stockholm in which the plaintiff was clearly lusting for blood. There were very few of the settlements so common elsewhere at that time between the relatives and the accused in homicide cases.[62] The hard line can be seen, for example, in a homicide trial in 1573 in which the killer begged the widow of the victim for mercy. But the widow "did not wish for any [settlement], and entreated the court, saying that his [i.e., the killer's] life was no better than that of her departed husband." Again, in 1600, the widow of a milliner who had been killed deposited "an executioner's fee" with the court, just to be on the safe side.[63] Such cases disappeared in the early seventeenth century, mainly as a result of the influence of the court of appeal and the state executive. The absence of formal (i.e., approved by the court) and informal settlements and the prevalence of sentences that conformed strictly to the law are a reflection of the harsh discipline prevailing in the capital. Throughout the seventeenth century, Stockholm continued to pass the most severe sentences of the towns studied here.[64]

Vadstena adopted a completely different policy during the early Vasa period. In petty cases, and sometimes even in more serious cases, the court either passed a conditional sentence (a repetition of the deed would lead to the forgiven crime being punished) or it merely threatened the offender with punishment (a new offense would incur the enforcement of a conditional fine). This lenient pacification of those who broke the law succeeded, at least in Vadstena, for there is not a single instance of recidivism as far as crimes of violence are concerned in the 1590s and early 1600s.[65]

In the settlement of disputes in Vadstena, emphasis was placed on reconciliation, which was often made a condition of a reduction in the fines imposed. Thus in 1624, the governor ordered two men who had been engaged in a fight to pay a conditional fine of one hundred thalers because they would not be reconciled.[66] Even at the end of the second decade of the seventeenth century, the court reduced the fines of those who were convicted of crimes of violence by half "on the intercession of the good men."[67] In accordance with this policy, exceptionally lenient punishments were awarded even in cases of grievous violence. Thus in 1587, one Sven Nilsson was found guilty of breach of domiciliary peace and defamation, having gone to a house, slandered the inhabitants, and finally pushed the mistress of the house to the floor. He got off with a caution "this time," although according to the law the deed should have incurred a harsh punishment.[68]

Another example of Vadstena's lenient judicial policy is provided by a case of breach of domiciliary peace that occurred in 1596. It also offers insight into the community's attitude toward such cases. A widow accused one Anders Gärtsson, a foot soldier of Duke Charles, of breach of domiciliary peace because he had assaulted two schoolboys who were living in her house. The incident began in a street in the town; Anders knocked down one of the boys and threatened him with his sword. The boy drew his own sword, and the soldier fled. A burgher's wife, who had seen the incident, urged the boys to go through her house so that the soldier would not have an opportunity to attack them again. But when the young lads returned to the street, the soldier charged at them with his sword drawn. The boys ran back into the house where they were living. The soldier left, but as soon as the boys reemerged, Anders advanced on them in a threatening fashion. This time Anders's father arrived and took his son away. But Anders refused to give in. He arrived at the widow's house a third time, and with his sword in his hand he tried to pick a fight with the boys. A man who was visiting the house thrashed him and threw him out. The soldier shouted to the boys to come out, and in the scuffle that ensued, Anders's mother(!) arrived and struck the boys with a sharp weapon. Despite all this, the court discharged Anders, although it strongly admonished him about the consequences of a recurrence of the deed.[69]

The judgment represented an attempt to protect the schoolboys from the violence, but it also exhibited consideration for the soldier. One might easily conclude that the town court was reluctant to convict a soldier of Duke Charles, but it was probably really a question of the lenient policy adopted by the local community of Vadstena. Ironically, Charles was the ruler who first really took issue with judgments like this which contravened the provisions of the law.

In the late sixteenth century, the situation in Arboga was similar to that in Vadstena: the court was lenient even in its judgment of serious cases. In one such case, a soldier assaulted the mayor with a sword in his own home. The soldier apologized and confessed to having done wrong. The "good men" of the town interceded for him, and the mayor forgave him, so the case was dropped and the crime was thus atoned for.[70]

Even in the 1590s, many cases of homicide were dealt with by settlement. For example, in spring 1599 the court noted that the plaintiff did not demand the life of the accused killer, and therefore the case was referred for settlement. However, the situation soon changed, when the sentences for crimes of homicide began systematically to be submitted for ratification by the king.[71]

The change reflects the tighter grip of the state executive, which wished to get rid of "informal" settlements of homicidal crimes. Even so, it was not just a case of stricter state control, because in principle the lenient punishment of other kinds of violence could have continued. In the early seventeenth century, Arboga experienced an internal crisis. The public had lost its respect for the town court, and councilors were frequently the victims of violent assaults and slanders. The councilors tried to reassert their authority by passing out sentences that strictly conformed to the letter of the law and may have been excessively severe as a result. This caused even more problems, which did not cease for many years until changes were made in the town's administration.[72] It was not until the late 1650s that "lenient" sentences were given again in cases of petty violence.[73]

It is probable that the punishment of violence in Turku in the sixteenth century was extremely tolerant, for even during the seventeenth century, the town's general penal policy could hardly be called very harsh. The town court encouraged the parties involved in crimes of violence, petty and grievous alike, to strive for a settlement among themselves. Almost without exception a settlement was reached, even when the crime was considered heinous (e.g., breach of domiciliary peace or aggravated assault). The settlement of cases of homicide was not, however, permissible until the court of appeal had made its decision. The intervention of the state authority could also be seen in the fact that in many cases of violence in which a settlement was reached with the plaintiff, the court asserted that the compensation due to the town and the Crown was still not settled and required that it be so. Usually, however, the settlement was conducted in good order, and the court of appeal did not adopt a particularly severe stance in its judgments of such cases: the views of the community, the town court, and the court of appeal coincided.[74]

■

Therefore, we see that differences between the executive and the local communities in their attitudes to the way in which violence should be punished only began to appear in the seventeenth century. The jurists of the courts of appeal did not normally demand strict conformity with the Mosaic and divine laws, but they did enforce judgments that were in accordance with the law of Sweden. The problem cases were mainly "ordinary" homicides, in which the king's subjects preferred to settle for a modest compensation rather than prosecute their case to the end. But did these cases ultimately constitute such a big problem for the state, the church, and the local communities?

After the courts of appeal were founded, it was required in principle that every case of homicide be referred by the lower court to the court of appeal for judgment without any prior settlement between the plaintiffs and the accused. The private settlement of homicide cases *before* the court of appeal passed its final judgment ought not to have been possible in the seventeenth century. In practice, however, this state of affairs was not achieved until the end of the century. Before that, of the homicide cases that were committed in the towns under the jurisdiction of the Göta Court of Appeal, for example, over one-third were settled beforehand. The Göta Court of Appeal made no protest about this; on the contrary, it tried to gradually "legalize" the procedure.[75]

Thus, even over ordinary cases of homicide, there was very little disagreement between the towns and the state. The courts of appeal adapted themselves to the job of slowly molding local practices and did not attempt to achieve any fast or radical change. On the other hand, there were considerable discrepancies between the ways in which the different courts of appeal handled the matter; in the towns under the jurisdiction of the Turku and Svea Courts of Appeal, there are considerably fewer premature settlements (i.e., agreed before the judgment of the court of appeal) than in the area covered by the Göta Court of Appeal.[76]

Since the state and the church intervened strongly in the affairs of the towns, the civilizing process cannot have been a completely spontaneous phenomenon. On the other hand, attitudes toward violence and its proper punishment were in many cases ultimately very much the same, and thus the idea of control, a strict order, a disciplining process, or an acculturation, all imposed from above, does not by itself seem very likely.

There are some important questions which have so far been totally ignored: Did registered crime generally decrease at all in the towns under investigation? What was the situation like in the other towns of Sweden? And do our observations reflect the real situation? At least with regard to the study of everyday violence, the validity of the source materials has often been called into question.

A Decrease in Homicide, an Increase in Other Violence

In figures 2.1–2.4 describing violent and homicidal crime, the number of cases has been made proportionate to the population. Because there are no exact statistics available, it has been necessary to estimate both the number of cases of violent crime and the populations for all the towns.[77] Even so, the material yields a very reliable picture of the quantitative development of crime. There

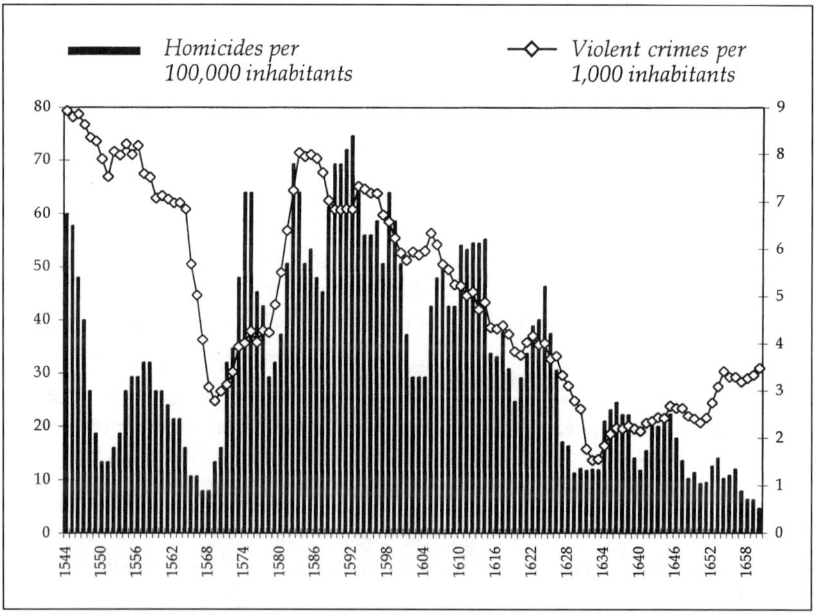

Fig. 2.1. Violent crime in Stockholm, 1544–1660. Five-year sliding average (missing years estimated). *Sources:* ST 1544–1627; SSA judgment books and fine rolls of the town court and treasurer's courts 1627–60; Lindström 1988a; Vuorela 1997, 143–47.

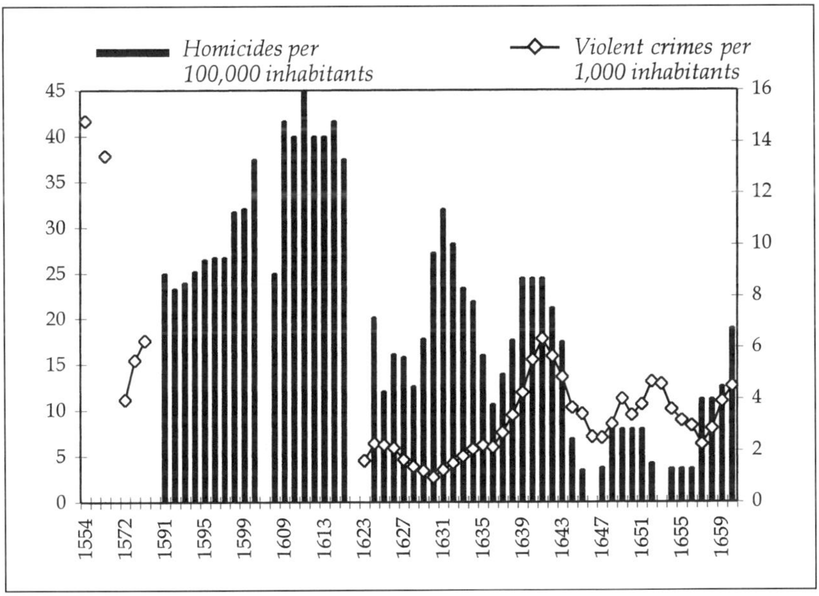

Fig. 2.2. Violent crime in Turku, 1544–1660. Five-year sliding average (missing years estimated). *Sources:* KA bailiffs' accounts, fine rolls; Turku R and Turku K 1623–60; BÅH 1: I.

are major defects only in the material for Turku in the sixteenth century, in that the figures for homicidal crime have been taken from the Turku Cathedral lists of persons buried, which certainly did not mention all those persons who had been murdered in the town. Nevertheless, the data make it possible to compare the situation at the end of the sixteenth century and the beginning of the seventeenth with that of later times.[78]

When we examine homicide and violent crime generally over a long period, we can observe a clear correspondence in the towns in Sweden proper: in Stockholm, Arboga, and Vadstena they follow a parallel development (when one rises, so does the other, and so on) right up to the end of the period of this research. On the other hand, in Turku there is no correspondence between homicide and violent crime, especially in the 1620s and 1630s. The treasurer's court, which was established there in 1629, evidently handled many of the cases of petty crime in the 1630s, but because there are no sources at all for this period, we have not ventured to try and estimate the number of cases.[79]

In all the towns, the absolute number of registered crimes of violence grew toward the end of the period. This development may perhaps be attributed

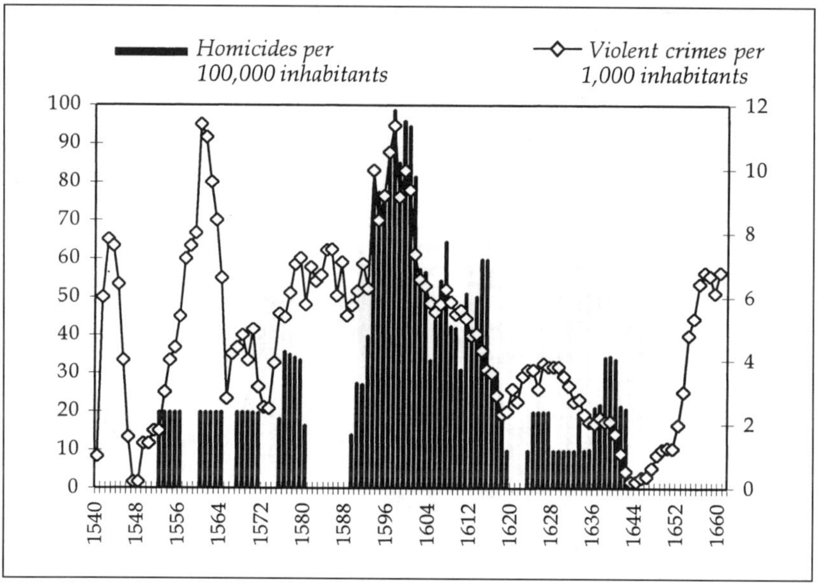

Fig. 2.3. Violent crime in Arboga, 1540–1660. Five-year sliding average (missing years estimated). *Sources:* Noreen 1941–50; ULA Arboga R 1569–1613; RA Arboga R and Arboga K 1615–60.

partly to the harsh conditions of war in the late 1650s. That alone, however, does not offer a sufficient explanation, for a state of war was rather a part of everyday life than an exceptional circumstance. In the towns of Finland, homicide decreased, but the total amount of violent crime increased.[80] This permits us to assume that it was not just a coincidental phenomenon in some towns but a sign of a more general growth in the cases of violence that came before the courts.

Homicide did not decrease steadily in any of the towns. In some cases there were several intervening rises. This may partly result from problems caused by the heterogeneity of the sources, but such deficiencies can only explain a fraction of the changes, for the use of sliding averages evens out the discrepancies. Between 1540 and 1660 there was no unbroken process of "pacification." The curve describing the development in Stockholm looks like a roller coaster: in the 1550s and 1560s there were fewer homicides than in the 1630s.[81]

In spite of everything, homicidal crime really did decrease in Turku, Stockholm, and Arboga in the first half of the seventeenth century. In Turku the decline was considerable when one takes into account the gaps in the sources for the sixteenth century. In the capital, too, there was a clear fall from the 1620s

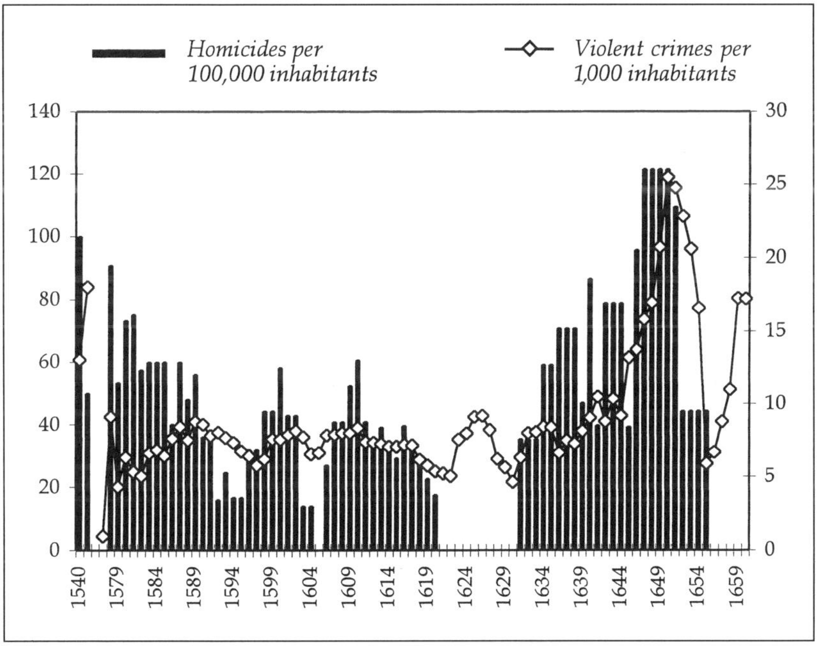

Fig. 2.4. Violent crime in Vadstena, 1540–1660. Five-year sliding average (missing years 1542–76). *Sources:* RA KA LH, Östergötland 1540–41; GHA Vadstena 1618–60; Eriksson 1952.

on. The situation in Arboga is more difficult to discern. The apparent total absence of homicide from the 1640s on may be a result of deficiencies in the source material, but this is impossible to verify.[82] In Vadstena, contrary to what one might expect, the figures rose sharply during the seventeenth century. The number of murders in Vadstena during the *sixteenth* century has been considered exceptionally high, but a comparison with Turku, Stockholm, and Arboga shows that this was not the case. During the earlier Vasa period, it was actually less violent than in these large towns.[83]

An analysis of homicide in Stockholm and Arboga reveals that the worst period in both towns was the 1590s and the early 1600s. The same also seems to hold true for violent crime as a whole. The situation in Vadstena was not so bad, but there, too, as well as in Turku, the homicide rate was about forty per 100,000 capita. Although this figure is astonishingly high, it is still only half of the rates in Stockholm and Arboga.

The fact that homicidal crime peaked at the end of the sixteenth century is not a coincidence. It can be considered part of a general European crisis that took place in the 1590s, although it is difficult to find common denominators for the problems that then occurred in different parts of the Continent. However, at that time economic, political, and military problems became exacerbated.[84] Sweden experienced particularly great problems because, in addition to a prolonged war, the economy was shaky and the country was torn by an internal power struggle. The sharp rise in violence in Stockholm and Arboga is probably connected with this power struggle and the more general crisis. In Turku and in Vadstena, which was further away from the centers of the crisis, the situation does not seem to have been quite as bad. It therefore seems that the growth of violence was concentrated mainly in politically central areas. It is probably not too far-fetched to connect the decision of Duke Charles to adopt the Mosaic and divine laws with an attempt to pacify the domestic situation.[85]

Above we referred to the administrative reforms that were made during the seventeenth century. The most important of these with regard to this subject was the foundation of the courts of appeal. It is possible to analyze the decrease or increase in homicidal crime by examining the judgments of the Svea and Göta Courts of Appeal.[86] In addition to these, figure 2.5 includes data about Stockholm provided by Johan Söderberg, although at first sight there would seem to be a considerable difference between these data and those concerning the capital presented in figure 2.1. These figures permit us to compare Stockholm in terms of peacefulness or dangerousness with the other towns of the kingdom.[87]

With the exception of Stockholm, homicide decreased in the towns under the jurisdiction of the Svea and Göta Courts of Appeal during the period 1635–1700. The decline was not, however, an uninterrupted one.[88] Even so, these towns were generally safer than the capital. This is interesting in view of the fact that Stockholm has been considered the cradle of the "Swedish civilization process," one important indicator of which has been held to be a significant decline in homicidal crime.

Thus homicide dropped significantly between 1540 and 1700, but at the same time registered crimes of violence as a whole first waned and then increased. The statistical growth of violence at the end of the period 1540–1660 can to a great extent be put down to differences between the towns in penal policy and the associated increase in official control. Vadstena, the smallest of the towns, was the one where by far the largest number of crimes of violence were brought to trial relative to the population. This does not necessarily mean that it was the most violent of the towns under investigation: it is conceivable that it was customary in Vadstena to bring cases of petty violence before the court, and thus that even the most insignificant of affrays were all brought to trial. The

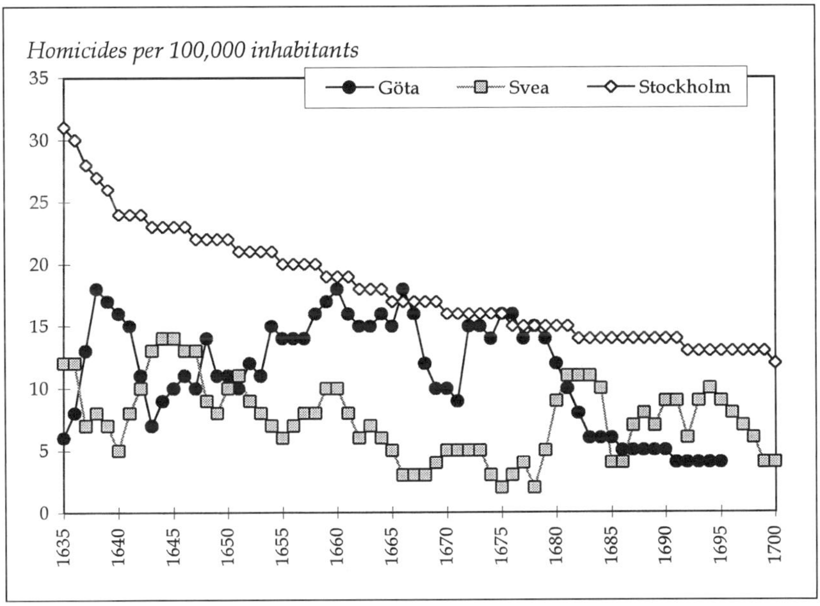

Fig. 2.5. Homicide in Stockholm and the towns in the judicial districts of the Göta and Svea Courts of Appeal, 1635–1700. Five-year sliding average (missing years estimated). *Sources:* ULA, KSHB 1635–1700; GHA GHC 1635–88; BU 1693–95. Data for Stockholm have been calculated according to Söderberg 1993, 90.

figures for both homicide and violent crime generally are distorted to some extent by the fall in population that followed upon the decline of the town. Statistically, Vadstena may have been a dangerous town, but this does not necessarily mean that the citizens there were afraid to walk in the streets. The prosecution of petty cases is more a reflection of the fact that the "soft" settlement and the expiation of sins were commonplace for the people there.

In Arboga, the growth of violence at the end of the period was mainly a result of the fact that it was not until the latter half of the seventeenth century that the administration and judiciary of the town began to function properly. The provision and availability of judicial services improved markedly because the treasurer's court, the town's lower court, began more and more frequently to try petty cases. Confidence in the court was restored, and the authority of the judges, which had been compromised earlier, was now reasserted. At the same time the justice system was more frequently able to pass "lenient" sentences and avoid applying the harshest sanctions.

The two-level court system in Stockholm, Turku, and Arboga made it possible to bring cases of violent crime to trial quickly and cheaply. In Stockholm there had been a system of this kind since the early sixteenth century, and thus the city had longer traditions in this respect than the other towns. The "strict law" policy pursued by the Stockholm Town Court ensured at least in the beginning that the lower courts, of which there were as many as three in 1654, kept to an equally strict line. The lower courts in the other towns, which were established in the seventeenth century on the Stockholm model, however, operated on different principles. In an important ordinance on urban administration issued by the chancellor of state, Axel Oxenstierna, in 1619, the function of the treasurer's courts was defined as a judicial process that was swift, economical, and based on settlement. The aim of getting disputes and petty crimes settled was central.

The settlement in court of disputes and cases involving the infliction of insignificant bruises partly explains why registered violence grew at the end of the period, although homicidal crime declined significantly.[89] Cases that previously would never have come to the notice of the courts were now ever more frequently settled there: the settlements thus became official. Settlement had for a long time been difficult for the poor and the disadvantaged because the methods by which the town courts operated had become slower and more bureaucratic in the early seventeenth century.[90] It was a prime purpose of the state to reform the systems of administration and justice because it realized that it was the only way to increase the amount of taxes paid by the towns to the Crown.[91] Unlike the town courts, the lower courts operated with a small number of officials, they were cheap, and they handled cases in a less bureaucratic way. With the foundation and establishment of the lower courts, the people learned to use the court system more than they had done previously and to have various decisions ratified in court.[92]

■

We shall now consider the question of whether the social composition of the groups involved in crimes of homicide (the perpetrators and the victims) changed during the period under investigation. The sources do not permit us to analyze the social background over the whole period, so for the sixteenth century we have taken the situation in Stockholm and for the seventeenth all the crimes of homicide referred to courts under the jurisdiction of the Göta Court of Appeal.

According to tables 2.2 and 2.3, the social structure of the groups involved in homicidal crime was similar in the sixteenth and seventeenth centuries. In

Table 2.2. Social Status of the Parties Involved in Crimes of Homicide in Stockholm, 1544–80

	Perpetrator											
Victim	Burgher	Servant	Functionary	Clergyman	Peasant	Soldier	Student	Nobleman	Other	Not known	Total	Percent
Burgher	13	0	1	1	0	1	0	0	0	3	19	28
Servant	2	5	0	1	1	0	0	0	0	1	10	15
Functionary	0	1	0	0	0	1	0	0	1	1	4	6
Clergyman	0	0	0	0	0	0	0	0	0	0	0	0
Peasant	1	0	0	0	2	0	0	0	1	2	6	9
Soldier	3	1	2	0	1	3	1	0	0	3	14	21
Student	0	0	0	1	0	0	0	0	0	0	1	1
Nobleman	0	0	0	0	0	1	0	0	0	0	1	1
Other	0	0	0	0	0	1	0	0	1	0	2	3
Not known	2	1	0	0	0	0	0	0	0	8	11	16
Total	21	8	3	3	4	7	1	0	3	18	68	100
Percent	31	12	4	4	6	10	1	0	4	26	100	

Source: ST 1544–80.

both Stockholm and the towns under the jurisdiction of the Göta Court of Appeal, a third of all killers and victims were burghers. Killings among the townsfolk were mostly confined to those of the same social rank or to servants. In other words, group-internal killings were general: peasants most often killed other peasants, and servants murdered fellow servants.[93]

The proportion of soldiers among the *victims* was exceptionally high in the mid-sixteenth century; nearly 20 percent of homicide victims were in the army. Of the killers, on the other hand, only 10 percent were soldiers. In the seventeenth century, the number of soldiers among the killers doubled, but the relative number of soldiers who were victims remained almost at its previous level.

The killings and other acts of violence committed by soldiers have received a considerable amount of attention, but in the material used here their number does not seem to be strikingly high. Partly this may be a result of the fact that in the seventeenth century soldiers were tried and sentenced directly in courts-martial, and consequently there are no records of such cases in the judgment books of the town courts. However, these cases probably did come before the courts of appeal, so most homicides in which soldiers were involved are represented in table 2.3.[94]

Table 2.3. Social Status of Parties Involved in Crimes of Homicide in the Göta Court of Appeal, 1635–95

	Perpetrator											
Victim	*Burgher*	*Servant*	*Functionary*	*Clergyman*	*Peasant*	*Soldier*	*Student*	*Nobleman*	*Other*	*Not known*	*Total*	*Percent*
Burgher	13	9	4	0	3	6	0	0	0	0	35	28
Servant	13	6	1	0	1	2	1	0	1	0	25	20
Functionary	3	0	4	0	0	3	0	0	0	1	11	9
Clergyman	0	0	1	1	0	1	0	0	0	0	3	2
Peasant	2	3	0	0	4	3	0	0	1	1	14	11
Soldier	5	3	1	1	1	7	1	1	1	0	21	17
Student	0	0	0	0	0	0	1	0	0	0	1	1
Nobleman	0	0	0	0	0	0	0	0	0	0	0	0
Other	1	1	0	0	0	0	0	0	0	0	2	2
Not known	2	0	3	0	0	4	0	0	0	3	12	10
Total	39	22	14	2	9	26	3	1	3	5	124	100
Percent	31	18	11	2	7	21	2	1	2	4	100	

Sources: GHA GHC 1635–88; BU 1693–95.

Even so, it is possible to cite highly sensational examples of the atrocities committed by soldiers in all the towns. An extreme example happened in Arboga in 1613, when some soldiers of the castle who were billeted in the town under the so-called burglager system slew the mayor and two citizens and assaulted dozens of others. The fact that the king set up a special commission to investigate the incident indicates its gravity and exceptional nature.[95]

The killings carried out by soldiers drew considerable attention among the people of the time. For the townsfolk there was something unfamiliar and therefore frightening about the acts of violence perpetrated by soldiers and sailors. The soldiers usually ran riot in large numbers, whereas the form of violence that the townspeople were accustomed to was a fight between two men who were acquainted with one another.[96] Spierenburg's observation that in other parts of Europe fighting among young men served as a means of bringing shame on their adversaries rather than injuring them does not hold true for Sweden; when groups fought there, they always meant business.

There regularly followed a thorough investigation whenever more than two persons were involved in a fight. Such incidents were described as "disturbances" and even uprisings, and they disturbed the peace and harmony of the community and thus brought the wrath of God upon the town. That is why they received a considerable amount of attention, more perhaps than their real significance justified.

Other social groups were only rarely represented among both the victims and the perpetrators,[97] so most of the killings took place between acquaintances or at least members of the same social group. This explains why there survive few indications that people lived in fear of violence. It is only toward the end of the period that this kind of fear is expressed more clearly. We shall return to this subject in the final section.

The large number of those involved in homicide cases who came from outside the urban communities distorts the figures for homicidal crime in the towns, because the total number of homicides is always made proportionate to the population of the town in question. However, the removal of "outsiders" from the statistics is not appropriate or even possible.[98] In the seventeenth century, the towns of Sweden and Finland were much more dangerous than the countryside. Previously there had been a higher incidence of killing in the larger Swedish towns than in the small ones, but in the seventeenth century this situation was reversed. Sweden, too, entered the age of the "peaceful big cities."[99]

Violence and Civilization: Did Pacification Take Place from Above or Below?

Why did homicidal crime in the towns of Sweden and Finland decrease in the seventeenth century? One can distinguish two main trends in the interpretations of scholars concerning the decline in killing: according to one it was a result of a policy of pacification imposed from above by the state; the other sees a spontaneous decrease in violence stemming partly from economic development and differentiation. Common to both models is the assumption that the concept of honor changed so as to diminish the need for the practice of violence. Another significant factor was the removal of restless elements from the town communities by conscripting them into the army in time of war and the fact that generally there were fewer "angry young men" on the loose.[100]

The lack of an aggressive male element and concomitant factors causing a decrease in violence did not appreciably affect the towns, which were not obliged to supply men for the army as the country districts were. The burden of conscription lay less heavily on the towns, for they were mainly expected to provide money, and it was the main object of the Crown's policy in developing their administration to increase the amounts they provided. On the other hand, the towns were often obliged to billet soldiers, and this situation, as we saw above, sometimes resulted in disturbances and unrest.[101]

The concept of honor certainly changed and became more diverse. The honor concept of some groups, like the artisans, remained a collective one, but other groups in the towns began to shed the traditional way of thinking. In this respect economic differentiation and the resultant financial independence were crucial factors behind the decline in violence. A man whose good name had been offended could no longer be quite sure whether he was justified in hitting his loud-mouthed neighbor or whether he should take the matter to court. "Honor" itself did not disappear, however, and its significance particularly in cases concerning chastity was considerable.

Signs of the change in attitudes toward honor in cases of violent crime can be seen in some instances of assault and intimidation in Stockholm in the 1650s. In 1653, the lower court of the town dealt with an assault on Nils Skunck, the town clerk, by a master builder by the name of Adrian, who had "shamefully in the presence of a large crowd and without . . . cause" thrashed Skunck on the public highway. The deed cost the master builder fifty silver thalers. The magnitude of this sum is apparent from the fact that the fine for homicide was a hundred silver thalers.[102] Three years later, Jakob Momma, a powerful merchant and industrialist who was later ennobled, made a complaint about one Måns Persson, who before a large group of people had wounded his honor and threatened to kill him. Witnesses testified to the fact that he had threatened to strike the merchant on the head so that "he'd have to carry his brains in his hat." This time the fine was considerably lower, but Måns was given a severe warning and a conditional fine of one hundred silver thalers if he did it again.[103] What was particularly incriminating in addition to the actual acts of violence was the public insult and intimidation involved, which indicates a change in attitude regarding the use of violence. In neither case did the victim take the law into his own hands and set out to defend his honor on the spot; instead, he took the matter directly to court. It appears then that there was confidence in the judicial system. In each case the victim had been a man who belonged to the elite of the town's society, and it was this group that first adopted peaceful means of settling conflicts, although Skunck, for example, demanded that his assailant receive a punishment "as a warning to others."[104]

The most important question behind the decline in violence concerns the roles of the state executive and the church in bringing about a change from homicidal crime to less serious forms of violence. The significance of both in this process was considerable. The increased involvement of the executive and the representation of the Crown in town courts and the council chambers weakened the autonomy of the towns and altered the earlier social order. Certainly, this influence must not necessarily be regarded as unfortunate. The in-

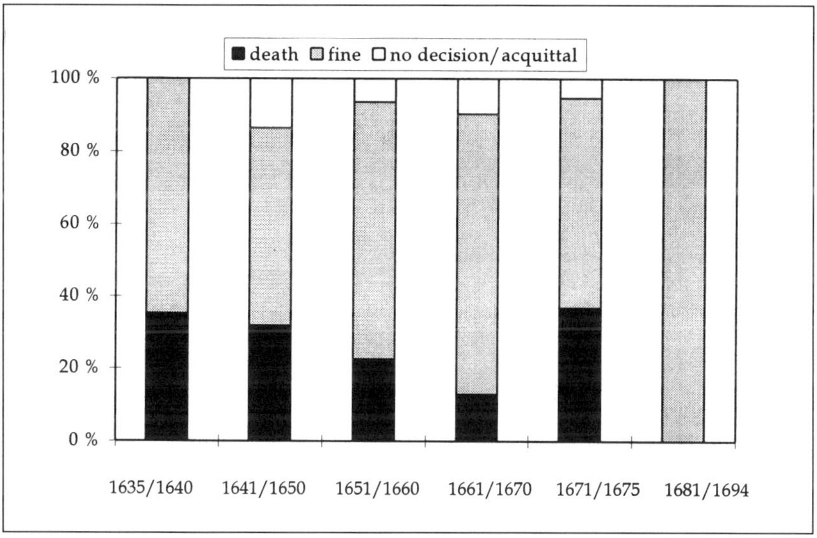

Fig. 2.6. Judgments of the Göta Court of Appeal concerning cases of homicide in towns under its jurisdiction, 1635–95 (relative distribution). *Source:* see fig. 2.5.

tervention of the state in the affairs of the local communities was apparent in the legal sphere mainly in the strict control that the courts of appeal maintained over the activities of the local courts. The scope of the town courts for independently making their judgments harsher or more lenient was curtailed. From the end of the sixteenth century, legislation was tightened up with the adoption of the Mosaic and divine laws. In practice, however, the new judicial sources had very little influence on the adjudication of cases of violence. They had a greater effect on the punishment of theft and sexual crimes.

The courts of appeal in different parts of the country passed practically the same sentences for crimes of homicide,[105] which means that judicial practice became more uniform. With the coming of the courts of appeal, the punishments for homicide actually became *more lenient.* We can see this by comparing the judgments passed by the Stockholm Town Court in cases of homicide in the period 1544–80 with the sentences of the Göta and Svea Courts of Appeal in the seventeenth century (figs. 2.6 and 2.7). At most, four out of ten killers were sentenced to death. The relative proportion of capital sentences in the area under the Göta Court of Appeal fell to as low as 10 percent in the 1660s. There was a temporary sharp increase in the harshness of sentences in the 1670s, but this was the only decade in which more than 50 percent of murderers received the death penalty in the Svea district.[106] On the other hand,

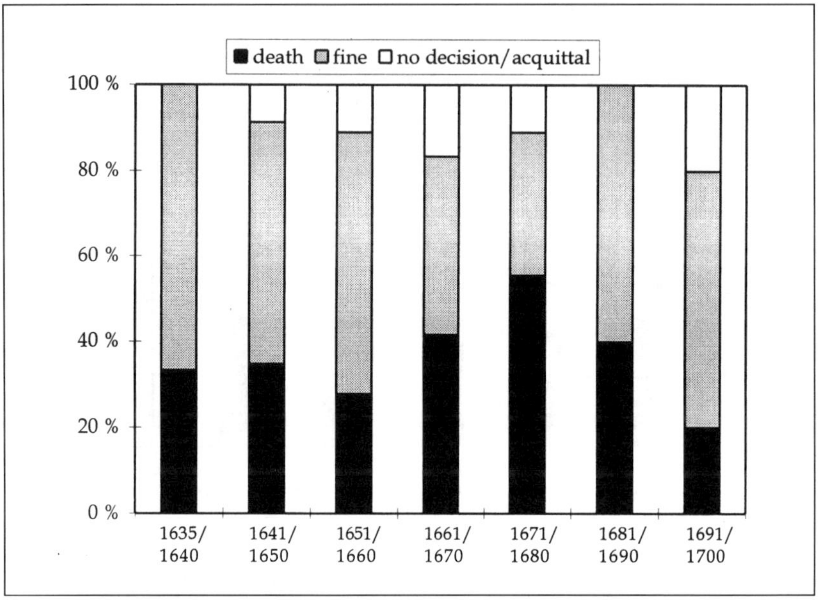

Fig. 2.7. Judgments of the Svea Court of Appeal concerning cases of homicide in towns under its jurisdiction, 1635–1700 (relative distribution). *Source:* see fig. 2.5.

back in the sixteenth century in Stockholm, 60 percent of killers were sentenced to death.[107]

It can clearly be seen, therefore, that sentences became more lenient in the seventeenth century.[108] But even then, those who were guilty of the most heinous crimes did not get off any more lightly than before. If a case fulfilled the criteria of the church, the state, and the local community for a particularly heinous deed, then there was no hesitation in using the wheel and other harsh forms of punishment. On the other hand, completely "irrational" homicide decreased in the seventeenth century, but then there was no increase in premeditated homicide either.

The involvement of the state in ratifying the sentences passed for cases of violent crime, which had been handled mainly within the local communities, did not take place in one fell swoop. It evolved. The executive infiltrated the local justice systems and influenced the norms of the towns, operating on their terms while gradually molding them to its own ends. Consequently, there were no major conflicts between the views of the state and the towns. The courts of appeal were an important factor in bringing down the rate of gross violence, for their control and above all their commuting of capital sentences to fines or other forms of punishment had a "civilizing" effect on society. Alongside enforcement of the "strict law," the court of appeal was also able to show mercy. In this task the role of the church as a disseminator of targeted propaganda was emphasized, for the clergy preached not only the wrath of God but also the doctrine of the expiation of sin. In the seventeenth century, the blood-lusting a-life-for-a-life cases that occur so frequently in the sixteenth-century source materials are almost completely absent. In many cases of homicide, the killer still attempted to settle with the relatives. In fact, the perpetrator was in a better position than before because he normally had the support of the court of appeal; a settled homicide meant an expiated sin. The restoration of harmony was in the interests of all parties.[109]

The doctrines asserted by the ministers in their sermons certainly did not fall on deaf ears. The message was drilled in through repetition, and slowly but surely the dogma began to have an effect. The importance of religion and its doctrines is demonstrated by the fact that some people even considered slaying another person to save their own souls—people believed that the absolution given by the priest on the scaffold would save their souls—and in the capital a few actually committed such "suicidal murders." In this light it seems exaggerated to speak of a weakening of the church's grip in Stockholm in the latter half of the seventeenth century,[110] when suicidal murders began to increase. The significance of religion was certainly as great in the capital as in all the other towns of the kingdom. Quite another matter is the fact that the clergy had little say in deciding about lay matters in the town councils.[111] But this does not affect the importance of religion in any way.[112]

Although the attitude in Stockholm toward violence was clearly stricter than in the other towns under consideration, this naturally does not mean that there was no concern for human life. This is proved, for example, by the case of Anders Bengtsson cited at the beginning of this article as well as many other cases quoted here. Even so, some of the acts of violence committed in Stockholm were of a kind not found elsewhere. It appears, therefore, that Stockholm was not the cradle of the Swedish civilization process. If a decrease in violence is to be considered an indication of the progress of civilization at all, then we must look to the small towns of the realm. It is necessary to make this observation because many of the cases mentioned above show that the excessive use of violence was not common among the inhabitants of small towns. Violence was acceptable only within certain limits.

The state executive and the urban community cooperated with regard to violent crime. Neither wished to disregard the views of the other. The state tolerated the existence of different forms of judicial practice. Of course, their existence was partly a question of the state's own contradictory orders. The towns, too, gradually came to realize that the settlement of gross violence required the court of appeal's approval. Town dwellers also began to take greater advantage of the services offered by the courts for dealing with even petty cases. This had been made possible by the vigorous efforts of the state executive to develop local administrative and judicial systems. Consequently, direction from above must be considered to be a powerful factor behind the decrease in serious violence. The influence of the state in the towns did not, however, consist just in the use of power or "the pedagogy of fear."

Notes

1. Translator's note: Quotations from the original sources have been rendered as literally as possible.

2. The Town Law of King Magnus Eriksson contained two separate homicide codes: the Intentional Homicide Code (*dråp med vilja*) and the Accidental Homicide Code (*dråp med våda*).

3. ST 1584–88, 30 October 1584, pp. 102–4; see also Lindström 1988a, 105–6; Österberg n.d., 109–10.

4. On the relations between the modern state and the towns, see esp. Tilly 1990, 1994; Bonney 1991.

5. On the decrease in violence, see Stone 1987; Cockburn 1991; Spierenburg 1994; Heikki Ylikangas's article in the present work; Næss 1994; Österberg 1991b, 1991c; Söderberg 1993; Ylikangas 1994.

6. On the research problems connected with the subject and the concentration of the research, see Knafla 1996; Emsley 1996; Rousseaux 1996; Lüdtke and Reinke 1996; King 1996. Muir and Ruggiero 1994b adopt a different approach (above all microhistorical and oriented toward qualitative analysis). Other articles in Emsley and Knafla 1996 also frequently refer to the level of violent crime and problems connected with the source material. See particularly Knafla 1996.

7. See, however, Spierenburg 1994; Adler 1997.

8. See, e.g., Finch 1997; Dean and Lowe 1994, 4–6. Cf. Fumagalli 1994, 20, 39–45; his basic premise is the violence of the towns and the fear of their inhabitants. On concepts of time, see Ågren 1998, 224–25.

9. See Lindström 1994; Sharpe 1990; Spierenburg 1984; Sharpe 1986; Jaakkola 1995; Matikainen 1996, 29–32; Muir and Ruggiero 1994a, 226, 230–31, 235; Katajala 1995; Vilkuna 1996a.

10. Elias 1978, 1982. See also Lindström 1994, 519–22.

11. Muchembled 1984, quotation p. 58; Muchembled 1985; for a criticism, see Wirth 1984, esp. 67, 76–77.

12. The "from violence to robbery" theory, according to which there is a change from homicide to property crime, has also received a lot of attention. Its significance for the present subject, however, is slight. For criticisms of the various explanatory models, see, e.g., Sharpe 1986; Lindström 1994; Frank 1995; Rousseaux 1996.

13. See, however, Liliequist 1992; Jansson 1994; Vilkuna 1996b; Karonen 1997.

14. See also Duerr 1988.

15. See Jarrick and Söderberg 1993; Söderberg 1993; Jarrick and Söderberg 1994a. For criticism, see Andersson 1996, 283–86 (Andersson is critical of linking tolerance and

empathy with the decline in violence). According to Jarrick and Söderberg 1993, important factors in the spontaneous civilizing process in Sweden were a decrease in violence, an extension of economic networks, emigration, secularization, enlightenment, and an understanding of these. Elsewhere (1994a, 9–10) they condense these under four headings: (1) respect for life and human dignity and attitudes toward violence and brutality; (2) care of weak groups; (3) the right to equal treatment; (4) personal autonomy and tolerance, "the citizen's constitutional liberties and rights are crucial here." Of these, it is mainly the first two categories that are relevant to research into the early modern age. Certainly, it is possible to distinguish a wide variety of significant aspects of the civilizing process. Elias concentrated to a great extent on changes in table manners and other forms of etiquette. Kustaa H. J. Vilkuna (1995) again studied the phenomenon through the state's intervention in the excessive drinking of the common people.

16. The study is limited to cases of violence alone.

17. Translator's note: Åbo is the Swedish name of the town.

18. As elsewhere in Europe, in Finland and Sweden the research has also concentrated on the countryside or at most limited itself to a few towns. For example, Österberg 1996a reviews Swedish, Norwegian, Danish, and Icelandic research on the subject. There have been previous studies of crime in Vadstena, Arboga, and Stockholm, but the approaches or the periods studied have been different. See particularly Lindström and Österberg 1988; Jarrick and Söderberg 1994b; see also Sundin 1992.

19. Criminological research has been criticized on the one hand for problems connected with the comprehensiveness of the source material and on the other hand for being limited to sources from the higher courts alone or being restricted to local sources. See, e.g., Knafla 1996, 35; Rousseaux 1996.

20. In Stockholm, the treasurer's court operated regularly from the 1580s on. The advantages resulting from this system in the capital led the administration in the seventeenth century to establish lower courts in other towns around the kingdom. Of the towns under investigation here, there were treasurer's courts in Turku (established in 1629) and Arboga (established in 1629), as well as in the capital. See Karonen 1994b, 61; Karonen 1995b (both works have English summaries).

21. In addition, the fine rolls (*saköreslängder*) have been preserved in Stockholm, and they have been quoted here in the form of the figures presented by Dag Lindström (1988a, 1988b). It is assumed in this article that the figures for crimes of violence in the fine rolls, which are often considerably higher than those indicated by the "notebooks" (*tänkeböcker*), are a result of the operation of the treasurer's court. Obviously, it is not possible to arrive at any absolute figures through a process of estimation, but I believe that we can get sufficiently close to the "true" amount of crime that came to the cognizance of the courts.

22. The fine rolls can be considered fairly accurate indicators of overt crime. Ylikangas (1976a, 107–8; 1988, 108–11) has carried out a comparison between the fine rolls and the judgment books in sixteenth-century Finland and found that, in addition to other grievous crimes, homicides were also entered into the fine rolls. The practice was very probably the same in the towns as well.

23. The judgment books of the towns can be considered a sufficiently comprehensive source for overt crime. See esp. Karonen 1994b, 35n. 85.

24. GHA GHC, BU. The material covers the period 1635–95, after which the next judgment books on microfilm are not until 1716. There are no data for 1676–80, 1682–86, and 1689–92. See further, e.g., Thunander 1993, 19–20; Sundin 1992, 40–50.

25. ULA KSHB. The index covers the following provinces: Uppsala län (data not available for 1664–68), Gamla Stockholms län (data available for the years 1640–46), Kopparbergs län, Gävleborgs län (data not available for 1673–77), Örebro län (data not available for 1690–95), Västmanland (from 1664). The judgments of the Turku Court of Appeal for the city of Turku (Åbo) have been preserved sporadically up until the 1690s. See further Karonen 1996a, 1998a.

26. The population estimates for the towns are based on the rolls of burghers and various taxation sources (for the sixteenth century) and on the census lists (from the 1630s on). The population figures for the sixteenth century are generally less accurate than those for the seventeenth. It is not possible here to go into the methods used to estimate the populations of the different cities in detail. For the seventeenth century, the populations have been calculated as double the census figures. For the population of Stockholm, see esp. Lager 1962; Lager-Kromnow 1992; Lilja 1995, 308, 315. For Åbo (Turku), see Grotenfelt 1887; Kaukiainen 1980, 105; Kerkkonen 1945, 81; Karonen 1994b, appendix 6. For Arboga, see Forssell 1872–83; Kumlien 1971, 180; Lundqvist 1974, 222; Corin 1978, 175, 178; RA Eli F. Heckscher Collection; RA YA, Boskaps m. fl. längder; Mantalslängder; Verificationer. The population figures for Vadstena in the sixteenth century have been calculated mainly from the skott taxation lists: see Ericsson 1952, 79–82, 86–97, 144–54, 174–77, 187–90, 226–30, 251–53, 446–51; Forssell 1872–83; RA Eli F. Heckscher Collection; RA KA, Boskaps- m. fl. längder; Mantalslängder; Verificationer.

27. The decline of Vadstena was real, for a monastery that was important to the town was closed as a result of the Reformation. Sandström 1996, 150.

28. See, e.g., Corin 1978; Stadin 1993.

29. MESL Högmålsbalken; Edsörebalken; Dråpamålsbalken 1 (om dråp med vilja); see Hemmer 1928; Renvall 1949; Ylikangas 1971; Lindström 1988c, 25–32.

30. "Och så vpwecker Gudh oss örlifh och krigh eller andra skadeligha bekostningar, ther skeer oss rett vthinnan." Norri 1987, sec. 4, p. 36.

31. For the distribution and adoption of the "Instructions for Judges," see particularly Ylikangas 1982; Blomstedt 1987.

32. See Takala 1993; Thunander 1993, 72, 90; Andrén 1990; Normann 1948; Pleijel 1951; Vilkuna 1996b; Karonen 1997; generally, e.g., Roberts 1968; Kirby 1994.

33. See Spierenburg 1994.

34. See, e.g., Lindström 1994, 539–41; Ylikangas 1971; Matikainen 1995.

35. Andersson 1995, 152–53; "Desse såges wara ehrelöse och måge ey lag gå eller wittne bära" (Schmedeman 1706, 7–9). Johan Söderberg (1990, 246–48) also emphasizes the individual concept of honor in Swedish society at the beginning of the modern age.

36. Ylikangas (1994) has linked the change in the concept of honor with the weakening in the position of the kin as the state executive took a firmer hold on society in the seventeenth century.

37. On this see Laine 1996, 16–24; Englund 1994; Österberg 1992.

38. Vadstena 30 August 1641.

39. Vadstena 20 June 1642.

40. ST 1556, pp. 149–50.

41. See, e.g., Österberg and Lindström 1988, 153; Finch 1997, 258.

42. Spierenburg 1994, 704–5.

43. See further MESL, Högmålsbalken (the Grievous Crimes Code) I; Renvall 1949, 17–19; Hemmer 1928.

44. ST 1544–1548, pp. 72–73 (for 1545), 133–34 (1546), 172 (1546), 242–44 (1547); see also ST 1576, pp. 4–5, 6–7, 17–19, 24; ST 1596, p. 12.

45. Jansson 1994, 24. Jonas Liliequist (1992) has observed similar characteristics in cases of bestiality.

46. Between 1623 and 1660, only one murder was recorded in the towns of Finland. See KA Turku R 1643: 393–407; Karonen 1996a; GHA GHC, Värmlands and Dals län 3.12.1673: 5 (Filipstad); ULA KSHB, Uppsala län 19.6.1650, 3.7.1650 (Upsala); 27.6.1662 (Upsala).

47. GHA CHC, Kalmar län 15 May 1650: 22, 2 October 1650: 1 (Västervik).

48. "Orsak," SAOB 19, columns 1347–51; ST 1547, p. 254; ST 1587, pp. 334–35; see also, e.g., Vadstena 1608, 422; GHA GHC, Östergötland 19–21 October 1652: 9 (Norrköping).

49. ST 1575, p. 402; see also ST 1582, pp. 304–5 (the culprit had struck a person on the ground several times).

50. ST 1600, pp. 97, 101.

51. GHA GHC, Skaraborgs och Västergötlands län 6 November 1645: 24 (Falköping). On the harsh punishments meted out by the court of appeal, see also GHA GHC, Värmlands och Dals län 4 November 1640: 4 (Filipstad); Skaraborgs ja Vätergötlands län 29–30 May 1643: 17 (Mariestad); Östergötland 14 September 1639: 4 (Norrköping); see also Thunander 1993; Karonen 1998a.

52. See Lindström 1988a, 99–100; Sundin 1991, 249–52; Sundin 1992, 340–44; Karonen 1996b, 87–88, also n. 5 and the references cited therein.

53. Lindström 1988a; the towns of Finland 1540–1660: Karonen 1996b; towns under the jurisdiction of the Göta and Svea Courts of Appeal 1635–1700: GHA GHC BU; ULA KSHB.

54. Thunander 1993, 153.

55. On the harshness of the punishments, see also Lindström 1988a, 100; Sundin 1991, 249.

56. "Wällachtade gode männ, efter det iagh förnimmer, att jagh shall döö för mennes skuldh så bedejag ödmiukligen, att iagh icke må sittie länge i fängelsedtt." Arboga R 1 June 1625: 514; 15 June 1625: 515v; 30 September 1625: 516–516v.

57. The culprit first claimed that "God had killed and raped her," after which statement the recorder added, "Ah, you liar." Stockholm R 21 May 1627: 83–83v; 26 May 1627: 85v; 28 May 1627: 87–87v; 9 June 1627: 89–90; 18 June 1627: 94; ST 1627, p. 75.

58. Stockholm R 27 August 1656: 436–37.

59. See, e.g., Renvall 1949; Liliequist 1992.

60. According to Eva Österberg, the intervention of the state in "new types of crime" increased at the expense of earlier crimes: Deeds of violence were replaced by cases of financial abuse and surveillance of the people's morals. This view is open to criticism, because Österberg's conclusions are based on scant and even one-sided material. Outside the central localities (above all), there is little evidence of such a development, at least in the early seventeenth century. For the latest version of this interpretation, see Österberg n.d., 121–22. For the development of the thesis, see also Österberg 1988, 62–64; 1991a, 155, 157, 163–64; 1991c, 21–22. For a criticism of this proposed development of crime, see Karonen 1994a, 1995a. Sandström 1996 came to the same conclusion, particularly with regard to financial crime.

61. On the professionalization of the administrative and judicial functionaries in the towns in the seventeenth century, see Karonen 1995b; 1996c, 242–52 and the references cited therein; Karonen 1998a.

62. Settlements were not, however, completely unknown in Stockholm. See Lindström 1988a, 131–35.

63. ST 1573, p. 230; 1600, pp. 60, 65–66, 71, 72–73. See also ST 1599, pp. 260–61, 291.

64. Studies of the congregational life in the city also show that the church court (the Consistory) complained about the harsh judgments passed by the lay courts. Although the criticism concerned cases connected with sexual morality and there are statements with a contrary bearing, the mention of such cases and the extremely harsh punishments in cases of sexual crime dealt out by the Consistory itself indicate the "tough" atmosphere that prevailed in the city of Stockholm. See Bogren 1953, 82–83; Murray 1949; figure 2.1 and the sources mentioned therein.

65. Ericsson 1952. Recidivism was rare in Stockholm too. Lindström 1988a, 99.

66. Vadstena 28 September 1624.

67. For example, Vadstena 2 August 1619, 6 December 1619. Similar instances can be found in the Finnish towns in the 1620s, e.g., in the small towns (particularly Pori) of the Province of Turku and Pori. Karonen 1994a, 92.

68. Vadstena 9 April 1587, p. 118; see also Vadstena 28 April 1605, p. 373.

69. Vadstena 9 October 1596, pp. 221–22; 22 November 1596, p. 226.

70. Arboga 3 July 1599: 515. According to Österberg (1988, 62–63), as many as 90 percent of the fines imposed for minor crimes of violence in Arboga in the early sixteenth century were reduced.

71. Arboga 18 April 1599: 479; 7 July 1599: 483.

72. This interpretation is based on research currently being carried out by the present writer and covering nearly thirty Swedish and Finnish towns during the Vasa period. The state authorities also reacted to the problems of Vadstena, e.g., by appointing royal mayors from outside the town community, but these measures, which weakened the town's independent authority, only served to exacerbate the situation. See Karonen 1995b, 51; cf. Corin 1978, 228.

73. Especially the Arboga Treasurer's Court began to impose lenient punishments for cases of petty violence and slander in the late 1650s. See, e.g., Arboga K 29 March 1658: 208v.

74. See, e.g., Turku R 31 August 1639: 259; 24 March 1641: 220, 29 March 1641: 233–34, 5 April 1641: 246–47, 7 April 1641: 251–52; 6 November 1641: 49–50; 22 January 1642: 112, 24 January 1642: 116–17, 5 February 1642: 124–25, 7 February 1642: 125–26, 14 February 1642: 138, 19 February 1642: 148, 26 February 1642: 152, 2 March 1642: 163–64, 5 March 1653: 51; Karonen 1996a, 77–78.

75. Karonen 1997, 250–55.

76. There are some indications that the Turku Court of Appeal was rather stricter about settlements in homicide cases. These cases, however, concern killings that took place in the countryside. See Aalto 1997, 183.

77. For the basis of the statistics in figures 2.1 through 2.4, see n. 26, above, and the sources mentioned therein. Dag Lindström (1988a) has calculated the number of homicides from the judgments in the "notebooks," which produces a slightly lower figure than that given here. For crimes of petty violence, Lindström's data have been supplemented with material compiled by Piia Vuorela (1997) according to slightly different principles. See also Söderberg 1993, 90–91.

78. The data on both persons who were undoubtedly victims of homicide and those who were executed in Turku (although not all of them received their punishment for homicide or even for crimes committed in the city of Turku) have been taken from the Turku Ca-

thedral list of persons buried. However, those who were executed in connection with the political crisis of the 1590s have not been included. BÅH l:I; Karonen 1995c.

79. The records of the Turku Treasurer's Court from the year 1639 on have been preserved, which may partly explain the increased number of violent crimes recorded at the beginning of the 1640s.

80. The Finnish material covers all of the thirteen "old" (i.e., founded before 1632) towns. See Karonen 1995c, 9.

81. It has generally been held that there was a fairly uninterrupted decline in homicidal crime in Stockholm from the fifteenth century right down to the 1750s at least. See esp. Söderberg 1993, 90 (figure); Jarrick and Söderberg 1993; Andersson 1996. According to Lindström, who used other methods to achieve his results, violent crime was more prevalent in the 1580s than earlier in the same century. Lindström (1988b, 84, 85, and n. 55) has taken punished crimes of violence as the object of his research.

82. The decisions of the Svea Court of Appeal concerning Arboga for the period under investigation have not been preserved.

83. Cf. particularly Österberg 1988; 1991b, 73; 1991c; see also Karonen 1995c, 7n. 19. At the end of the sixteenth and the beginning of the seventeenth centuries in Vadstena, numerous killings that were committed elsewhere were investigated. Naturally, these should not be included in the homicide figures for Vadstena.

84. See, e.g., Bonney 1991.

85. Cases directly connected with warfare and politics, such as the executions ordered by the courts under Duke Charles, have not been included in the homicide figures for the towns. There is a considerable body of literature on the political problems in Sweden in the sixteenth century: see, e.g., Anthoni 1935, 1937; Odén 1966; Roberts 1968; Renvall 1939; Ylikangas 1996.

86. While there are deficiencies in the source material, the data are nevertheless indicative. The material only includes cases from the towns of "Old" Sweden within the area under the jurisdiction of the Göta Court of Appeal, and thus does not include killings that took place in towns captured from Denmark. These towns observed the law of Denmark for most of the period of this study.

87. The differences between Söderberg's figures and those presented here are partly a result of different population estimates. Here the population of Stockholm has been calculated according to the data of Sven Lilja (1995).

88. The populations of the towns in the area (except Stockholm) have been estimated as follows:

	Towns in Judicial District of Svea Court of Appeal	*Towns in Judicial District of Göta Court of Appeal*	*Total*
1635–50	17,000	17,000	34,000
1650s	22,000	23,000	45,000
1690s	28,000	27,000	55,000

Sources: RA KA Boskaps- m.fl. Längder; Mantalslängder; Verificationer; Eli F. Heckscher Collection; Lilja 1994, 1990.

Note: Lilja's population estimates have been partly modified because his classification does not follow the borders of the judicial districts of the courts of appeal.

89. It has been noted in studies concerning the countryside that cases of minor violence are no longer to be found in the judgment books in the seventeenth century. Minor cases were settled out of court; in other words, the development in the countryside was exactly the opposite of what is suggested here as taking place in the towns. Judicial procedures were less well developed in the countryside, where there were court sessions only two or three times a year, while in the towns the courts might sit that often in one week. See, e.g., Matikainen 1996, 34; Aalto 1996, 59–62; Aalto 1997; cf. more generally Lenman-Parker 1980, who points out that petty crime gradually began to disappear from the courts.

90. Cf. Andersson (1994, 70), according to whom the strong growth of the state executive in Stockholm happened at the same time as "the establishment of more peaceful relations between people." Andersson links this with the development of civil justice. Financial disputes now began to be settled peacefully.

91. See esp. Karonen 1994b; Karonen 1995b; Karonen 1996c.

92. On this subject, see esp. Karonen 1994b, chap. 6. Shoemaker (1991, 92–93) notes that in London in the latter half of the seventeenth century there was evidently little settlement of criminal cases. There would have been a need for informal mediation, however, because the poor could not afford to prosecute their cases officially in court.

93. On this see also Lindström 1989b, 90–91.

94. According to Arne Jansson (1991, 220), cases of violence perpetrated by soldiers in Stockholm at the end of the 1650s were automatically referred to courts-martial.

95. Another appeal made by the people of Arboga refers to as many as four victims: see ULA Arboga R as an appendix to the judgment book for 1613, fols. 1042–43; "kortt memorial . . . om dhe klagemåls puncter some borgerskapit wthi Arboga Stadh hafua emott Welam Von Saltzburgz Soldater," fols. 1052–53; Corin 1978, p. 103. On the appointment of a special commission of investigation, see RA RR 5 March 1613: 221, 223, 224.

96. For example, in 1605 almost a score of German cavalrymen ran riot in Stockholm, causing a general uproar, wounding the city guards, and shooting a miller's assistant. Lindström (1988b, 90) has also drawn attention to rioting by groups of soldiers. ST 1605, pp. 55–58, 58–61.

97. However, 25 percent of the perpetrators in Stockholm went undiscovered.

98. By using this method, the level of homicidal crime in Stockholm, for example, could be made to appear much more "civilized" in the sixteenth century as well, as the method of presentation below shows:

The minimum numbers of outsiders—victims and perpetrators—from outside the urban communities in Stockholm and the towns within the judicial district of the Göta Court of Appeal (source: tables 2.2 and 2.3):

	Victims	*Perpetrators*
Stockholm 1544–80	30	16
Towns in the judicial district of the Göta Court of Appeal	28	35

99. Österberg 1991b; Söderberg 1992, 25; Karonen 1995c, 7, 10; Karonen 1996a, 79; see also Spierenburg 1994, 706–7 (the annual homicide rate in Amsterdam in the sixteenth century was 20–30/100,000 inhabitants and in the latter half of the seventeenth century un-

der 10); Schwerhoff 1991, 282–86 (at the turn of the sixteenth and seventeenth centuries on average 9 persons per 100,000 per annum died violently in Cologne).

100. See, e.g., Ylikangas 1994; Aalto 1997; Jarrick and Söderberg 1993, 1994a; Andersson 1994, 1995; Österberg 1996b.

101. On the subject of billeting and other military burdens on the towns, see Sandberg 1991, 320–27; Jansson 1991, 208–14; Karonen 1996a, 94.

102. Stockholm K 20 August 1653: 298–298v.

103. Stockholm K 8 December 1656: 390v–391v; 10 December 1656: 394.

104. For a similar case, see Södra förstadens K 15 July 1659: 88v–89 (Laurentius Klingelius accused Olof Bengtsson of committing violence on the public highway and in a harbor).

105. See Karonen 1998a; Thunander 1993.

106. The sources for the Göta Court of Appeal for the 1680s and 1690s are sadly inadequate.

107. Although harsher than average punishments were meted out in the capital, it can still be maintained that sentences became more lenient in the seventeenth century. Of the cases handled in Stockholm between 1544 and 1580, 21 percent were settled with fines. In 19 percent of the cases, there was no sentence or it is not known. Probably, however, the number of executed killers was somewhat lower than the number of those who were given capital sentences, for some of the cases were referred to the king, who could commute the sentence. See table 2.2 and the sources mentioned therein.

108. This is indicated by results obtained by Thunander (1993). Likewise Johan Söderberg (1993 and elsewhere) has emphasized the decrease in capital sentences.

109. Karonen 1997.

110. See Jansson 1994, 29; Jarrick and Söderberg 1994a, 15.

111. One important exception to the rule is the town of Kokkola (Gamla Karleby) in Ostrobothnia in Finland, where in the 1650s and 1660s it often seemed as if the town was run by the church minister. It is hardly a coincidence that Gamla Karleby was one of the most peaceful towns of the time in terms of registered violence. Karonen 1998b.

112. Cf. Jansson 1994, 21, 29, 31.

Sources

Archive Sources

Göta hovrätts arkiv (GHA) [Göta Court of Appeal Archives], Jönköping

Criminalia (GHC), 1635–88, EVAA: 1–66, consulted on microfiche in the Swedish State Archives in Stockholm.

Brottmålsutslag (BU), BIIA: 2 4, 1693–95.

Vadstena rådstuga 1618–60 (Vadstena).

Kansallisarkisto (KA) [Finnish National Archives], Helsinki

Åbo rådstuvurättsprotokoll and Åbo kämnersrättprotokoll 1623–60 (Turku R and Turku K), consulted in the microfilm collection of Jyväskylän yliopiston historian laitos [Dept. of History of Jyväskylä University] (JYHL)

Landsarkiv i Uppsala (ULA) [Uppsala Provincial Archives]

Arboga rådstuvurättsprotokoll 1569–1613 (Arboga).

Kortregister över Svea Hovrätts brev till länstyrelserna. Svea Hovrätts kriminaldomar (KSHB).

Riksarkivet (RA) [Swedish State Archives], Stockholm
Ekonomisk-historiska föreningens vid Stockholms högskola arkiv
Eli F. Heckschers arkiv, Låda 16. Mantalskriven befolkning 1633–1820 (Eli F. Heckscher Collection).
Kammararkivet (KA) [Chamber Archives], Stockholm
Landskapshandlingar (LH), Östergötland, consulted on microfilm in RA. Vols. 1, 3 (1540–41).
Boskaps- m. fl. längder.
Länsräkenskaper. Mantalslängder (Mantalslängder).
Verifikationer 1628–50 (Verifications).
Riksregistratur [Swedish National Records] 1613 (RR) (JYHL).
Svea hovrätts arkiv [Svea Court of Appeal Archives]
Consulted on microfiche.
Arboga rådstuvurättsprotokoll ad Arboga kämnersrättsprotokoll 1615–60 (Arboga R and Arboga K).
Norrmalms (Stockholm) kämnersrätt 1644–45 (Norrmalm).
Stockholms stadsarkiv (SSA) [Stockholm City Archives], Stockholm
The Stockholm material is not referred to in detail.
Borgmästare och råds arkiv före 1636
Tänkeböcker i renskrift.
Vols. 40–44, Stockholms stads tänkebok 1626–35.
Saköreslängder vol. 95, 1623–37.
Stockholms magistrats och rådhusrätts arkiv 1636–1849.
Renskrift av tänkebok vols. 1–20.
Stockholms stads tänkebok 1636–60.
Stockholms stads huvudböcker.
Originalhuvudböcker. Vols. 26–47 (1637–60).
Norra förstadens kämnärsrätt.
Protokoll i civil- och kriminalmål (renskrift). Vols. 1–7 (1635–54).
Stockholms stads kämnersrätt vols. 1–16 (1640–60).
Södra förstadens kämnersrätt vols. 1–7 (1654–60).
Turun kaupunginarkisto (TKA) [City Archive of Turku] (Åbo)
Åbo rådstuvurättsprotokoll (koncept).

Published Sources and Official Documents

BÅH 1: I. *Utdrag ur Åbo domkyrkas räkenskaper 1553–1634. Bidrag till Åbo stads historia.* Första serien. I. Published by R. Hausen. Helsingfors, 1884.

Ericsson, Georg J. V. 1952. *Vadstena stads äldsta tänkeböcker ("domboken") 1577–1610.* Published by Georg J. V. Ericsson. Uppsala.

Noreen, Erik. 1941–50. *Arboga stads tänkebok IV. Fjärde delen 1534–1569. Utgiven av Erik Noreen samt register till Arboga stads tänkebok av Sven Ljung.* Collections published by Svenska Fornskrift-Sällskapet. Bd 53. Uppsala.

Norri, Matti, trans. 1987. Olavus Petri, *Tuomarinohjeet.* Jyväskylä.

Schmedeman, Joh. 1706. Kongl. *Stadgar, Förordningar och Resolutioner Ifrån Åhr 1528 in till 1701 angående Justitie och Executions-Åhrender.* Published by Joh. Schmedeman. Stockholm.

Stockholms stadsböcker från äldre tid. Andra serien. Tänkeböcker. Ny följd. 1–8. 1544–91. Published by Joh. Ax. Almquist. Stockholm, 1936–48.

Stockholms stads tänkeböcker från år 1592. Utgivna av Stockholms stadsarkiv. Del I–XVI. 1592–1627. Edited by Daniel Almquist, Folke Sleman, Göran Setterkrans, Nils Staf, Lars Wickström, Sven Olsson, and Naemi Särnqvist. Stockholm and Uppsala, 1939–94.

References

Aalto, Seppo. 1996. *Kirkko ja kruunu siveellisyyden vartijoina. Seksuaalirikollisuus, esivalta ja yhteisö Porvoon kihlakunnassa 1621–1700.* Bibliotheca Historica 12. Helsinki.

———. 1997. "Miksi rikosrakenne muuttui? Väkivalta-ja seksuaalirikokset 1500- ja 1600-luvulla." In Koskivirta 1997.

Adler, Jeffrey S. 1997. "'My Mother-in-Law Is to Blame, but I'll Walk on Her Neck Yet': Homicide in Late Nineteenth-Century Chicago." *Journal of Social History* 2.

Ågren, Henrik. 1998. *Tidigmodern tid. Den sociala tidens roll i fyra lokalsamhällen 1650–1730.* Studia historica Upsaliensia 185. Stockholm.

Andersson, Hans, 1994. "Rättssäkerheten i stormaktstidens Stockholm." In Jarrick and Söderberg 1994b.

———. 1995. "Genus och rättskultur. Kvinnlig brottslighet i stormaktstidens Stockholm." *Historisk tidskrift* (Sweden) 2.

———. 1996. "Heder och civilisering." *Historisk tidskrift* (Sweden) 2.

Andrén, Åke. 1990. "Den andliga domsrätten i Sverige under reformationstiden." In *Reformationens konsolidering i de nordiska länderna 1540–1610,* ed. Ingmar Brohed. Otta.

Anthoni, Eric. 1935. *Konflikten mellan hertig Carl och Finland. Konfliktens uppkomst och hertigens seger.* Helsingfors.

———. 1937. *Konflikten mellan hertig Carl och Finland. Avvecklingen och försoningen.* Skrifter utgivna av svenska litteratursällskapet i Finland CCLXII. Helsingfors.

Blomstedt, Yrjö. 1987. *Esipuhe, Olavus Petri, Tuomarinohjeet.* Translated into Finnish by Matti Norri. Jyväskylä.

Bogren, Yngve. 1953. *Kampen om Stockholms kyrko- och skolstyrelse 1640–1668.* Lund.

Bonney, Richard. 1991. *The European Dynastic States 1494–1660.* The Short Oxford History of the Modern World. Avon.

Cockburn, J. S. 1991. "Patterns of Violence in English Society: Homicide in Kent 1560–1985." *Past & Present* 130.

Corin, Carl-Fredrik. 1978. *Arboga stads historia. Från 1500-talets mitt till 1718.* Köping.

Dean, Trevor, and Kate Lowe. 1994. "Writing the History of Crime in the Italian Renaissance." In *Crime, Society, and the Law in Renaissance Italy,* ed. Trevor Dean and K. J. P. Lowe. London.

Duerr, Hans Peter. 1988. *Nacktheit und Scham.* Frankfurt am Main.

Elias, Norbert. 1978. *The Civilizing Process.* Vol. 1: *The History of Manners.* Translated by Edmund Jephcott. New York.

———. 1982. *The Civilizing Process.* Vol. 2: *State Formation and Civilization.* Translated by Edmund Jephcott with some notes and revisions by the author. Worcester.

Emsley, Clive. 1996. *Albion's Felonious Attractions: Reflections upon the History of Crime in England.* In Emsley and Knafla 1996.

Emsley, Clive, and Louis A. Knafla, eds. 1996. *Crime History and Histories of Crime: Studies in the Historiography of Crime and Criminal Justice in Modern History.* Westport, Conn.

Englund, Peter. 1994 (1989). *Det hotade huset. Adliga föreställningar om samhället under stormaktstiden.* 3d ed. Stockholm.

Finch, A. J. 1997. "The Nature of Violence in the Middle Ages: An Alternative Perspective." *Historical Research* (October).

Forssell, Hans. 1872–73. *Sverige 1571. Försök till en administrative-statistisk beskrifning öfver det Egentliga Sverige, utan Finland och Estland.* I–II. Äldre bidrag till Sveriges officiella statistik I. Stockholm.

Forsström, Sari. 1996. "Laittomuuden laitatiellä." In *Laittomuuden laitatiellä. Rikos Suomessa 1500-luvulta nykypäiviin*, ed. Sari Forsström. Helsinki.

Frank, Michael. 1995. *Dörfliche Gesellschaft und Kriminalität: Das Fallbeispiel Lippe, 1650–1800.* Paderborn.

Fumagalli, Vito. 1994. *Landscapes of Fear: Perceptions of Nature and the City in the Middle Ages.* Translated by Shayne Mitchell. Cornwall.

Greyerz, Kaspar von, ed. 1984. *Religion and Society in Early Modern Europe, 1500–1800.* Chatham.

Grotenfelt, K. 1887. *Suomen kaupasta ja kaupungeista ensimmäisten Vaasa-kuninkaiden aikana.* Helsinki.

Hemmer, Ragnar. 1928. *Studier rörande straffutmätningen i medeltida svensk rätt.* Helsingfors.

Jaakkola, R. 1995. *Kriminologian teoriat.* Encyclopaedia Iuridica Fennica. IV. Rikos- ja prosessioikeus. Jyväskylä.

Jansson, Arne. 1991. *Bördor och bärkraft. Borgare och kronotjänare i Stockholm 1644–1672.* Stockholmsmonografier utgivna av Stockholms stad 103. Uppsala.

———. 1994. "Mörda för att få dö." In Jarrick and Söderberg 1994b.

Jarrick, Arne, and Johan Söderberg. 1993. "Spontaneous Processes of Civilization: The Swedish Case." *Ethnologia Europaea: Journal of European Ethnology* 23, no. 1.

———. 1994a. "Inledning." In Jarrick and Söderberg 1994b.

———, eds. 1994b. *Människovärdet och makten. Om civiliserings-processen i Stockholm, 1600–1850.* With the participation of Hans Andersson, Börje Bergfelt, Eva Eggeby, Arne Jansson, Arne Jarrick, Johan Söderberg. Monografier utgivna av Stockholms stad vol 118. Uppsala.

Karonen, Petri. 1994a. "Brottsligheten i städerna i Egentliga Finland och Satakunta i början av 1600-talet." *Historisk tidskrift för Finland* 1.

———. 1994b. *Kämnerinoikeudet Suomen kaupungeissa suurvalta-ajan alkupuolella (noin 1620–1660).* Studia Historica Jyväskyläensia 48. Jyväskylä.

———. 1995a. "Brottsligheten i Norden på 1500- och 1600-talet. *Historisk tidskrift* (Sweden) 1.

———. 1995b. *"Raastuvassa tavataan." Suomen kaupunkien hallinto- ja oikeuslaitoksen toimintaa ja virkamiehiä suurvalta-aikana.* Studia Historica Jyväskyläensia 51. Saarijärvi.

———. 1995c. "Trygg eller livsfarlig? Våldsbrottsligheten i Finlands städer 1540–1660." *Historisk tidskrift för Finland* 1.

———. 1996a. "Pohjolan vaarallisimmat asuinpaikat. Rikollisuus, pelko ja turvattomuus Suomen kaupungeissa uuden ajan alussa (noin 1540–1660)." In Forsström 1996.

———. 1996b. "Raiskaus—lähes tuntematon rikos 1500- ja 1600-luvulla?" In Forsström 1996.

———. 1996c. "Kronan och borgmästarna under stormaktstiden." *Historisk tidskrift för Finland* 2.

———. 1997. "Rahakkaista sovinnoista valtiovallan väliintuloon. Henkirikosten sovittelu Ruotsin kaupungeissa suurvalta-ajalla." In Koskivirta 1997.

———. 1998a. "The Worst Offenders in the Provincial Towns: Serious Urban Crime and Its Perpetrators in the Early Years of Sweden's Period as a Great Power." *Scandinavian Journal of History* 3–4.

———. 1998b. *Väkivalta, kunnia ja oikeuskulttuurit Pohjanmaan kaupungeissa puhdasoppisuuden ajalla. Kokkola ja Vaasa 1620–1670.* Published on the Web by Chydenius Institute <http://educa.kpnet.fi/kpkeko/chydeni/digiluku/petrik/karoalku.htm>.

Katajala, Kimmo, ed. 1995. *Manaajista maalaisaateliin. Tulkintoja toisesta historian, antropologian ja maantieteen välimaastossa.* SKS. Tietolipas 140. Jyväskylä.

Kaukiainen, Yrjö. 1980. "Suomen asuttaminen." In *Suomen taloushistoria 1. Agraarinen Suomi,* ed. Eino Jutikkala, Yrjö Kaukiainen, and Sven-Erik Åström. Helsinki.

Kerkkonen, Veikko. 1945. *Etelä-Suomen kaupunkien kruunun-verot 1614–1650.* HTutk XXX. Helsinki.

King, Peter. 1996. "Punishing Assault: The Transformation of Attitudes in the English Courts." *Journal of Interdisciplinary History* 27, no. 1 (Summer).

Kirby, David. 1994. *Östersjöländernas historia, 1492–1772.* Uddevalla.

Knafla, Louis A. 1996. "Structure, Conjuncture, and Event in the Historiography of Modern Criminal Justice History." In Emsley and Knafla 1996.

Koskivirta, Anu, ed. 1997. *Tie tulkintaan. Juhlakirja akatemiaprofessori Heikki Ylikankaalle 6. marraskuuta 1997.* Juva.

Kumlien, Kjell. 1971. *Västerås till 1600-talets början. Västerås i gamla tiderna 2.* Västerås.

Lager, Birgitta. 1962. *Stockholms befolkning på Johan III:s tid.* Stockholm.

Lager-Kromnow, Birgitta. 1992. *Att vara stockholmare på 1560-talet.* Stockholmsmonografier utgivna av Stockholms stad vol 110. Uppsala.

Laine, Esko M. 1996. *Yksimielisyys—sota—pietismi. Tutkimuksia suomalaisesta papistosta ja yhteiskunnasta kolmikymmenvuotisesta sodasta pikkuvihaan.* Saarijärvi.

Lenman, Bruce, and Geoffrey Parker. 1980. "The State, the Community and the Criminal Law in Early Modern Europe." In *Crime and the Law: The Social History of Crime in Western Europe since 1500,* ed. V. A. C. Gatrell, Bruce Lenman, and Geoffrey Parker. The Europa Social History of Human Experience. Rochester.

Liliequist, Jonas. 1992. "Brott, synd och straff. Tidelagsbrottet i Sverige under 1600- och 1700-talet." Dissertation, Historiska Institutionen, Umeå.

Lilja, Sven. 1990. "Urbanisering i långtidsperspektiv. Några teorier och ett empiriskt exempel." *Scandia* 2.

———. 1994. "Swedish Urbanization c. 1570–1800: Chronology, Structure and Causes." *Scandinavian Journal of History* 4.

———. 1995. "Stockholms befolkningsutveckling före 1800: problem, metoder och förklaringar." *Historisk tidskrift* (Sweden) 3.

Lindström, Dag. 1988a. "Crime and Control in the Capital: Stockholm 1475–1625." In Österberg and Lindström 1988.

———. 1988b. *Våld,förtal och förlikningar i Stockholm 1475–1625.* Rättshistoriska studier. Vol. 14. Serien II. Lund.

———. 1988c. "The Law and the Courts." In Österberg and Lindström 1988.

———. 1994. "Oärliga mästare och kivande makar. Ett och annat om rättskipning, kriminalitet och normsystem i 1500-talets Norden." *Historisk tidskrift* (Sweden) 4.

———. 1995. "Kvinnor, våld och vardagskriminalitet. Teman inom tysk kriminalitetsforskning." *Scandia* 2.

Lundqvist, Sven. 1974. "Rörlighet och social struktur i 1610-talets Sverige." *Historisk tidskrift* (Sweden).

Lüdtke, Alf, and Herbert Reinke. 1996. "Crime, Police, and the 'Good Order': Germany." In Emsley and Knafla 1996.

Matikainen, Olli. 1995. *Iskuin ja lyönnein. Väkivalta ja käräjät Käkisalmen läänissä 1618–1651*. Jyväskylän yliopisto. Historian laitos. Suomen historian julkaisuja 22. Jyväskylä.

———. 1996. "'Miksi näkisimme vaivaa vanhan miehen veren takia?' Näkökulmia arkipäivän väkivaltaan 1600-luvun Karjalassa." In Forsström 1996.

MESL. 1996. *Magnus Erikssons stadslag i nusvensk tolkning*. Edited by Åke Holmbäck and Elias Wessén. Rättshistoriskt bibliotek. Skrifter utgivna av institutet för rättshistorisk forskning grundat av Gustav och Carin Olin. Lund.

Muchembled, Robert. 1984. "Lay Judges and the Acculturation of the Masses: France and the Southern Low Countries, Sixteenth to Eighteenth Centuries." In Greyerz 1984.

———. 1985. *Popular Culture and Elite Culture in France, 1400–1750*. Translated by Lydia Cochrane. Baton Rouge.

Muir, Edward, and Guido Ruggiero. 1994a. "Afterword: Crime and the Writing of History." In Muir and Ruggiero 1994b.

———, eds. 1994b. *History from Crime*. Translated by Corrada Biazzo Curry, Margaret A. Gallucci, and Mary M. Gallucci. Selections from Quaderni Storici. Baltimore.

Murray, Robert. 1949. *Stockholms kyrkostyrelse intill 1630-talets mitt*. Samlingar och studier till Svenska kyrkans historia 20. Lund.

Næss, Hans Eyvind. 1994. "Vold." In *Det 22. nordiske historikermøte. Oslo 13.–18. august 1994*, ed. Kåre Tønnesson. Rapport II. *Normer og sosial kontroll i Norden ca. 1550–1850. Domstolene i samspill med lokalsamfunnet*. Oslo.

Normann, Carl-E. 1948. *Prästerskapet och det karolinska enväldet. Studier över det svenska prästerskapets statsuppfattning under stormaktstidens slutskede*. Samlingar och studier till svenska kyrkans historia 17. Lund.

Odén, Birgitta. 1966. *Kronohandel och finanspolitik 1560–1595*. Skrifter utgivna av vetenskapssocieteten i Lund 56. Lund.

Österberg, Eva. 1988. "Crime and Punishment in the Provincial Towns of Sweden: Swedish Criminality in a Comparative European Perspective." In Lindström and Österberg 1988.

———. 1991a. "Brott och social kontroll i Sverige från medeltid till stormaktstid. Godtycke och grymhet—eller sunt förnuft och statskontroll?" *Historisk tidskrift* (Norway) 2.

———. 1991b. "Kontroll och kriminalitet i Sverige från medeltid till nutid. Tendenser och tolkningar." *Scandia* 1.

———. 1991c. "Social Arena or Theatre of Power? The Courts, Crime and the Early Modern State in Sweden." In *Theatres of Power: Social Control and Criminality in Historical Perspective*, ed. Heikki Pihlajamäki. Publications of the Matthias Calonius Society I. Jyväskylä.

———. 1992. "Folklig mentalitet och statlig makt. Perspektiv på 1500- och 1600-talets Sverige." *Scandia* 1.

———. 1996a. "Gender, Class, and the Courts: Scandinavia." In Emsley and Knafla 1996.

———. 1996b. "Våld och ära, böter och skam.—Kriminalitet och straff i Sverige från medeltid till nutid." In *Kriminalitet, Kultur, Kontroll—en antologi*, ed. Malin Åkerström. Stockholm.

Österberg, Eva, and Dag Lindström. 1988. *Crime and Social Control in Medieval and Early Modern Swedish Towns*. Lund.

———. 1988. "Conclusion." In Lindström and Österberg 1988.

Pleijel, Hilding. 1951. *Från hustavlans tid.* Kyrkohistoriska folklivsstudier. Lund.

Renvall, Pentti. 1939. *Klaus Fleming und der finnische Adel in den Anfangsphasen der Krise der neunziger Jahre des 16. Jahrhunderts.* Turun yliopiston julkaisuja B: 24. Turku.

———. 1949. Suomalainen 1500-luvun ihminen oikeuskatsomustensa valossa. Turun yliopiston julkaisuja. Sarja B. Osa 33. Turku.

Roberts, Michael. 1968. *The Early Vasas: A History of Sweden, 1523–1611.* Cambridge.

Rousseaux, Xavier. 1996. "From Medieval Cities to National States, 1350–1850: The Historiography of Crime and Criminal Justice in Europe." In Emsley and Knafla 1996.

Sandberg, Robert. 1991. *I slottes skugga. Stockholm och kronan 1599–1620.* Stockholmsmonografier utgivna av Stockholms stad vol 105. Stockholm.

Sandström, Åke. 1996. *Plöjande borgare och handlande bönder. Mötet mellan den europeiska urbana ekonomin och vasatidens Sverige.* Studier i stads- och kommunhistoria 15. Published by Lars Nilsson. Stockholm.

SAOB 19. *Ordbok över svenska språket utgiven av Svenska Akademien.* Nittonde bandet. Lund 1952.

Schwerhoff, Gerd. 1991. *Köln im Kreuzverhör. Kriminalität, Herrschaft und Gesellschaft in einer frühneuzeitlichen Stadt.* Hirschberg.

Sharpe, J. A. 1986. *Crime in Early Modern England, 1550–1750.* Themes in British Social History. Singapore.

———. 1990. "Quantification and the History of Crime in Early Modern England: Problems and Results, Historical Social Research." *Quantum Information—Interquant Newsletter* 15, no. 4. Special issue on Quantification and Criminal Justice History in International Perspective, guest editor Eric A. Johnson.

Shoemaker, R. B. 1991. *Prosecution and Punishment: Petty Crime and the Law in London and Rural Middlesex, c. 1660–1725.* Cambridge Studies in Early Modern British History. Cambridge.

Spierenburg, Pieter. 1984. *The Spectacle of Suffering: Executions and the Evolution of Repression from a Preindustrial Metropolis to the European Experience.* Cambridge.

———. 1994. "Faces of Violence: Homicide Trends and Cultural Meanings: Amsterdam, 1431–1816." *Journal of Social History* 27 (Summer).

Stadin, Kekke. 1993. Maktkamp på Arboga redd. *Sjöfart inom skrå och aktiebolag.* Opuscula Historica Upsaliensia 11.

Stone, Lawrence. 1987. *The Past and the Present Revisited.* Worcester.

Sundin, Jan. 1991. "Världslig pragmatism och religiöst nit. Om sexualitets gränser i Sverige 1600–1850." *Historisk tidskrift* (Norway) 2.

———. 1992. *För Gud, staten och folket. Brott och rättskipning i Sverige 1600–1840.* Rättshistoriskt bibliotek. Vol. 47. Lund.

Söderberg, Johan. 1990. "En fråga om civilisering. Brottmål och tvister i svenska häradsrätten 1540–1660." *Historisk tidskrift* (Sweden) 2.

———. 1992. "Rättsväsendets utbyggnad i Sverige. Lokala konsekvenser och reaktioner 1550–1750." In *Lokalsamfunn og øvrighet i Norden ca. 1550–1750,* ed. Harald Winge. Skrifter fra Norsk lokalhistorisk institutt, publikasjoner nr. 27. Oslo.

———. 1993. *Civilisering, marknad och våld i Sverige 1750–1870. En regional analys.* Acta universitatis Stockholmiensis—Stockholm Studies in Economic History 18. Edsbruk.

Takala, Martti. 1993. *Lex De—Lex Politica: Lex Politica Dei -teos ja Kaarle IX:n lainsäädäntö.* Suomen Kirkkohistoriallisen Seuran toimituksia 160. Tampere.

Thunander, Rudolf. 1993. *Hovrätt i funktion. Göta hovrätt och brottmålen 1635–1699.* Rättshistoriskt bibliotek. Vol. 49. Lund.

Tilly, Charles. 1990. *Coercion, Capital, and European States, A.D. 990–1990.* Studies in Social Discontinuity. Cornwall.

———. 1994. "Entanglements of European Cities and States." In *Cities and the Rise of States in Europe A.D. 1000 to 1800,* ed. Charles Tilly and Wim P. Blockmans. Oxford.

Vilkuna, Kustaa H. J. 1995. "Alkoholin nauttimispaikka, juopottelijat ja juomisen ajankohta 1500–1700-luvun Suomessa." In *Sisä-Suomen tuomiokirjat tutkimuslähteinä ja elämän kuvaajina,* ed. Heikki Roiko-Jokela and Timo Pitkänen. Jyväskylän historiallinen arkisto. Jyväskylän yliopiston historian laitos, Jyväskylän maakuta-arkisto, Jyväskylän historiallinen yhdistys. Jyväskylä.

———. 1996a. *Arkielämää patriarkaalisessa työmiesyhteisössä. Rautaruukkilaiset suurvalta-ajan Suomessa.* HTutk 196. Helsinki.

———. 1996b. "Jumala elä rankase minua. Yksilöllisen subjektin synty." In *Siperiasta siirtoväkeen. Murrosaikoja ja käännekohtia Suomen historiassa,* ed. Heikki Roiko-Jokela. Jyväskylä.

Vuorela, Piia. 1997. "Raadin vallassa, kruunun varjossa. Tukholman kaupungin hallinto- ja oikeuslaitos kasvavien vaatimusten puristuksissa 1580–1627." Master's thesis, Department of Finnish History, University of Jyväskylä, Finland.

Wirth, Jean. 1984. "Against the Acculturation Thesis." In Greyerz 1984.

Ylikangas, Heikki. 1971. *Väkivaltarikosten motivaatiopohja 1500-luvulla Suomessa.* HArk 65. Loviisa.

———. 1976a. "Henkirikos keskiajan lopun ja uuden ajan alun Suomessa." In *Oikeustiede—Jurisprudentia. Suomalaisen lakimiesyhdistyksen vuosikirja VIII.* Vammala.

———. 1976b. "Major Fluctuations in Crimes of Violence in Finland: A Historical Analysis." *Scandinavian Journal of History.*

———. 1982. *Olaus Petrin tuomarinohjeet.* Helsinki.

———. 1988. *Valta ja väkivalta keski- ja uuden ajan taitteen Suomessa.* Juva.

———. 1994. "Ätten och våldet. Våldsbrott i Norden vid övergången till nya tiden." *Historisk tidskrift för Finland* 1.

———. 1996. *Nuijasota.* Keuruu.

CHAPTER 3

Homicide Trends in Estonia, 1971–1996

MARTTI LEHTI

Translated by Eva Lehti and Henry Fullenwider

SINCE 1978, THE HOMICIDE RATE IN ESTONIA HAS FLUCTUATED sharply.[1] This period, which can be regarded as very violent, differs from the period lasting from the early 1950s until 1978, which was characterized by a stable level of violence.

The conclusions in this article are based on a survey of the structure of present-day homicides in Estonia. It was carried out in 1996–97 as a part of two research projects, "History of Criminality" (Heikki Ylikangas, Academy of Finland) and "Eastern European Criminality" (National Research Institute of Legal Policy, Helsinki) and was mainly financed by the NSfK (Reykjavik, Iceland).[2]

Sources

The primary sources for studying homicide trends during this period in Estonia are official statistics, the investigation and legal documents of individual crimes, and news material available in the mass media. The most important of the statistical sources are crime statistics, recorded by the police, and cause-of-death statistics, compiled by the health authorities (in this case, of the number

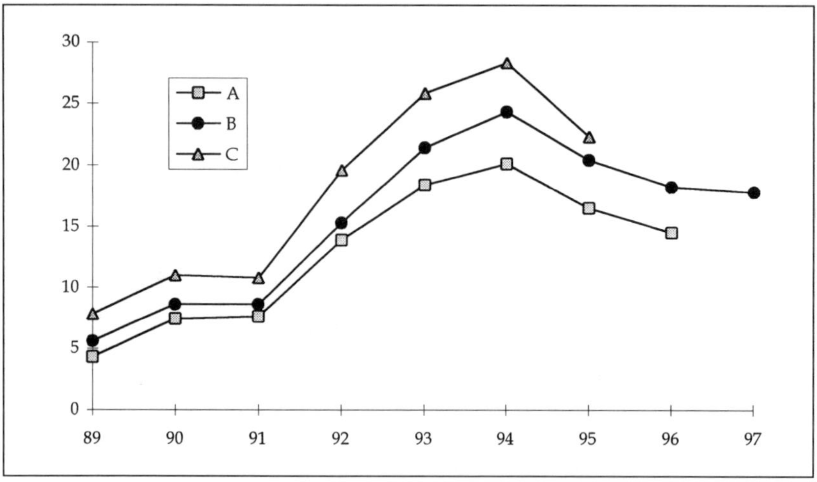

Fig. 3.1. Level of homicides in Estonia per 100,000 inhabitants, 1989–96.

Key: A = crime statistics (excluding attempts); B = crime statistics (including attempts); C = cause-of-death statistics.

of homicide victims). The crime statistics from the Soviet era are even more unreliable than crime statistics usually are. The contents of the Soviet statistics, not only of those published but also of those produced exclusively for use by the authorities, were determined in part by political expediency, which sometimes led to systematic distortion of information.[3]

However, even the older statistical material is relatively reliable regarding Estonian homicide trends. As Estonia was a politically insignificant border area, the pressures to fabricate information were less urgent than in the central areas of the USSR. In addition, homicide is by nature hard to conceal.

The crime statistics and the cause-of-death statistics give a relatively uniform picture of homicides since the late 1980s (see fig. 3.1). Using information from these two sources side by side will thus involve no great problems, although homicide is understood by the police and health authorities to some extent in different ways.

The cause-of-death statistics are practically the only source of information about homicide victims, since before 1996 police authorities often registered only the name of the victim, and the prosecution and legal documents contain very little information in this respect. On the other hand, crime and court statistics, as well as the documentary material, contain plenty of information about homicide offenders.

The most important documents used in this essay are the indictments (*süüdistuskokkuvõte*) from the years 1994–96. They contain a short description of the deed and background information about the offenders. The greatest problem involved in their use is, of course, that they don't give any information on unsolved crimes. On this score, attempts were made to obtain the missing information from investigation protocols and from the files of the Keskuurimisbüroo (the Central Investigation Unit for Serious Crimes in Estonia). In fact, most of the data on homicides committed in 1994–96 are based on Keskuurimisbüroo files for 713 crimes (76 percent of the homicides recorded).

Estonian Homicide Trends in a European Context

In the course of the twentieth century, the trends in Estonian criminality were shaped not only by the country's own social and cultural factors but also by developments in the Soviet Union and Europe in general. Although the Soviet Union passed into history in the early 1990s, the criminality of its successor states is still strongly marked by old common traditions and experiences.

Estonia's Own Tradition of Violence

In the 1900s Western and Central Europe had low homicide rates, and Eastern Europe had high homicide rates. Veli Verkko noted this in his research into European violence during the 1920s and 1930s, and the situation has changed little.[4] However, the area of low violent crime has somewhat enlarged and now includes Southern Europe with the exception of Italy. On the other hand, Eastern Europe can be divided into two parts: the eastern zone (Russia) with its very high rates (more than 6 killings per 100,000 inhabitants per year) and the central zone (2–6 killings per 100,000 inhabitants per year). Before 1990, the central zone consisted of Finland, Italy, the Baltic countries, Hungary, Bulgaria, Slovenia, and Croatia as well as the other Balkan states (with the exception of Greece). Because of their homicide levels, I now include the Baltic countries in the eastern zone, and I consider Poland and the Czech Republic part of the central zone.

In principle, Finland and Estonia share the Eastern European tradition of high violent crime. They have had the same general level of homicide as well as sharp changes in the homicide rate. Developments of short duration have occasionally been very different but at other times similar (see fig. 3.2).

Before 1990, Estonia had three periods of high violence. The first followed World War I and the second followed World War II. The third wave of violence began in the latter half of the 1970s, and it continues to this day. A common feature of the first two was their occurrence at a time of social and political crisis. They were also connected with a preceding period of war. According to Archer

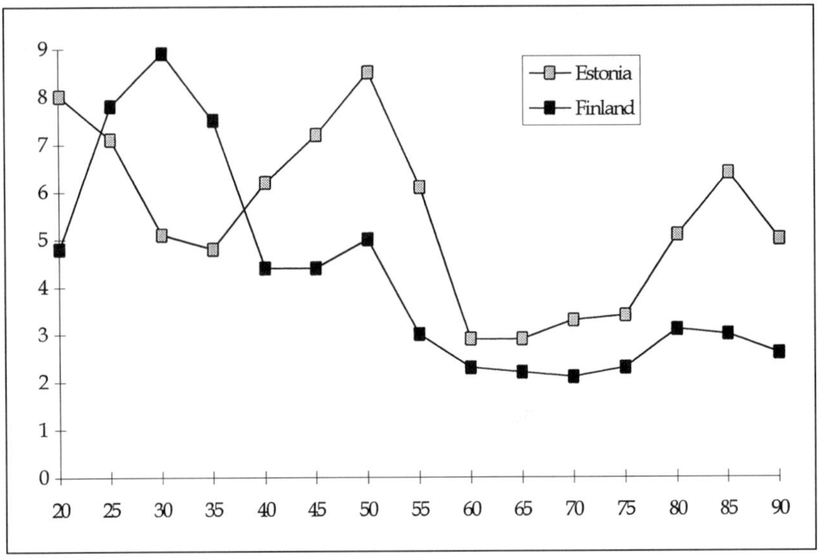

Fig. 3.2. Recorded homicides (excluding attempts and infanticides) per 100,000 inhabitants in Estonia and Finland, 1915–90. Figures are the average figure from the previous five years, except for Estonia in 1920, which is the average value of 1919–21. *Sources:* For Estonia: Leps 1991; Tõnismägi 1995; Eesti Arvudes 1920–35; for Finland: Pajuoja, 1987, 184.

and Gartner, most countries involved in the world wars experienced increased homicide immediately after the war. One of the most significant reasons they found for this was that violent behavior is legitimized by wars.[5] Besides this, in Estonia the increase of violence was related to the lack of a functioning administration both in the early 1920s and in the late 1940s, which created not only favorable conditions but also sometimes a direct need for taking the law into one's own hands and which no doubt contributed to the justification of violent behavior. During both periods, firearms were easy to obtain, and it was common for private citizens to arm themselves.

Crime statistics report only a fraction of the violence in the late 1940s, namely, only the mutual violence of Estonian civilians. Homicides committed by the Red Army, the security organizations, and the party functionaries (even the ones with purely criminal motives) are not included in the statistics. In Latvia, research has been done on nonpolitical violence practiced against the civilian population in the latter half of the 1940s by the Red Army and the NKVD.[6] Although the situation in Estonia was somewhat different—the war went on in Latvia for about six months longer owing to the battles in Kurzeme—the results can be considered similar as far as Estonia is concerned. In Latvia, soldiers of the Red Army committed about ten purely criminal murders a month during 1945 (the population of Latvia was then less than two million). The situation improved in the late 1940s, but total discipline had not yet been restored in the Red Army squads even by the autumn of 1952, despite sporadic efforts.[7]

The personnel of the NKVD and NKGB committed atrocities of the same kind and extent, although accurate statistics regarding their nonpolitical crimes are not available. In Latvia, the level of postwar violent crime was also increased by criminal groups (partly Latvian, partly those extending their activities from Russia to the Baltic countries) roaming the country. According to the reports of the Ministry of the Interior of the Latvian SSR, in 1945 and 1946, over four hundred people belonging to groups of this kind were arrested and accused of homicides. Even though the number of their crimes was probably not equally high, since their deeds were usually committed in groups, in proportion to a population of about two million it was nevertheless considerable.[8]

The above applies only to nonpolitical violence. In addition there was the political violence of the occupation forces and partisan groups waging resistance war.

When examining the homicide trends between 1918 and 1939 in Estonia, Finland, and Hungary, three countries belonging to the same violence zone, there are similarities as well as differences. All three of these countries had to endure a civil war at the end of World War I. In Estonia, the war's social impacts were slight; in Finland and Hungary, deep social divisions resulted. In all three countries, a relative political liberalization was characteristic of the 1920s, especially at the end of the decade. The Great Depression was accompanied by right-wing radicalism and social unrest in the 1930s. The governments in Hungary and Estonia became authoritarian and the social atmosphere more intolerant; in Finland, democracy was more or less preserved, though not without considerable strain.

As to its main features, the fluctuations in homicide in Estonia and Hungary in the 1920s and 1930s are similar, whereas in Finland almost the opposite can be seen (see fig. 3.3). In Estonia and Hungary, the level of homicide was remarkably stable in the 1920s. With the exception of the years immediately following World War I, the homicide rate in Estonia was about five and in Hungary about 3 per 100,000 inhabitants per year—thus in both the countries substantially lower than in Finland. A bloody civil war, as well as the great unrectified inequities of the landowning conditions, hardly seem to have affected the rate of homicide in Hungary during the 1920s.[9] On the other hand, Finland, especially following the civil war (which ended in 1918), had an exceptionally high homicide rate. Yet, even in Finland, the peak was paradoxically reached only in 1927–33.[10] Homicides suddenly doubled in 1927, and

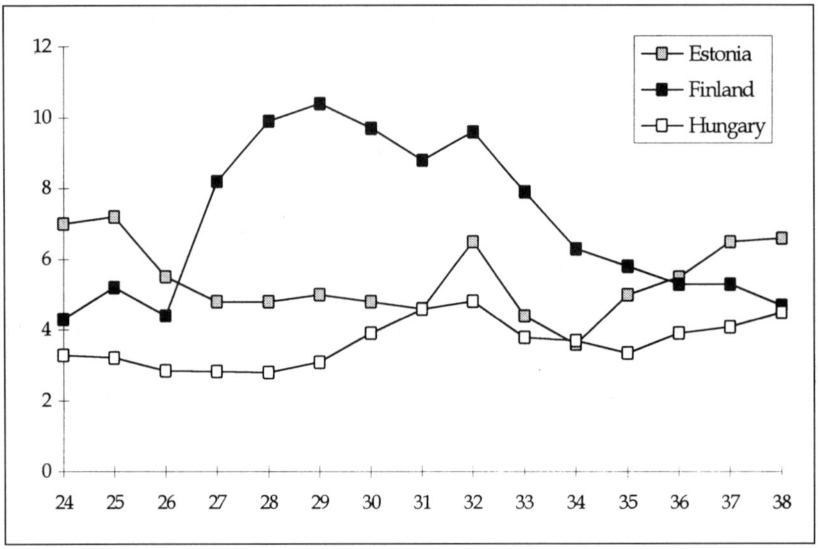

Fig. 3.3. Recorded homicides (excluding attempts and infanticides) per 100,000 inhabitants in Estonia, Finland, and Hungary, 1924–38. *Sources:* For Estonia and Finland, see fig. 3.2; Hungary: Archer and Gartner 1984, appendix.

they peaked in 1929 at 10.4 killings per 100,000 inhabitants. In the most dismal places, like Huopalahti and Kuusankoski, the level was as high as 30–40 per 100,000 inhabitants.[11] After this the homicide rate began to fall, and by 1934 it reflected the situation in the early 1920s.

The Great Depression put a great strain on the Estonian and Hungarian economy and society in particular; although the crisis was serious in Finland, too, its effects there were lighter and of shorter duration. Homicide increased considerably in Hungary but not in Estonia and Finland. As a whole, violent crime in Estonia remained stable and low between 1929 and 1933, as the right-wing Vapsi Movement rose and fell.[12] Homicide also decreased in Finland in 1930–31, when the right-wing Lapua Movement was most active.

In the latter half of the 1930s, during the autocratic administration of Konstantin Päts, when strict police control over the population was gaining in effectiveness, homicide rates were steadily increasing in Estonia.[13] The same phenomenon was also registered in Hungary, where the 1930s saw a gradual increase in administrative autocracy and violent crime. For Finland, the opposite was true. In those years, the social and economic development in Estonia was similar to that in Finland: prosperity and living conditions were rising rather evenly in all population groups, and the social atmosphere was at least superficially calm. The main difference between the situation in Finland, on the one hand, and in Estonia and Hungary, on the other, in the latter half of the 1930s is to be found in the political domain. In Finland the acceptance of the administration among the population was on the increase; in Estonia and Hungary the reverse was true. It is possible that this had some influence on the opposite trends of the homicide rate.

Estonia and the Homicide Trends in the Soviet Union

From 1945 until 1991, Estonia was de facto part of the Soviet Union. Besides having social and economic factors in common that influenced the trends of criminality, the Estonian underworld itself was a part of the northwestern Russian underworld. The expansion process was rapid: the criminal groups operating from Russia extended their activities to the Baltic countries as early as spring 1945, following on the heels of the occupation army.[14]

In the 1950s, Estonian society began to be transformed by a process whose long-term consequences might possibly account for the differences between the present-day homicide trends in the Baltic countries and Russia, on one hand, and in Eastern Central European countries, on the other: namely, the Soviet policy of internal immigration and the russification of the non-Russian republics, the Baltic countries in particular. The policy created immigrant towns with artificial economic and social structures, where the normal social networks were developing slowly and where the behavior of inhabitants was primarily controlled only by the authorities.

The systematic russification of Estonia took place between 1956 and 1987. In the 1960s and the 1970s, an average of 27,000 people were immigrating annually (principally from Russia and the other Slavonic republics) to Estonia. On the other hand, only one immigrant out of seven settled down permanently in the country, so the process resembled transit traffic to a considerable extent.[15] The immigrants were mostly young adults, and they settled down in Tallinn as well as in the industrial centers of the oil-shale mining areas in northeastern Estonia. The immigrant population was at its largest in the 1980s; by 1987 the policy had been abandoned.

The large group of young people, recently arrived and with loose social connections, might be supposed to have increased the homicide rate in Estonia since the 1960s. The picture was, however, anything but unambiguous. From the end of the 1950s until 1977 the homicide rate was very stable in Estonia. All in all, in the years 1951–60 the number of reported homicides increased during three years and decreased during seven years; between 1961 and 1970 the rate rose in five years and fell in five years; and the situation was the same between 1971 and 1980 (see fig. 3.4).

Table 3.1. Nationality of the Offender for Solved Homicides, 1994–96 (%)

	East Virumaa[a]		*Tallinn*[b]		*Rest of Estonia*		*Estonia*	
	p	*t*	*p*	*t*	*p*	*t*	*p*	*t*
Estonian	11	11	30	29	71	68	38	36
Non-Estonian	89	89	70	71	29	32	62	64
% of Estonians in total population Jan. 1, 1996	19		57		87		65	
N	242	145	330	234	272	158	844	537

Note: p = Politseiameti Teabebüroo; t = Keskuurimisbüroo.
[a] East Virumaa and Narva.
[b] Tallinn, Harjumaa, and West Virumaa.

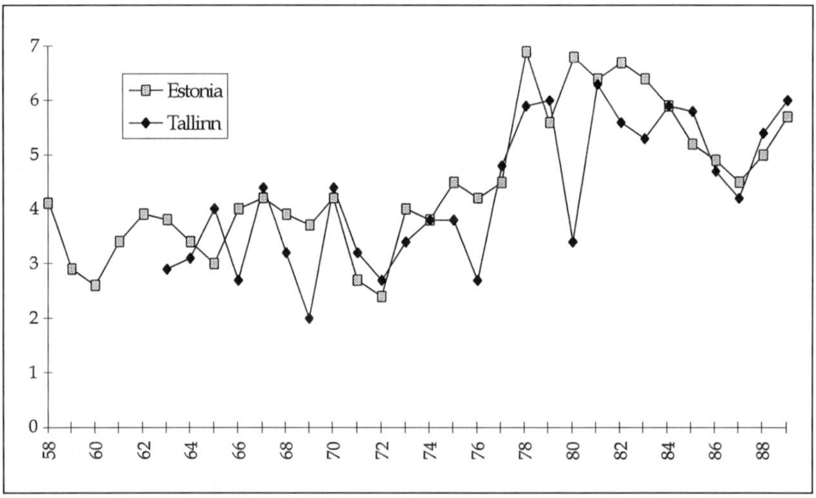

Fig. 3.4. Recorded homicides (including attempts) per 100,000 inhabitants in Estonia and the city of Tallinn, 1958–89. *Source:* Politseiameti Teabebüroo.

Although immigration does not directly show in the crime statistics, it seems to have increased violence in Estonia from the 1950s onwards. That is to say, the level of violent crimes among the immigrant population and their offspring has been considerably higher than among Estonians at least since 1980, and it still is.[16] The overall criminality of the non-Estonian population is at the moment somewhat higher than that of Estonians (see table 3.1).[17] The difference is, however, not essential and is largely accounted for by the different age structure of the population groups. Among those suspected of all crimes that were solved in 1995, 58 percent were Estonians and 42 percent were non-Estonians. On the contrary, the discrepancy in violent crimes is considerable: in the same year, 65 percent of those suspected of robberies were non-Estonians; the percentage in aggravated assaults was 55 percent, and in homicides, 66 percent.[18] To a great extent, the situation in Estonia thus resembles that in many other immigrant communities.[19] What is abnormal is the large proportion of immigrants among the total population.

The non-Estonian overrepresentation among the perpetrators of homicides is accounted for neither by regional factors nor by the concentration of the killings in cities or in northern Estonia. The Russian population is indeed distinctly urban: on January 1, 1996, 91 percent of Russians and 58 percent of Estonians in Estonia lived in cities or towns; however, homicide rates in rural areas and in cities are practically identical in Estonia; murders are not specific to towns. On the other hand, in northern Estonia, where the bulk of the non-Estonian population lives, the homicide rate is considerably higher than elsewhere in the country. The overrepresentation of the Russian population among the homicide perpetrators is, however, to be seen throughout the country. It is not limited only to Estonia, as the corresponding phenomenon is also perceptible in Latvia.[20] In Estonia the disproportion is by far the sharpest in the region of Tallinn, the slightest in East Virumaa.

The difference between the age structure of the Estonians and that of the non-Estonians is not a sufficient explanation either. The latest statistical information available on the age structure dates back to 1989 and is thus somewhat out of date (see fig. 3.5). In general, the situation is still, however, the same. The proportion of the Russian population is largest in the age group of twenty-five to thirty-nine year olds, i.e., the age group that committed about 40 percent of all the homicides in Estonia in 1994–96 (see fig. 3.6).

It is also interesting to notice the distinct difference between the ages of non-Estonian and Estonian offenders. The non-Estonians convicted of homicide are considerably younger than their Estonian counterparts (see fig. 3.7).

The fact that the age structure of Russians in Estonia differs from that of the native population as well as the different age division of Russian and Estonian homicide perpetrators (that is, strengthening its effects) will certainly increase the homicide rates of Russians compared with those of Estonians. Nevertheless, the fact that two-thirds of homicides in Estonia are committed by non-Estonians cannot be accounted for by demography alone, as their overrepresentation among the offenders is too great.

In Estonia, homicide is largely an interethnic phenomenon, though regional

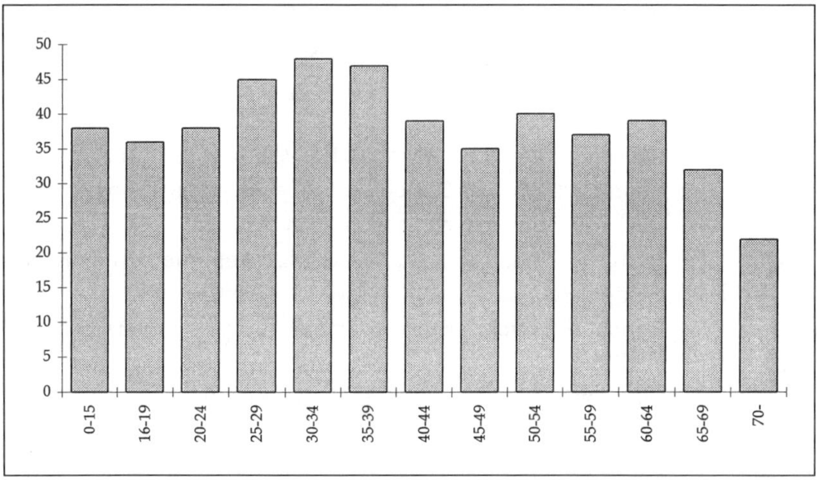

Fig. 3.5. Proportion of non-Estonians (%) living in Estonia in 1989, by age groups (N = 1,565,662).

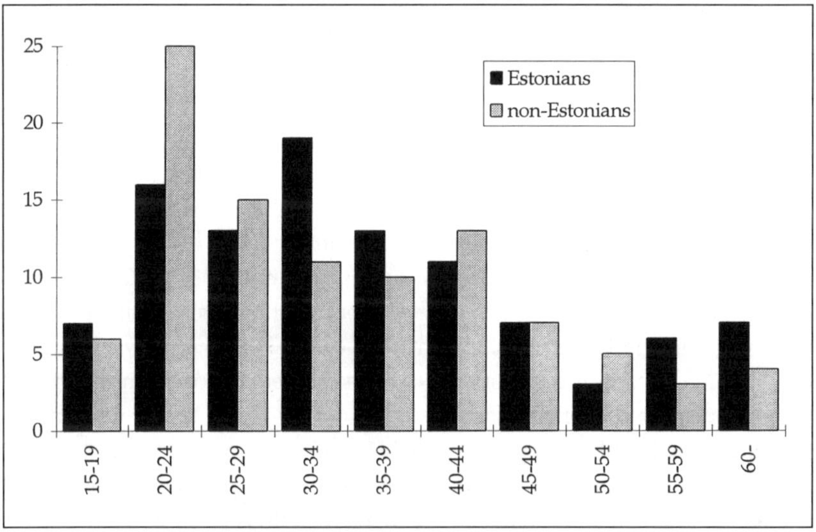

Fig. 3.6. Age structure (%) of Estonians (N = 184) and non-Estonians (N = 304) suspected of homicide in Estonia, 1994–96. *Source:* Keskuurimisbüroo.

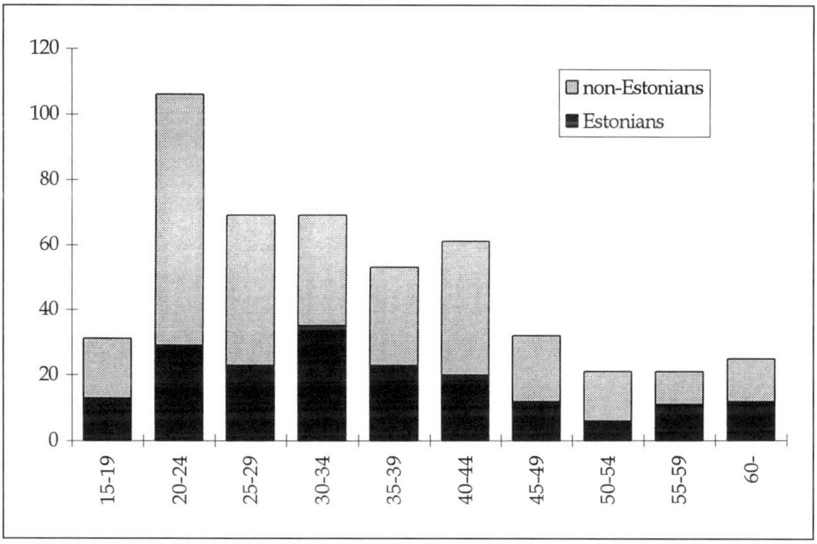

Fig. 3.7. Number of Estonians and non-Estonians convicted of homicide, by age group, 1994–96. *Source:* Keskuurimisbüroo.

differences are great. As is natural, the smaller the national minority in the area is, the greater the risk that those belonging to the main population will be victimized by the minority.[21] While in the whole of Estonia three-fourths of the victims of homicides committed both by the Estonians and the non-Estonians belong to the same nationality as the perpetrator, one-third of the victims of murders committed by Estonians in the province of East Virumaa are Russians and more than half of the victims of homicides committed by non-Estonians in central and southern Estonia are Estonians (see table 3.2).

The types of homicide among the Estonians and the non-Estonians are practically identical. The only significant exception is the almost exclusively inter-Russian violence of criminal groups, which to a large extent takes place in cities. In the same way, the proportion of drinking quarrels (another form of violence concentrated in cities) is slightly greater among the Russians. On the other hand, murders committed for profit are equally common in both groups of population (see fig. 3.8). The younger age structure of the Russian offenders would not therefore seem to be a result of differences in the nature of the committed crimes. The proportion of women and men among the offenders is the same among Estonians and non-Estonians.

The homicide level of the immigrant population, because it is considerably higher than that of Estonians (the homicide level per 100,000 inhabitants

Table 3.2. Nationality of Victim and Perpetrator in Homicides in Estonia, 1994–96

	East Virumaa[a]	*Tallinn*[b]	*Rest of Estonia*	*Estonia*
Estonian perpetrators	16 (11%)	67 (29%)	108 (68%)	191 (36%)
Victim:				
Estonian	10 (56%)	40 (61%)	93 (91%)	143 (77%)
Russian	6 (33%)	18 (27%)	9 (9%)	33 (18%)
Other nationality	—	5 (8%)	—	5 (3%)
Foreigner	—	2 (3%)	—	2 (1%)
Unknown	2 (11%)	1 (2%)	—	3 (2%)
Russian perpetrators	126 (87%)	157 (67%)	47 (30%)	330 (61%)
Victim:				
Russian	93 (78%)	107 (79%)	19 (45%)	219 (74%)
Estonian	20 (17%)	15 (11%)	22 (52%)	57 (19%)
Other nationality	—	1 (1%)	1 (2%)	2 (1%)
Foreigner	—	4 (3%)	—	4 (1%)
Unknown	6 (5%)	8 (6%)	—	14 (5%)
Other perpetrators	3 (2%)	10 (4%)	3 (2%)	16 (3%)
Victim:				
Estonian	1	2	—	3 (18%)
Russian	2	8	—	10 (59%)
Other nationality	—	1	3	4 (24%)

Source: Keskuurimisbüroo.
[a] East Virumaa and Narva.
[b] Tallinn, Harjumaa, and West Virumaa.

among the non-Estonian population was three times greater than that of Estonians in Estonia in 1994–96) and because the difference seems to be a stable phenomenon of longer duration (as the statistical information for the last twenty years suggests), is bound to have had an effect on the fluctuations in homicide rates in the country for the whole postwar period, namely, in direct proportion to the increase in the number of immigrants. As the total level of homicide was stable between 1960 and 1975, one comes to the conclusion that the homicide rate among the Estonian part of the population was decreasing over a longer time and more steeply than the figures concerning the whole population show. The fact that the homicide level in Estonia has been slightly higher than in Finland during the whole postwar period is very much due to immigration.

The reasons for the large volume of homicides among Russians in Estonia are probably largely the same as those which are responsible for violence in immigrant groups in general (loose social relationships, a high degree of urbanization, young age structure), but the cultural differences must also be taken into account. Russia has historically had significantly higher homicide rates

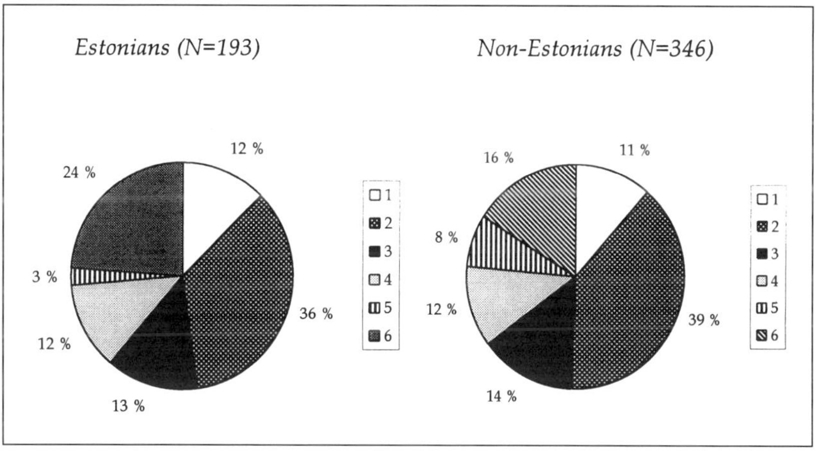

Fig. 3.8. Types of homicide for which the nationality of the offender was known, 1994–96. *Source:* Keskuurimisbüroo.

Key: 1 = family quarrel; 2 = drinking quarrel and other quarrel; 3 = robbery-murder; 4 = other profit; 5 = criminals' mutual violence; 6 = other or unknown. In cases in which several people committed a murder together, the deed was counted for each offender separately. When one person committed several murders, each crime was counted separately.

Note: These classifications are used throughout the article: "family quarrels" refers to impulsive homicides between members of the same family (except crimes committed during general drinking parties, which were included in drinking quarrels); "drinking quarrels" refers to impulsive crimes between drinking partners; "other quarrels" refers to impulsive crimes where the offender and victim were not family members and alcohol was not involved; "other profit" refers to instrumental homicides that were not robbery-murders (e.g., debt-related murders); "criminals' mutual violence" includes all homicides where both the offender and the victim were professional criminals and the motive of the crime was related to their criminal activity.

than the countries in the central zone. The reasons for this difference are not known, but it is possible that they are partly connected with national culture and the modes of behavior based on it.

The period of stable homicide rates came to an end in Estonia in 1977 (see fig. 3.9). It is, however, improbable that the factor which started the wave of violence in 1978 (or even one of the most essential factors) was immigration and the resulting upheaval of the demographic, social, and economic structure in northern Estonia. In fact, the increase in violence was an all-Soviet, partly even a general European phenomenon. All in all, the influence of mass immigration

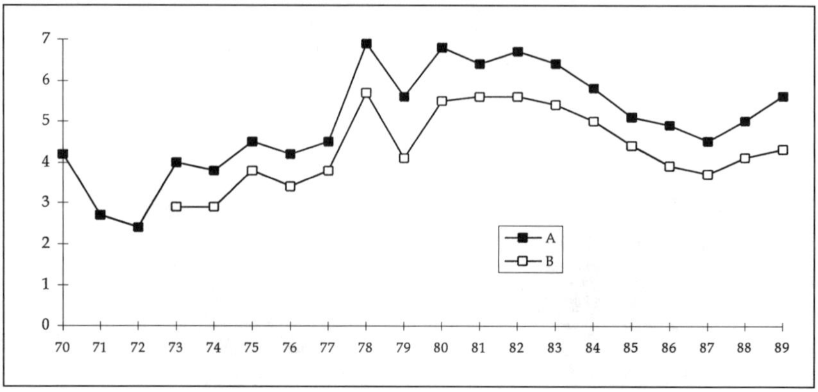

Fig. 3.9. Recorded homicides per 100,000 inhabitants in Estonia, 1970–89. *Source:* Politseiameti Teabebüroo.

Key: A = including attempts; B = excluding attempts.

on homicide rates would seem to have been a slow and lengthy process. It did increase the level of violent crime little by little, but it did not start any particular surge of violence. The trends in the late 1970s, as well as during the early to mid-1990s, do not seem to have influenced the Russian and the Estonian parts of the population in different ways; rather, the factors causing the increase in violent crimes have had approximately the same kind of influence on both population groups. On the whole, the cycles of Estonian homicide rates seem to have been more or less identical with those of European Russia since the 1950s.[22]

Estonia and the General Homicide Trends in Europe

The fluctuations in the Soviet homicide rates in the postwar era, on the other hand, appear at least partly to correspond to those in western countries. In most countries of Western Europe and North America violent crime was on the decrease from the late 1940s till the mid-1960s, but since the latter half of the 1960s the homicide rates have been growing steadily.[23] In Estonia, the general developments have chiefly followed this European pattern, although the increase began relatively late.

Herman Franke believes that the increase in homicides during the past few decades applies (at least in the Netherlands) to instrumental violence in particular, whereas the number of impulsive crimes has remained stable.[24]

A corresponding development is also referred to by reports from the United States, which show that the proportion of murders committed in connection with other crimes increased from 25 to 30 percent of all homicides between

1968 and 1992. At the same time, the percentage of young people among murder victims increased.[25] It should also be noted that a disproportionately large number of violent criminals are young immigrants in the Netherlands. According to Franke, this points to the fact that the increase in violence is due in part to the different culture of violence among immigrants, that it is directly related to postwar immigration. This pattern of explanation, however, seems to leave partly open the question of why the rise in the level of violence is connected with a structural change, in other words, why the homicides today are more related to profit seeking than before. In the United States, the causes for the change have been sought partly in demography: the fact that the postwar baby boom generation had reached the age when they were most likely to commit crimes.[26]

As was shown above, at least the large-scale immigration does not as such fit in as the catalyst of the increase in homicide rates that began in the latter half of the 1970s in Estonia. The following section will discuss changes in the structure of homicides in Estonia since 1978.

Homicide Trends in Estonia between 1971 and 1996

Regional Distribution of Homicides

Violent crime is not evenly distributed by region anywhere. In Western Europe and North America, homicide is largely an urban phenomenon.[27] But in Estonia, Finland, and Latvia, the homicide rates of urban and rural areas have traditionally been rather similar.[28] In Estonia in 1994–96, three-fourths of murders were committed in cities and towns and one-fourth in rural areas (see table 3.3). On January 1, 1996, 70 percent of Estonians lived in cities.

In 1994–96 the level of homicides in relation to the number of inhabitants was indeed somewhat higher in urban areas as a whole, but the sole reason for this was the higher degree of urbanization in northern Estonia (where the bulk of crimes was committed) compared with the rest of the country. When surveying crime rates province by province, it emerges that the homicide level in northern Estonia as well as in other parts of the country was in fact higher in rural areas than in cities (see table 3.4).

Despite the similarity of the volume, the structure of homicides in the rural communes seemed to differ significantly from that of cities between 1989 and 1996.[29] Impulsive violence was more common in urban than in rural areas. Especially homicides connected with the use of alcohol were proportionally more common in urban areas than in the economically less affluent countryside. When evaluating the results, however, one must pay attention to the fact that the location of the crime as recorded in the files of the Keskuurimisbüroo, on

Table 3.3. Recorded Homicides (including attempts) in Estonia, 1994–96, by Locality of Crime

	1994	*1995*	*1996*	*1994–96*
City[a]	262 (72%)	224 (74%)	185 (69%)	671 (72%)
Village	103 (28%)	80 (26%)	61 (23%)	244 (26%)
Uninhabited place	—	—	22 (8%)	22 (2%)
per 100,000 inhabitants				
Urban area	25.1	21.8	18.2	21.7
Rural area	23.0	17.9	18.6[b]	19.8
N	365	304	268	937

Source: Politseiameti Teabebüroo.

[a]The classification here and in table 3.4 is from Estonian crime statistics. Before 1996, they gave as locality of crime either city (*linn, alev*) or village (*küla*); the former category referred mainly to urban areas, the latter to rural areas. In 1996, a new category was added, uninhabited place (*väljas pool asustatud punkti*), which can include both urban and rural areas.

[b]The reports on villages and uninhabited places have been combined. The majority of crimes committed in uninhabited places took place in rural communes, but in part also in cities. Thus, the figure for urban areas is here somewhat smaller than in reality, and the one for the rural areas is correspondingly larger.

Table 3.4. Recorded Homicides (including attempts) in Estonia, 1994–96, by Locality of Crime and Region

	Tallinn[a]	*East Virumaa*[b]	*Rest of Estonia*	*Estonia*
City	311 (76%)	223 (86%)	137 (51%)	671 (72%)
Village	84 (21%)	33 (13%)	127 (47%)	244 (26%)
Uninhabited place	12 (3%)	3 (1%)	7 (3%)	22 (2%)
per 100,000 inhabitants per year[c]				
Urban area	20.4	41.1	13.4	21.7
Rural area	27.1	54.2	14.6	19.8
N	407	259	271	937

Source: Politseiameti Teabebüroo.

[a]Tallinn, Harjumaa, and West Virumaa.

[b]East Virumaa and Narva.

[c]Population on December 31, 1995. The figures for rural areas include homicides in villages and in uninhabited places.

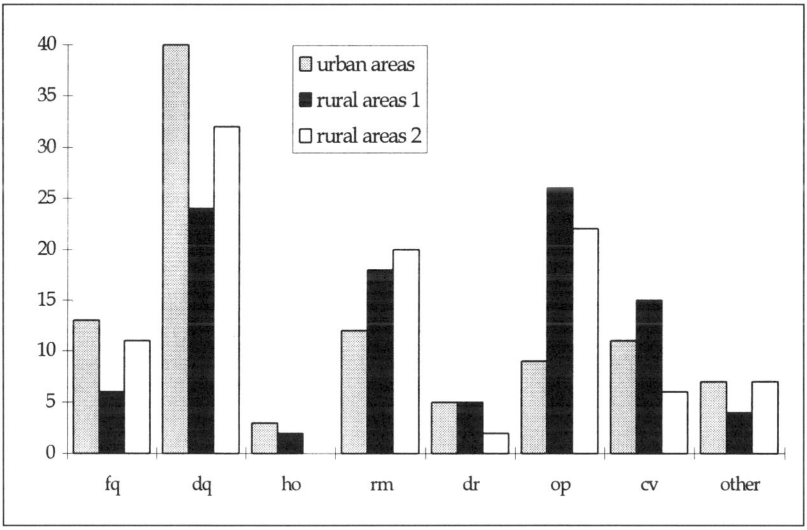

Fig. 3.10. Types of homicide (%) in urban (N = 425) and in rural areas, 1994–96. *Source:* Keskuurimisbüroo.

Key: Rural areas 1 = whole of Estonia (N = 161); rural areas 2 = Estonia excluding the provinces of Harjumaa and East Virumaa (N = 82); fq = family quarrel; dq = drinking quarrel and other quarrel; ho = hooliganism; rm = robbery-murder; dr = debt-related; op = other profit; cv = criminals' mutual violence. See figure 3.8 for description of classifications.

which the information is based, is in fact the place where the victim was found, and a great many victims of crimes committed in Tallinn or Narva and Kohtla-Järve were hidden in the surrounding rural communes of the provinces of Harjumaa and East Virumaa. Thus, the cases of instrumental violence in the rural areas include many crimes actually committed in cities or which are otherwise connected with urban violence. When the information concerning the rural communes of Harjumaa and East Virumaa is removed from the figures for rural areas, the structure of rural homicides changes significantly, especially the number of the crimes linked to the criminals' mutual violence, and organized crime becomes significantly smaller (see fig. 3.10). But the proportion of instrumental homicides is still greater in the countryside than in cities, and correspondingly the proportion of impulsive violence is smaller. The most important reason for this is the large number of robbery-murders in the countryside. These crimes, mostly victimizing old people and committed in connection with burglaries, constituted one-fifth of all homicides committed in the rural areas in 1994–96.

On the other hand, robbery-murders constitute that aspect of rural homicide that is not local in its origins, but committed usually by vagrants, who often come from nearby cities and towns.

While the association of robbery-murders is characteristic of rural crimes, urban homicides, particularly at present, are characterized by criminals' mutual violence and manslaughters committed in connection with drinking parties.

The proportion of homicides connected with family quarrels was the same in cities and in the countryside in 1994–96. This partly implies that the current structural differences are mainly the result of the trends of the 1990s. It is because the volume of interfamily homicides, which formerly made up the bulk of homicides committed in Estonia, has in the last few years remained very stable.

Even though the differences in the levels of violent crime are small between the urban and the rural areas, they are nevertheless considerable on the basis of comparisons between the provinces. In the 1990s, the extreme ends have been the islands of western Estonia, where homicide rates correspond to those in western Europe, and the northeastern border province of East Virumaa, with circumstances resembling the situation of the worst inner-city slums of North America.

Western Estonia has had a relatively low rate of violent crime at least since the early 1960s, whereas the exceptional situation of East Virumaa is to a large extent a phenomenon of the 1990s, although the changes of homicide level were usually more radical in the province than elsewhere in the country even before.

On the basis of the present level of homicide and the changes that have taken place in the course of the last seven years, Estonia can be divided into four geographical regions (see table 3.5).

1. On the western islands, the provinces of Saaremaa and Hiiumaa, the homicide rates are more or less identical with those of the Western European countries, and in the 1990s no essential changes have taken place. Considering the rates in the long run, the level has been rising to some extent; however, as very small absolute numbers (from one to three crimes a year) are involved, the effect of random factors on the yearly changes is considerable.

2. In central and southern Estonia, the homicide level has remained at 5–10 killings per 100,000 inhabitants on average. The annual variance in different provinces has been considerable, but homicide rates have clearly risen: the 1996 level averaged 130 percent higher than the 1990 level. On account of the annual variations, it is impossible to establish a high-water mark. So far the highest level of violence was reached in most provinces in 1993–95, but not until 1996 in Jõgevamaa and Raplamaa, for example.

Table 3.5. Recorded Homicides (including attempts) in Estonia, 1990–96, by Prefecture (per 100,000 inhabitants)

Prefecture	*1990*	*1991*	*1992*	*1993*	*1994*	*1995*	*1996*	*1990–96*	*A*	*B*
Tallinn area								16.9	81	44
Harju	8.6	8.9	13.3	22.4	26.3	24.2	22.6	18.0	38	34
West Viru	11.3	11.3	16.4	11.8	19.9	17.2	14.6	14.6	46	20
Tallinn	10.1	9.1	15.0	22.8	24.4	23.4	14.5	17.0	100	50
East Virumaa								31.0	89	81
East Viru	15.1	14.5	26.3	53.5	53.6	40.3	38.7	34.6	83	72
Narva	8.4	9.6	14.9	31.6	43.7	40.6	35.4	26.3	100	96
The islands								3.0	40	3
Hiiu	—	—	—	8.3	8.4	8.4	—	3.6	36	4
Saare	—	2.5	2.5	2.5	4.9	2.5	4.9	2.8	41	3
Western Estonia								10.2	52	13
Järva	4.6	9.1	4.6	16.0	13.7	6.9	6.9	8.8	40	7
Lääne	8.9	3.0	17.7	3.0	12.3	9.3	3.1	8.2	48	17
Pärnu	6.0	5.0	9.0	15.0	14.1	11.0	12.0	10.3	65	16
Rapla	12.5	5.0	—	12.5	10.0	20.0	20.0	11.4	38	9
Eastern Estonia								11.8	55	15
Jõgeva	2.3	2.3	4.7	9.4	7.1	9.6	11.9	6.8	32	11
Põlva	—	5.5	13.9	11.0	13.8	19.3	8.3	10.3	29	6
Tartu	8.6	4.9	16.0	22.5	22.0	15.7	21.5	15.9	72	21
Valga	4.8	2.4	9.7	7.4	12.5	15.2	12.6	9.2	56	21
Viljandi	1.5	4.6	6.2	7.7	15.5	3.1	15.7	7.6	48	8
Võru	2.2	4.4	13.2	4.4	13.4	15.9	9.1	8.9	41	7

Source: Politseiameti Teabebüroo.

Note: Column headings are as follows: A = percentage of urban population, January 1, 1996; B = percentage of non-Estonian population, January 1, 1996 (see map 3.1).

3. In Tallinn and the northwestern provinces of Harjumaa and West Virumaa, as well as in the city of Tartu and its surroundings, the average annual level of homicide was 15–20 killings per 100,000 inhabitants in 1990–96. In Tallinn and the northwestern provinces, the trend has been uniform: the most violent year was 1994, and since then violent crime has been rapidly decreasing; in 1996 the homicide rate in Tallinn was only 70 percent higher than in 1990. In Tartumaa the level of violence remained high and stable from 1992 to 1996. In 1996 the homicide rate was 150 percent higher than in 1990.

4. In East Virumaa and in the city of Narva, the level of homicides has been on an average 25–35 killings a year per 100,000 inhabitants during the 1990s. The trend differed from that in the rest of Estonia in 1993, and the homicide

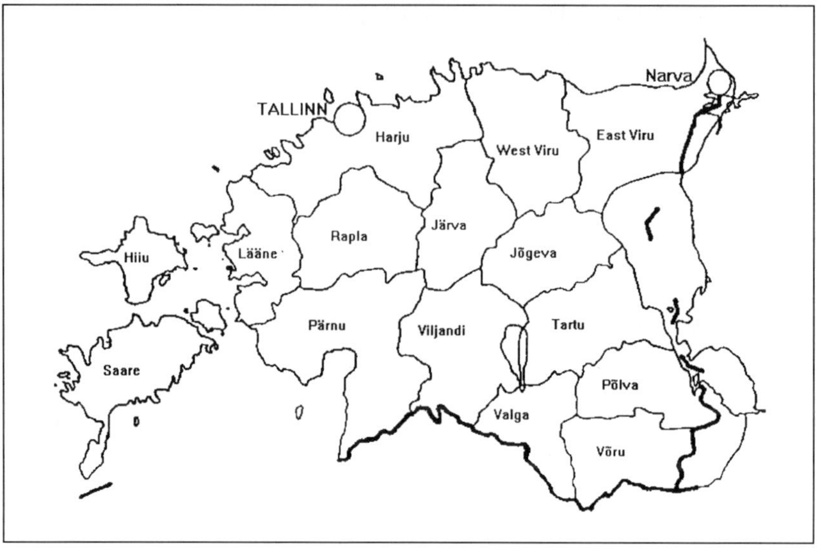

Map 3.1. The prefectures of Estonia, January 1, 1996.

rate was at its highest in 1994. It fell in 1995–96, but it was still 215 percent higher than in 1990.

When surveying the trends on the basis of the cause-of-death statistics, the picture becomes more accurate. Although it is impossible to determine a clear-cut trend for the individual provinces of southern and central Estonia, by classifying them into eastern and western groups[30] it may be noted that in the east (Jõgevamaa, Põlvamaa, Tartumaa, Valgamaa, Viljandimaa, and Võrumaa) the increase in homicide rates culminated in 1993, in the west (Hiiumaa, Järvamaa, Läänemaa, Pärnumaa, Raplamaa, and Saaremaa) in 1993–94. The increase in the number of homicides in eastern as well as in western provinces has been not only less pronounced but also of shorter duration than in northern Estonia.

A situation like the one in East Virumaa is not found anywhere else in the Baltic area. In Latvia, for example, where the homicide picture has otherwise been virtually identical with that of Estonia, the fluctuations by region have been considerably less abrupt. On the other hand, there is no region in the neighboring countries where the proportion of native population has been reduced below one-fifth of the total population, as in East Virumaa, where 80 percent of the population (and almost the entire population in Narva) consists of recently arrived immigrants and their offspring.

In East Virumaa, the increase in the number of homicides has been directed simultaneously toward the entire population, men as well as women.

Thus it cannot have been due to the increase in one certain type of homicide (for example, that involving the criminals' mutual violence), but it has included all kinds of homicides. This is also suggested by the fact that there are no great differences in the structure of crime between the different regions of Estonia. The level of other criminality in East Virumaa is not exceptionally high, even though it is above the average for the whole country (as is true in all the northern Estonian provinces).

The Different Types of Homicide and Their Reflections

The age of offenders and victims. The crimes of young (ages twenty-four and younger) homicide offenders, on the one hand, and middle-aged and older ones, on the other hand, differed radically in Estonia in 1994–96. In the same way the risk of being a victim of different types of homicide varied according to age groups, although somewhat differently from the offenders.

The homicides of young offenders were largely motivated by profit, whereas homicides related to drinking quarrels and, of course, to domestic violence were still unusual. This age group was responsible for less than 30 percent of all homicides committed in 1994–96 but for every second profit-motivated murder and for nearly 70 percent of robbery-murders (see fig. 3.12). Their crimes were directed more often than usual toward people they did not know (at least 30 percent of their homicides had strangers as their victims). The crimes were also very often committed in groups; there were an average of nine murders per ten offenders (0.88), while none of the older age groups had a ratio below one. The role of criminals' mutual violence was, however, small in the homicides of the youngsters. Even though they often committed their crimes in groups, they were neither professional nor systematic in nature.

Correspondingly, the homicides of the middle-aged and old people mostly occurred in the circle of acquaintances, in families and drinking parties. The crimes were generally impulsive, committed in a moment's burst of anger and with no great deliberation. They were mostly associated with lower social classes, and the risk of being victimized was restricted to a relatively small circle limited beforehand.

Homicides connected with criminal groups fell into a special category. The offenders were usually young adults and middle-aged men (though the poor clearance rates for these crimes left the general validity of the results to some extent open). In any case, 90 percent of those found guilty of this kind of homicide were age twenty-five to thirty-nine, whereas the criminals' mutual violence was responsible for nearly 15 percent of the homicides committed by this age group.

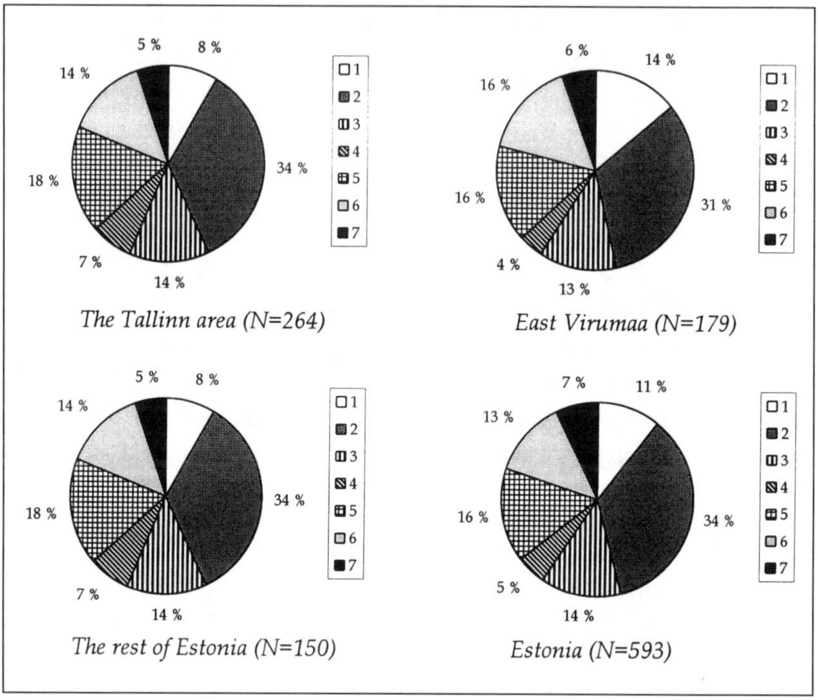

Fig. 3.11. Types of homicide in Estonia by region, 1994–96. *Source:* Keskuurimisbüroo.

Key: 1 = family quarrel; 2 = drinking quarrel and other quarrel; 3 = robbery-murder; 4 = debt-related; 5 = other profit; 6 = criminals' mutual violence; 7 = other.

Another question is how stable the differences between the types of homicide of different age groups are. This could not be examined here as the source material was confined to three successive years. In addition no corresponding analysis had been made in Estonia before, so there were no possibilities of comparison. Some of the differences (for instance, the proportion of homicides related to family quarrels) are to be traced straight to the different situation of life of the age groups; thus they are, no doubt, fairly permanent in nature. On the other hand, the most essential difference—that is, the prevalence of instrumental violence among young age groups compared with middle-aged and old people—has been noticed in surveys carried out earlier in various parts of Europe and North America.[31] In this case the Estonian situation is normal rather than exceptional. It is this difference which stands out in attempts to discover the changes which have taken place in the types of homicide in Estonia over the course of the last quarter century, because the available information con-

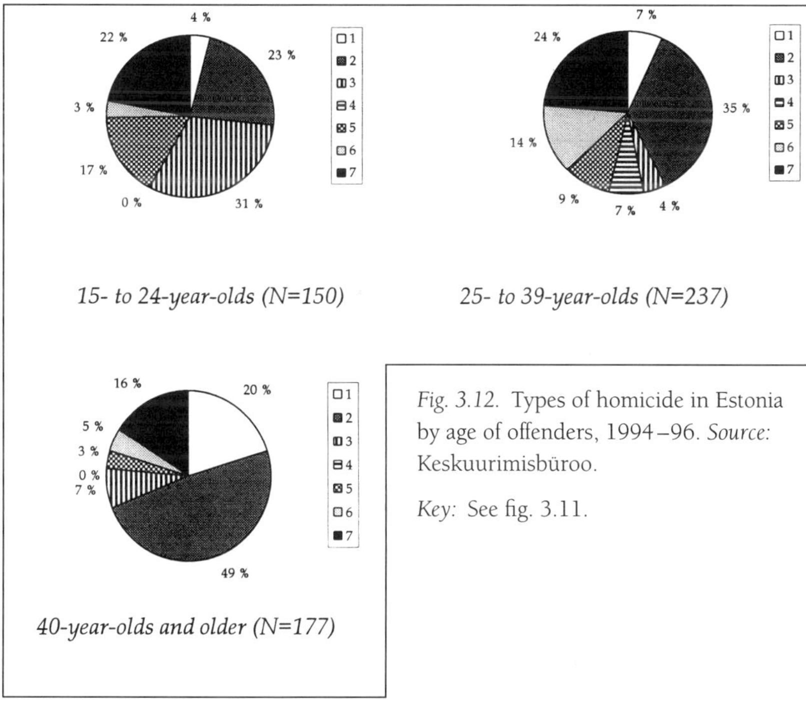

Fig. 3.12. Types of homicide in Estonia by age of offenders, 1994–96. *Source:* Keskuurimisbüroo.

Key: See fig. 3.11.

cerning offenders' age structure is far more accurate and objective than the few summaries that police authorities made from time to time dealing with the motives for murders in different years.

As a starting point, this study assumes that the differences noticed in 1994–96 between the crimes of different age groups were in their basic features the same for the whole period of time from 1971 to 1996.

The types of homicide varied considerably, depending not only on the age but also on the sex of the perpetrator. While the proportion of instrumental violence was about the same as that of impulsive violence among all investigated homicides in 1994–96, only a quarter of those committed by women were instrumental. And although a female perpetrator was responsible for only one-tenth of all the homicides, altogether one-third of the crimes connected with family quarrels were committed by women (see fig. 3.13).

Even the types of women's homicides varied greatly according to age groups. The crimes committed by those twenty-four years old and younger were mainly motivated by profit, as were those committed by young men. In the group of twenty-five to thirty-nine year olds, the most common type of homicide was a killing in a drinking quarrel, whereas the homicides committed by

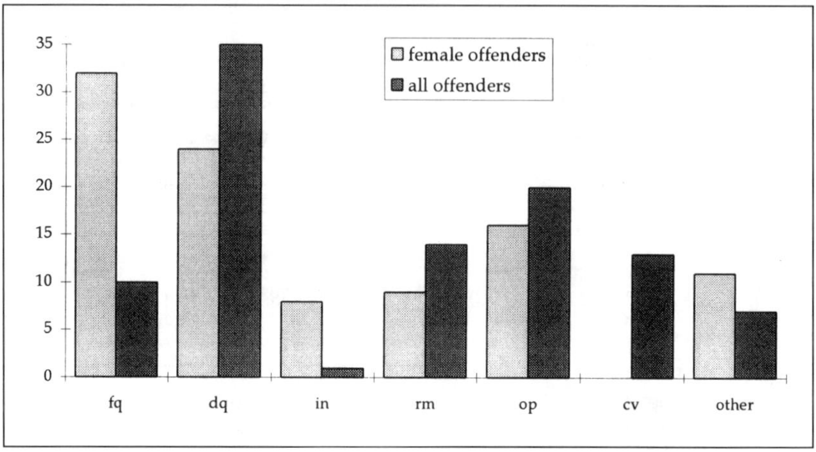

Fig. 3.13. Types of homicides (%) committed by women (N = 75) in Estonia, 1994–96, compared with all homicides (N = 593). *Source:* Keskuurimisbüroo.

Key: fq = family quarrel; dq = drinking quarrel and other quarrel; in = infanticide; rm = robbery-murder; op = other profit; cv = criminals' mutual violence; other = other or unknown.

those 40 and older were connected with family conflicts nearly without exception. The majority of the victims of the crimes belonged to the perpetrator's family circle (independent of the offender's age). One-third of the women under twenty-five and four-fifths of middle-aged women killed their spouses and/or children.

At present, crimes committed by women comprise 10 percent of all solved homicides in Estonia; in practice their proportion has remained stable at least since the 1960s.[32] Comparing the level of women's homicides in Estonia, it is thus only a fraction of homicides committed by men but, on the other hand, they have reacted to the changes of the last few decades in much the same way.[33]

The types of homicide also varied depending on the age and sex of the victim. On the basis of age and motive the victims could be divided into five distinct groups: (1) children, (2) teenagers, (3) people in their twenties, (4) middle-aged, and (5) old people. It is true, however, that no single type of crime in any of these groups could account for even half of all the homicides directed toward the group. Thus, the differences in the structure of motives were not as clear-cut concerning the victims as was the case with the culprits.

Crimes against children took place mainly in family circles and the slayer was nearly always one of the parents. The reason for the crime was most usu-

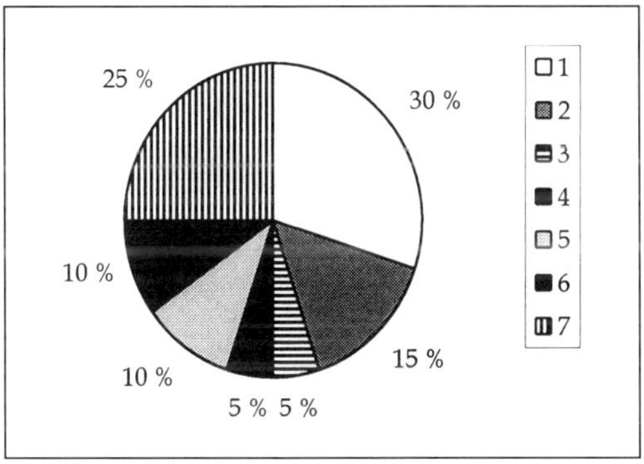

Fig. 3.14. Types of homicide directed against children under 15 in Estonia, 1994–96 (N = 20). *Source:* Keskkuurimisbüroo.

Key: 1 = infanticide; 2 = family quarrel; 3 = other quarrel; 4 = hooliganism; 5 = getting rid of burden of child rearing; 6 = fit of insanity; 7 = unknown.

ally the desire to free oneself from a child who was considered a burden—or to use the child as an instrument in a quarrel between the parents. Mothers were usually guilty of the former type, fathers of the latter (see fig. 3.14).

Studying the structure of violence directed against teenagers was made difficult by the very low clearance rate of these crimes. Sexual crimes, however, formed one of the most significant types of killing in this age group. Otherwise the crimes seemed usually to have been committed for profit. Domestic violence was a very unusual cause of death among teenagers, falling victim to a previously unknown attacker relatively common instead (see fig. 3.15).

People in their twenties and thirties were also most usually victimized by instrumental violence. Domestic violence was in this age group still relatively unusual, whereas drinking quarrels as causes of death increased steadily in direct proportion to the age of the victim. This age group was the object of the majority of criminals' mutual violence. One of every five male victims in 1994–96 was killed in conflicts between criminals.

Homicides directed at people in their forties and fifties were mostly committed on the spur of the moment, as a result of a family or drinking quarrel.

On average, fewer than 10 percent of victims of working age were killed at work. On the other hand, 41 percent of those who were murdered in 1994 were neither employed nor studying—the social situation of the victims was to a great extent identical with that of the culprits.[34] If the unemployed had been excluded, the proportion of those killed at work would thus have been considerably larger among those of working age and actually employed.

Violence directed against old people had its origin, again characteristically, in the seeking of material profit and was often committed by perpetrators unknown to the victims. In contrast to younger age groups, old people were most usually victimized in their own homes.

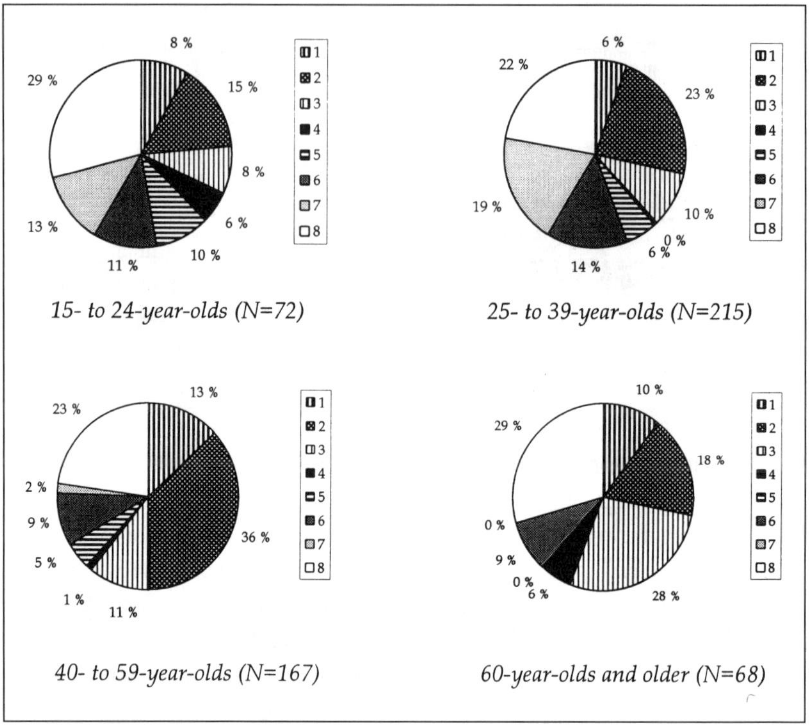

Fig. 3.15. Types of homicide in Estonia by victim's age, 1994–96. *Source:* Keskuurimisbüroo.

Key: 1 = family quarrel; 2 = drinking quarrel and other quarrel; 3 = robbery-murder; 4 = sexual crime; 5 = debt-related; 6 = other profit; 7 = criminals' mutual violence; 8 = other or unknown.

As in the case of homicides committed by women, a large percentage of female victims died as a result of domestic violence. One-fourth of female victims in Estonia in 1994–96 were killed as a result of family quarrels[35] and one-third were killed by a family member (see fig. 3.16). Women were also relatively frequently victimized by murders associated with robbery. The types of homicide varied considerably depending on the age of the victim. The proportion of domestic violence was by far the largest in the age group of twenty-five to fifty-four year olds. The majority of elderly women had been victimized by robbery-murders and correspondingly the role of instrumental violence in the youngest age groups was significant.[36] The most important types of homicides directed against young victims were related to sexual crimes or jealousy. In the groups

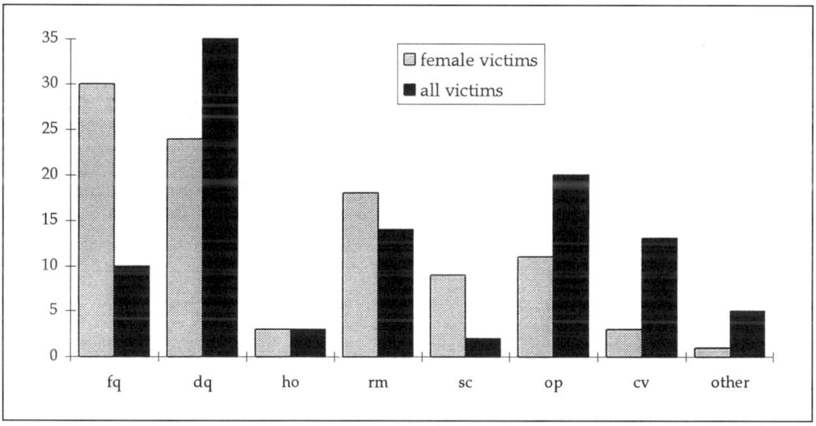

Fig. 3.16. Types of homicides (%) directed against women (N = 120), compared with all homicides (N = 593) in Estonia, 1994–96. *Source:* Keskuurimisbüroo.

Key: fq = family quarrel; dq = drinking quarrel and other quarrel; ho = hooliganism; rm = robbery-murder; sc = sexual crime; op = other profit; cv = criminals' mutual violence.

of young victims and pensioners, many of the perpetrators were unknown to victims (for those twenty-four years old and younger, 27 percent of offenders whose identity was determined; for fifty-five year olds and older, 20 percent). In the group of twenty-five to fifty-four year olds the spouse was the perpetrator in more than 60 percent of the crimes.

Assaults with life-endangering consequences. Published crime statistics in Estonia recognize only two intentional crimes of homicide: murder and attempted murder. These include the crimes listed in paragraphs 100–103 of the Estonian Criminal Code.[37] Some intentional violent crimes with fatal consequences are, however, dealt with as aggravated assaults with fatal consequence (Estonian Criminal Code, paragraph 107, article 2, clause 1) in law courts as well as in statistics.

The division of homicides into murders, attempted murders, and assaults with fatal consequences is reflected in Estonian crime statistics over the last few years, as shown in table 3.6.

About one-fifth of all intentional homicides were recorded as aggravated assaults, and their proportion seems to be increasing. The proportion of attempted homicides has, on the other hand, been rather steady: in 1994–96 attempts accounted for 15 percent of all recorded homicides, in the 1980s the

Table 3.6. Murders, Attempted Murders, and Assaults in Estonia, 1994–96

	1994		*1995*		*1996*	
	Total	*Attempts*	*Total*	*Attempts*	*Total*	*Attempts*
§ 100	233	22	187	28	172	30
§ 101	128	41	113	29	91	23
§ 102	3	—	2	—	5	1
§ 103	1	—	2	1	—	—
§ 107 art. 2.1	67	—	78	—	70	—
Total	432	63	382	58	338	54
Dead people	393		343		301	
Per crime	0.91		0.90		0.89	
Attempts	15%		15%		16%	
§ 107 art. 2.1	16%		20%		21%	

proportion was 17 percent and in the 1970s it was 21 percent. For example, during the 1990s in Hungary and Finland, attempted homicides annually accounted for more than 60 percent of all recorded homicides. From this we can draw the conclusion that, for one thing, the interpretation of the concept of intentional homicide has in Estonia (at least as used by police authorities) remained relatively unchanged for the last few decades and, for another, that the concept (in the case of attempted homicides) is considerably narrower than the one which is nowadays applied in Finland.[38] Violent crimes not resulting in the actual death of the victim are nearly without exception registered as assaults in Estonia. As for crimes resulting in the victim's death, the practice does not seem to differ much from that applied in Finland or the other Nordic countries.[39]

As a legacy of the Soviet era, the Estonian Criminal Code separates aggravated assaults into two categories: those with life-endangering consequences and other aggravated assaults. The former type of crime is important for homicide research because its characteristics leave relatively little room for interpretation (the characteristics are defined directly on the basis of the quality of injuries caused) and the injuries in these crimes are so grave that they will almost without exception come to the knowledge of the health authorities and through them be reported to the police. The level of unreported crime can thus be estimated to be very low in these assaults. Besides, it can be assumed that the proportion of assaults causing fatal injuries should be fairly stable regardless of the point in time.

Aggravated assaults together with impulsive homicides form a type of crime where the bases and causes of the deeds are usually the same, only the consequences are different. Accordingly, when impulsive crimes dominate, the trends of homicide should in principle be parallel to those for aggravated assaults. If again instrumental violence predominates, the lines of development will probably be more divergent.

The End of the Stable Period of Homicide Rates

A period of relatively stable homicide rates, which had lasted for a quarter of a century, came to an end in Estonia in 1978 when the number of homicides began to increase sharply.

The growth of violent crime starting in the West as early as the 1960s thus appears to have reached Estonia with ten years' delay. It seems, however, that the reasons for the increase were different from those in the West. The shift in the trend during the late 1970s in Estonia was due to an increase in impulsive violence rather than in instrumental homicides (see table 3.7).

Statistical information on the motives for homicides is available since the beginning of the 1960s from occasional summaries made by the Ministry of Internal Affairs of the Estonian SSR for its own use. The basic classification and the technique of drawing up homicide statistics have to a great extent been identical for the whole period from the 1960s to the present day; however, the classification has been rather offhand, and there is no knowledge about how it has been implemented on any given occasion.

In the 1960s and 1970s, when the homicide rates were stable, the volume of some types of crime seems to have been more or less constant: for example, the number of homicides connected with robberies and sexual crimes. On the

Table 3.7. Classification of Solved Homicides in Estonia, 1961–80, according to Heiman and Svaiko (%)

Motive	*1961–65*	*1966–70*	*1971–75*	*1976–80*
Robbery	5	4	5	5
Sexual crime	2	3	3	2
Hooliganism	10	13	9	8
Jealousy and other[a]	48	63	73	61
Total	65	83	90	76

[a] Consists mostly of homicides related to family or drinking quarrels. In 1981, 49% of these crimes (39 homicides) were connected with family quarrels.

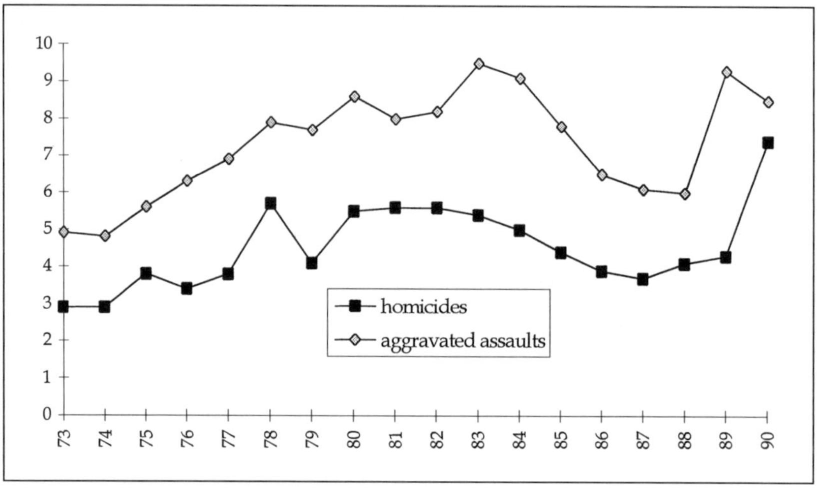

Fig. 3.17. Recorded homicides (including attempts) and aggravated assaults per 100,000 inhabitants in Estonia, 1973–90. *Source:* Politseiameti Teabebüroo.

other hand, for instance, the level of manslaughters related to family and drinking quarrels displays radical fluctuations. The problem in judging the authenticity of the latter is, however, the fact that it is not possible to determine whether or how the official division of motives was applied in different periods.

Comparing the information from the prosecutor's office on the motives for homicides in 1976–80 with that of the earlier five-year period, one can notice that the percentage of unclassified crimes has increased considerably. This doesn't necessarily indicate the emergence of new, previously unknown, or rare types of homicide in Estonia. Instead the possibility must be considered, based on the trend of the past few years, that with the increase in the number of crimes the shortcomings of the statistical information reported by the criminal investigators also increased. The rise in homicide rates during the latter half of the 1970s seems to have occurred mainly with regard to homicides related to drinking quarrels. Instrumental crimes (robbery-murders) also increased, but more slowly (their proportion with respect to all homicides remained unchanged).[40]

The impression that the rise in homicide rate took place in impulsive crimes, in particular, is also supported by the fact that the increase in the rate of life-endangering assaults was almost identical with that of homicide in the latter half of the 1970s (see fig. 3.17).

Another factor indicating an increase in homicides connected with drinking quarrels is the rapid rise in the percentage of homicides committed under

Table 3.8. Recorded Homicides (including attempts) in Estonia, 1970–82, by Region (per 100,000 inhabitants per year)

	1970–77	*1978–82*	*Change (%)*
Estonia	3.8	6.5	+71
Tallinn area	3.7	5.6	+50
East Virumaa	6.0	12.5	+108
The islands	1.3	1.2	−8
Western Estonia	3.1	4.8	+53
Eastern Estonia	3.2	5.7	+78

Source: Politseiameti Teabebüroo.
Note: Tallinn area = the city of Tallinn, Harjumaa, and West Virumaa; East Virumaa = East Virumaa and the city of Narva; the islands = Saaremaa and Hiiumaa; Western Estonia = Järvamaa, Läänemaa, Pärnumaa, and Raplamaa; Easter Estonia = Jõgevamaa, Põlvamaa, Tartumaa, Valgamaa, Viljandimaa, and Võrumaa.

the influence of alcohol. In 1961–65, 61 percent of those guilty of homicide were intoxicated when they committed their crimes, while in 1976–81 the corresponding proportion was 71 percent. Regionally the growth of homicide rates, even in the late 1970s, was concentrated in East Virumaa, that is, in an area where the proportion of immigrant population in Estonia was the greatest (see table 3.8). Nevertheless, as was already stated above, the increase in crime would seem to have occurred proportionately in both population groups, and the massive immigration cannot be considered to have triggered the rise in homicide, but was only one factor intensifying the change. The beginning of the growth of the homicide rate coincides with the period of the increasing disintegration of the Soviet social life and economy, the last years of the Brezhnev regime (see fig. 3.18).

One of the measures of the degree of social frustration is the fluctuation in the consumption of alcohol. The curves describing the number of alcohol poisonings, on the one hand, and that for homicides, on the other hand, show an almost identical development during the above period in Estonia. There are no usable statistics available on the consumption of alcohol in the former Soviet Union. Instead, fairly reliable information on the numbers of alcohol poisoning fatalities yearly is to be found in the cause-of-death statistics.[41] The number of alcohol poisonings per 100,000 inhabitants rose from fewer than 5 for the year 1970 to 10 in 1976 and as many as 17 in 1979 (the corresponding level was not reached again until 1992). In part the increase was related to a deliberate

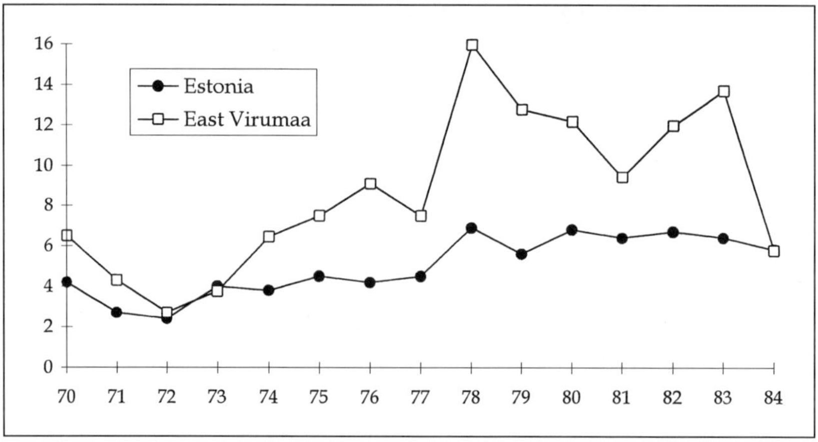

Fig. 3.18. Recorded homicides (including attempts) per 100,000 inhabitants in East Virumaa and Estonia, 1970–84. *Source:* Politseiameti Teabebüroo.

policy of the Soviet regime: when the ability to supply citizens with the daily necessities of life was diminishing rapidly, attempts were made to compensate by increasing the supply of alcohol intensively.[42]

The growth of violence in Estonia in the late 1970s has to be regarded primarily in the context of general Soviet trends, not as part of the current wave of violence in the western industrialized countries.

When examining the homicide rate by regions one can notice the same distinctions as in the 1990s. On the islands, which immigration did not reach and where the local communities remained more cohesive than elsewhere in Estonia, the level of violent crime was considerably lower than anywhere else and immune to the developments of the rest of Estonia. During the social reaction of the 1970s violent crime was on the decrease on the islands.

The Beginning of the Reforms in 1983–87

The increase in the homicide rate temporarily stopped in 1983–87, and the crime level slumped by an average of 18 percent. These events have been connected with the reform policy of the Gorbachev era, that is, with the new restrictions in the distribution of alcohol and the general liberalization of the social atmosphere.[43] It must be taken into account, however, that at least in Estonia the decrease in violent crime started as much as two years before the beginning of the Gorbachev era, not to mention the actual start of the reform policy. When the reforms really began to influence social life and the economy in 1987–88, homicide rates were again on the increase in Estonia.

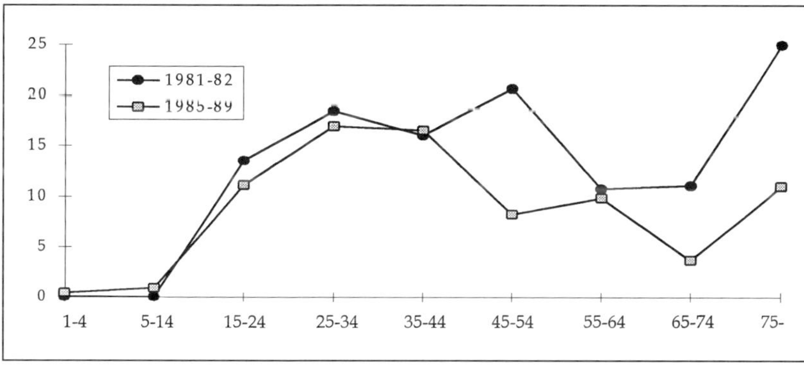

Fig. 3.19. Homicide death rate for men by age group per 100,000 inhabitants in Estonia, 1981–82 and 1985–89. *Source:* World Health Statistics Annual 1994–95.

The beginning of the slump in the crime level in 1983 coincides with the short regime of Yury Andropov and the measures taken by his administration to tighten social control in the Soviet Union, both over the common citizens and over the local authorities.[44] As a matter of fact, it seems as if the fall in violent crime was connected not so much with changes in social conditions or even in the social atmosphere, but with tightening discipline and control over the population.

There are no data available on the motives for homicides committed in 1983–87; however, there are data on the age distribution of the victims of the crimes. During the years in question, the homicide death rate for men diminished especially and almost exclusively among middle-aged and old men (see fig. 3.19).

Correspondingly, the women's death rate decreased the most sharply in the age group of twenty-five to forty-four year olds (see fig. 3.20). The decrease in death rates for men as well as women indicates the significance of the decrease in homicides related to drinking quarrels for the favorable trend of the crime level. In 1994–96 about 40 percent of homicides whose victims were men aged forty or older were committed in connection with drinking quarrels or family quarrels brought about more or less by alcohol. Correspondingly, among women aged twenty-five to forty-four the cause of homicide death was much more often an impulsive crime than among other age groups.

Homicide-related deaths in 1983–87 were thus decreasing precisely in those age groups where the percentage of crimes linked to alcohol consumption in one way or other is greatest and in which the changes in drinking habits could be supposed to have had the strongest effect on the death rate (at least for a while). This assessment is also supported by the decrease in the level of

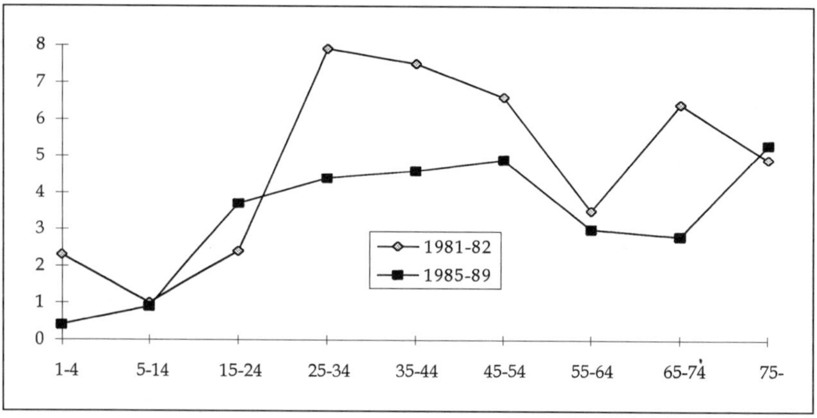

Fig. 3.20. Homicide death rate for women by age group per 100,000 inhabitants in Estonia, 1981–82 and 1985–89. *Source:* World Health Statistics Annual 1994–95.

aggravated assaults during the first half of the 1980s. The number of life-endangering assaults went down in 1983–87 in almost the same proportion as homicides.

The annual number of alcohol poisonings does not, however, suggest a decrease in the consumption of alcohol (nor does it thus indicate the disappearance of a single one of the causes of the exceptionally high level of consumption). The death rate by alcohol poisoning remained stable and very high through the whole period of time in 1978–85 (see fig. 3.21). The number of poisonings began to fall significantly only from 1986 on.[45] It would thus seem that the disciplinary campaign resulting in a reduction of the homicide rate had, above all, an effect on drinking habits: a decrease in public drinking and drinking during weekdays and thus a decrease in the number of conflict situations causing violence (by making the drinking sessions shorter and drinking parties smaller).

The fall in violent crime was centered in areas where the growth had been the most radical in 1978–82: East Virumaa and the provinces of eastern Estonia.[46] The reason for this was probably that the sort of violent criminality that had caused the growth of the previous years was falling the most sharply. On the other hand, in the Tallinn area and in western Estonia no significant changes took place (see table 3.9).

Trends of Homicide in 1987–96

From 1987 to 1994, homicide rates increased fivefold in Estonia. The rise was at its fastest in the years 1991–94, on an average 60 percent a year. Contrary to the earlier period of rising violent crime in 1978–82, it was not only the

Table 3.9. Recorded Homicides (including attempts) in Estonia, 1978–87, by Region (per 100,000 inhabitants per year)

	1978–82	*1983–87*	*Change (%)*
Estonia	6.5	5.3	−18
Tallinn area	5.6	5.5	−2
East Virumaa	12.5	7.3	−58
The islands	1.2	0.4	−66
Western Estonia	4.8	4.2	−13
Eastern Estonia	5.7	4.3	−25

Source: Politseiameti Teabebüroo.
Note: See table 3.8.

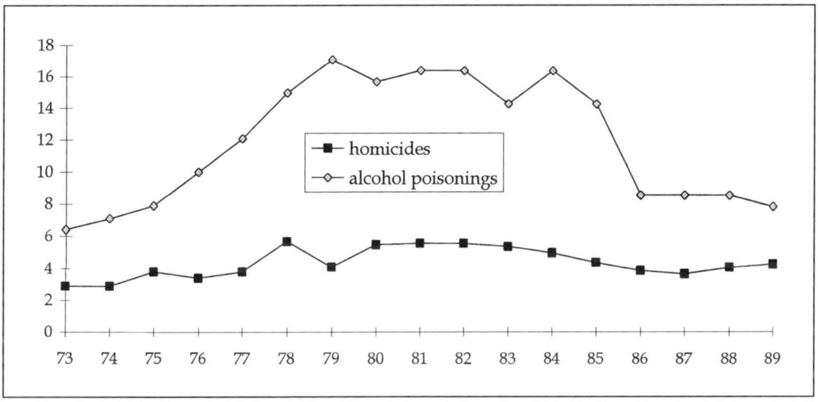

Fig. 3.21. Recorded homicides (excluding attempts) and deaths by alcohol poisoning per 100,000 inhabitants in Estonia, 1973–89. *Sources:* Politseiameti Teabebüroo; Värnik 1997, 37.

level of crime that changed this time; there were also considerable changes in the motive structure of homicides. Impulsive violence, mostly connected with family quarrels and the internal quarrels of drinking parties, led to nearly 80 percent of all homicides committed in Estonia in the early 1980s. The situation did not change significantly in this respect either during the period of increasing homicide rates in 1978–82 or during the slump of 1983–87; the changes took place mainly in the number of impulsive crimes, while the level of instrumental violence remained relatively stable.

Ascertaining the motives of homicides has become more difficult during

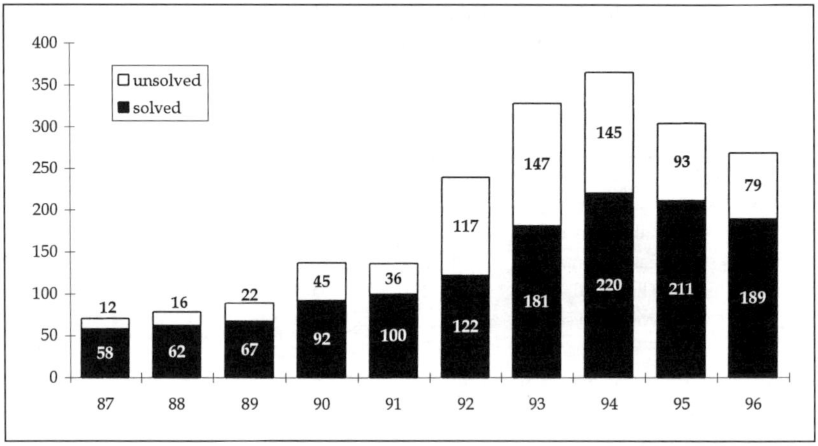

Fig. 3.22. The annual number of solved and unsolved homicides (including attempts) in Estonia, 1987–96. *Source:* Politseiameti Teabebüroo.

the last few years because of the sharp fall in the clearance rate. In Estonia from the 1960s to the late 1980s, 90–100 percent of all homicide cases were solved within a year; at present the situation is very different: in 1994–96 the annual clearance rate averaged 66 percent.

The situation was at its worst in 1993, when the clearance rate was as low as 50 percent; in 1996 it was already 71 percent (excluding attempted homicide). Thus, the situation in Estonia is no longer exceptional compared to the rest of Europe, but in regard to the earlier decades it is still rather poor. The bulk of unsolved crimes can be estimated to have most probably been committed with motives for profit or to have been connected with criminals' mutual violence. These types of crimes are thus underrepresented in the official summaries of motives made on the basis of solved crimes.

The decline of the clearance rate has also had some effect on the comparisons concerning the regional homicide trends in recent years. It has proved to be far more difficult to solve crimes in the provinces of northern Estonia than in other parts of the country: an average of 58 percent of homicides committed in 1993–96 were cleared up annually in East Virumaa[47] and in the Tallinn area,[48] 77 percent in the rest of the country (see figs. 3.22–25).

The main reason for the low clearance rate is the sharp and sudden rise in the number of homicides; the authorities have simply exhausted their resources. The problem is not so much a lack of manpower and technical resources, but it seems that the training of criminal investigators during the Soviet era was inadequate in some respects. Even as late as 1995–96 the

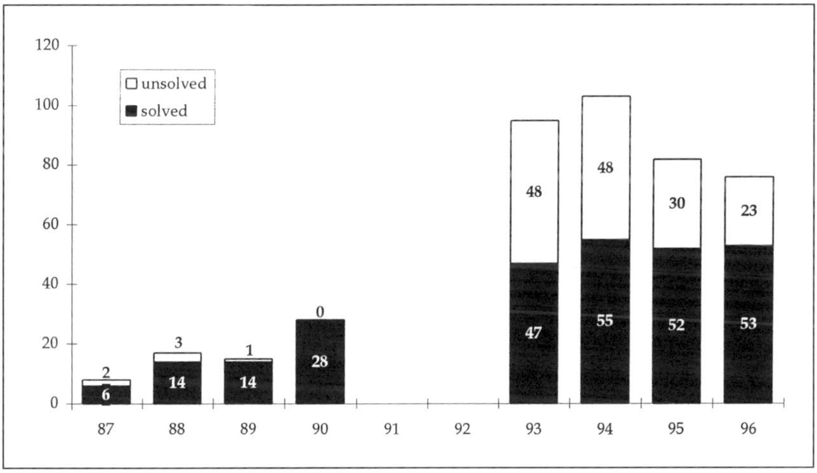

Fig. 3.23. Annual number of solved and unsolved homicides (including attempts) in East Virumaa and the city of Narva, 1987–96. *Source:* Politseiameti Teabebüroo. Reports on unsolved crimes before 1993 concern homicides whose investigation was interrupted, so the figures are not fully comparable with those from 1993 through 1996.

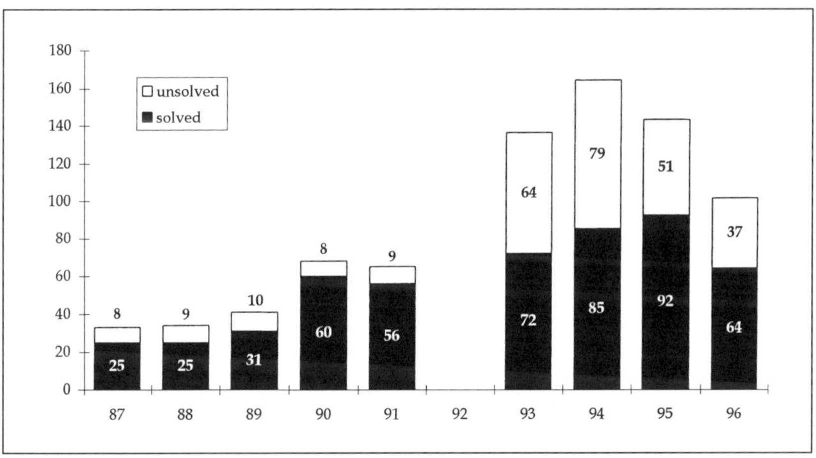

Fig. 3.24. Annual number of solved and unsolved homicides (including attempts) in Harjumaa, West Virumaa, and the city of Tallinn, 1987–96. *Source:* Politseiameti Teabebüroo.

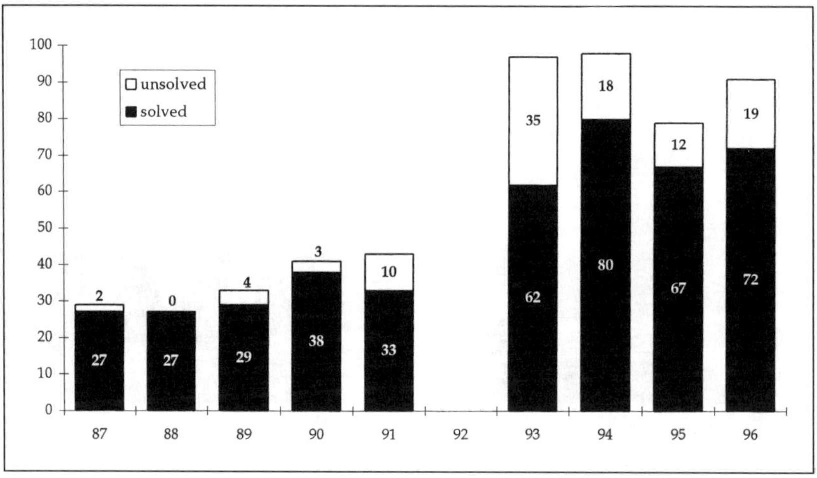

Fig. 3.25. Annual number of solved and unsolved homicides (including attempts) in the rest of Estonia, 1987–96. *Source:* Politseiameti Teabebüroo.

Keskuurimisbüroo had to interfere each month in the activity of some local investigators and restart preliminary investigations that had been interrupted without cause.[49] The reason for this was that some investigators had a very formal attitude to their work, which they considered completed not when the crime was solved but when all the regular technical investigations had been carried out. It is obvious that a criminal investigator with this sort of work ethic will be unable to clear up any but the very simplest of homicides.[50]

In spite of this problem, motive analyses done on the basis of solved crimes as well as of all homicides present a very similar picture of the present situation. The proportion of impulsive crimes has fallen from the previous 70–80 percent to about half of all homicides; especially the proportion of crimes within families has reduced. While more than 60 percent of homicides were connected with family quarrels in the 1970s and about 50 percent still in the 1980s, the proportion of this kind of crime was only 10–20 percent in 1994–96 (see fig. 3.26). The absolute number of homicides committed as a result of family quarrels has remained very stable in the course of the last fifteen years; in 1983 there were thirty-eight such crimes, in 1994–96 an average of forty a year. On the other hand, the relative proportion of homicides related to drinking quarrels would seem to have remained rather stable at 25–30 percent of all homicides. In the early 1980s twenty-five to thirty people a year died as victims of drinking quarrels; in the last three years there were on average eighty victims per year. In the 1990s, the number of such crimes thus trebled, growing more or less at the

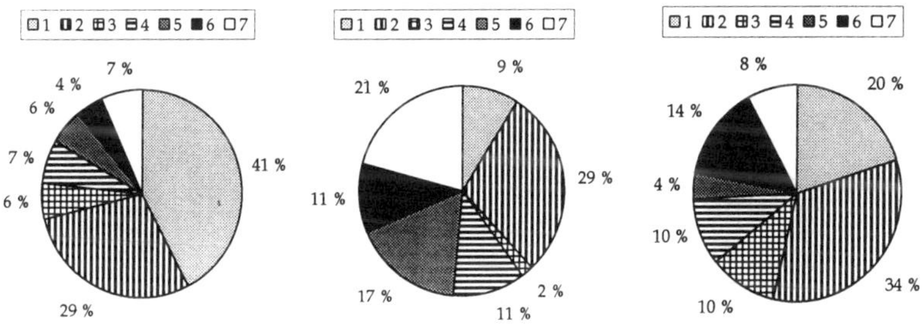

1983 (N=90) (Politseiameti Teabebüroo) | 1994-96 (N=713) (Keskuurimisbüroo) | 1994 (N=220) (Politseiameti Teabebüroo)

Fig. 3.26. Types of homicide in Estonia in 1983 and 1994–96.

Note: Information from the Politseiameti Teabebüroo from 1983 and 1994 refers to solved crimes. Information from the Keskuurimisbüroo from 1994–96 refers to all recorded homicides.

Key: 1 = family quarrel; 2 = drinking quarrel and other quarrel; 3 = hooliganism; 4 = robbery-murder; 5 = other motive for profit; 6 = criminals' mutual violence; 7 = other or unknown.

same pace as the total number of homicides. While the relative proportion of impulsive crimes has gone down, those committed with motives for profit have correspondingly increased.

While murders for profit comprised about 10 percent of homicides in the 1980s, the percentage of such crimes was more than 30 percent in 1994–96. The majority of these kinds of crimes were robbery-murders (in 1994–96 a minimum of 40 percent), up from the earlier 5 percent to 14 percent of all solved homicides; however, the number of various other types of homicide for material profit has also increased. On the other hand, instrumental crimes aiming at immaterial profit would seem to have remained stable or increased in the same proportion as the number of all homicides. (For example, in 1961–80 about 2 percent of all homicides were connected with sexual crimes; in 1994–96 the figures were unchanged). All in all, in the years 1994–96 homicides classified as instrumental were committed at the rate of 90 to 125 a year,[51] while in 1983 their number was 10. About 230 more homicides were committed annually in 1994–96 than in the previous decade; thus, the murders for profit were responsible at least for a third, at most for half of the increase (see fig. 3.27).

Another type of crime that has increased rapidly consists of homicides connected with criminals' mutual conflicts; their proportion has risen from 5

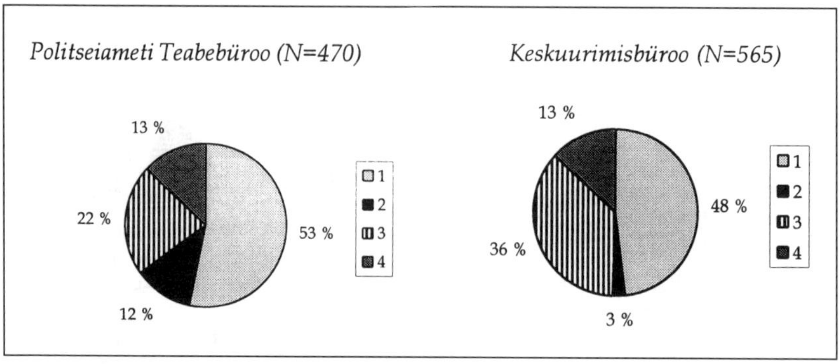

Fig. 3.27. Types of homicide in Estonia, 1994–96 (excluding infanticide and crimes committed in fits of insanity or in self-defense). *Sources:* Keskuurimisbüroo; Politseiameti Teabebüroo.

Key: 1 = impulsive crimes; 2 = hooliganism; 3 = instrumental crimes; 4 = criminals' mutual violence.

percent in the early 1980s to about 13 percent in 1994–96. The number of such crimes has in the last few years been forty-five to eighty a year; in 1983 it was five. Their proportion of the increase in homicide of the 1990s is thus 20 percent to 25 percent.

Because a third of the homicides committed in 1994–96 have not yet been solved, the estimates of the motive structure are really only estimates. The substantial increase in the proportion of homicides for profit, however, is also supported by other sources besides statistical motive summaries. Comparisons of the changes in the level of aggravated assaults and homicides during the last few years reveal that they are no longer parallel. The number of life-endangering assaults grew in the 1990s, though considerably more slowly than the number of homicides (see fig. 3.28). This can be considered to be indicative of the growth in homicide rates taking place in instrumental crimes in particular.

Because the types of homicide committed by the young differ from those of the middle-aged offenders, a rise in the proportion of instrumental violence ought to have made the age structure of homicide perpetrators younger in the course of the last few years, provided, of course, that the clearance rate had remained stable and the proportions of different types of solved homicides had also remained unchanged. In the present situation of Estonia the sharp fall in the clearance rate can be expected to have made the age structure of culprits, as presented in crime statistics, older than it actually was.[52] Indeed, the changes have been in the course of the decade altogether relatively small. Despite the lower percentages of solved crimes, however, the statistics support the data regard-

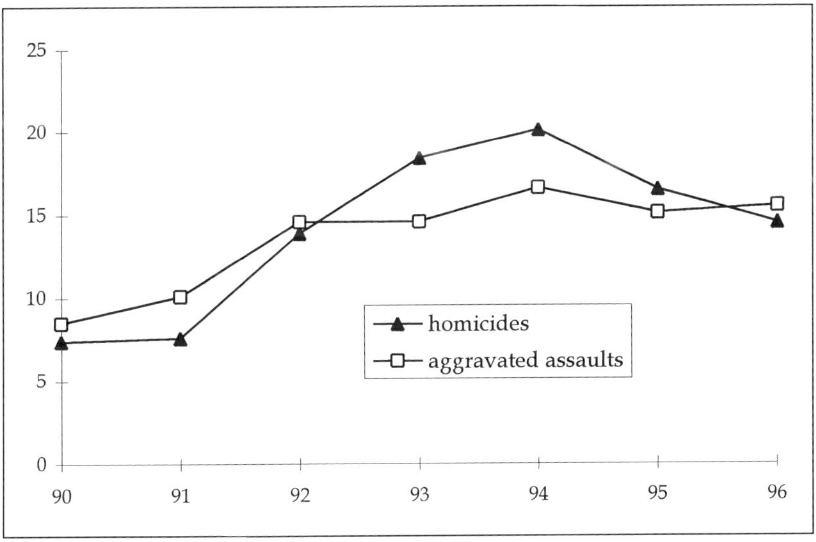

Fig. 3.28. Recorded homicides (excluding attempts) and aggravated assaults per 100,000 inhabitants in Estonia, 1990–96. *Source:* Politseiameti Teabebüroo.

ing the changes in the motive structure of homicide: the age structure of culprits has been getting steadily younger since 1990, even for solved homicides.

Even compared with the 1980s, the average age of offenders has become younger. In 1980, 70 percent of the culprits were over twenty-nine years old; in the 1990s, their proportion has been 56 percent on average (see table 3.10). The percentage of minors has, on the other hand, remained stable: in 1976–81 it was 6 percent, in the 1990s correspondingly 5 percent. The most vigorous growth has thus taken place in the age group of nineteen to twenty-nine year olds. A development which corresponds with that for all offenders can also be seen for women perpetrators. As table 3.11 shows, the age structure of female offenders has become younger with the increase in homicide rates. Presently the age profile of female and male homicide offenders is more or less identical in Estonia.

On examining the statistics for victims of crimes, the decline in the clearance rate does not cause problems. The victims of homicides are found out and identified almost without exception. However, it is true that a few victims are never discovered, and some are found only a long time after the crime was committed. In Estonia the number of missing people has steadily increased during the 1990s, and every year ten to sixty of them have been found dead (see fig. 3.29).[53]

In countries where the population registry is well developed, accurate

Table 3.10. Suspects, According to Age Group, 1990–96 (%)

Age	*1980*	*1990*	*1991*	*1992*	*1993*	*1994*	*1995*	*1996*	*1990–96*
<25	30[a]	25	28	24	24	28	32	24	27
<16		—	1	1	0.3	3	1	1	
16–17		4	5	2	2	5	3	4	
18–24		21	22	21	22	20	28	19	
25–29	—	11	15	18	17	15	14	22	17
30–	70	65	57	58	59	56	53	54	56
30–49		54	42	43					
30–39					25	24	22	25	
40–55					27	23	24	22	
50–		11	15	15					
55–					6	9	7	7	
Male	81	91	92	89	91	91	91	88	90
Estonians	45	42	37	39	49	44	34	36	40
N	30	102	106	134	253	278	297	269	1,439

[a] Younger than 30.

Source: Politseiameti Teabebüroo.

Table 3.11. Women Suspected of Homicides, by Age Group, 1990–95 (%)

	1990–92	*1993–95*	*1990–95*
<30	37	44	43
<15		3	2
16–17	6	1	3
18–24	22	22	22
25–29	9	18	16
30–	63	56	57
30–49	47		47
30–39		22	
40–55		25	
50–	16		10
56–		8	
Estonians	34	43	41
N	32	76	108

Source: Politseiameti Teabebüroo.

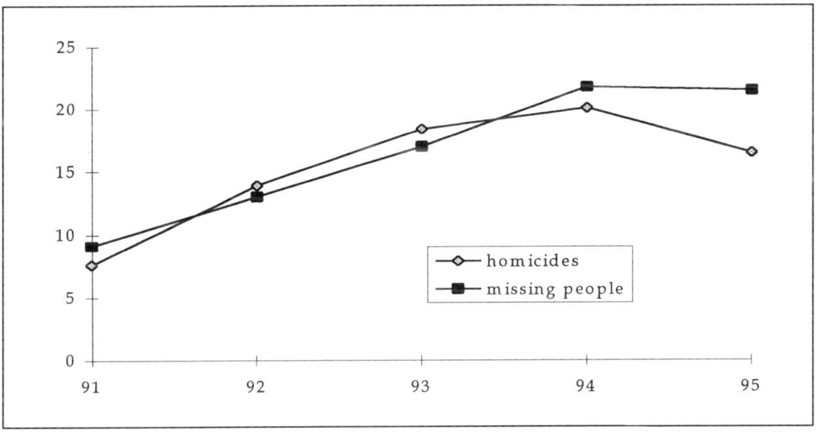

Fig. 3.29. Recorded homicides (excluding attempts) and those recorded as missing at the end of each year per 100,000 inhabitants in Estonia, 1990–96. *Source:* Kirs 1995.

information is annually obtained on missing people, and on the basis of experience it can be estimated how large a percentage of them are likely to have been victimized by homicide. In Estonia there are still certain problems attached to the population registry, even if the situation is continually improving. Besides, it must be assumed that the proportion of unregistered inhabitants is largest in the groups of people where the risk of being victimized is higher than average (for example, professional criminals and the homeless). This phenomenon is to be seen, among other things, in the rise in the number of unidentified victims. Also, people staying illegally in the country are not usually reported to the authorities in cases of disappearance, so the actual number of missing people is larger than the recorded one. Altogether the percentage of unreported crimes would, however, seem to be at the most only around 10 percent of all the homicides committed, which would hardly misrepresent the total picture obtained of the homicide victims.

The age structure of homicide victims has in the 1990s become substantially younger compared with the situation during the late 1980s. The most rapid rise in the homicide death rate for men has taken place in the age group of twenty-five to thirty-four year olds, for women in the age group of thirty-five to forty-four year olds (see figs. 3.30 and 3.31).

As far as twenty-five- to thirty-four-year-old men are concerned, one of the reasons for their high mortality is that deaths related to one of the three factors behind the increase in homicide (i.e., the criminals' mutual violence) fall almost totally within this age group. More than a quarter of the male victims of this age

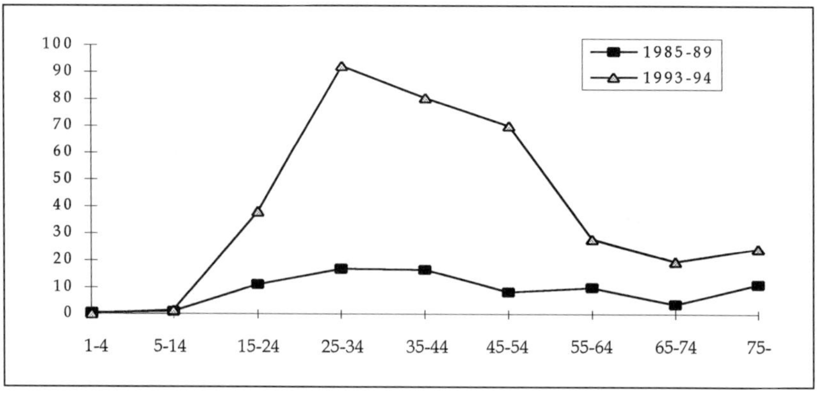

Fig. 3.30. Homicide death rate for men per 100,000 inhabitants in Estonia, 1985–89 and 1993–94. *Source:* World Health Statistics Annual 1994–95.

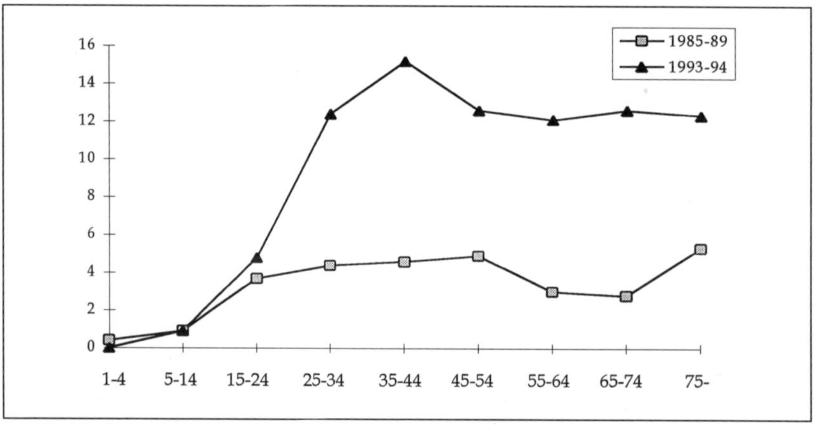

Fig. 3.31. Homicide death rate for women per 100,000 inhabitants in Estonia, 1985–89 and 1993–94. *Source:* World Health Statistics Annual 1994–95.

group die as a result of conflicts between criminals. The changes in the homicide death rates among men have actually concerned almost only the active population, the age groups of twenty-five to fifty-four. In these age groups the reason for homicide mortality in 1994–96 was impulsive violence in 33 percent of the reported cases and instrumental violence in 44 percent. (In 15 percent, the motive was not determined.)

As for female victims, the changes taking place recently have not been equally unambiguous. The increase in the death rate has been the most rapid in the same age groups in which they most sharply dropped toward the end of the previous decade. This development is not, however, a complete reflection of the earlier one, as the death rate of old women, too, has now increased almost as quickly as that of middle-aged women. Among those victims under twenty-five, who are victimized least of all by impulsive crimes, the growth has remained relatively slight.

Nevertheless, the changes in the statistics of female homicide victims support the view that instrumental violence, especially when connected with pursuit of material profit, has been increasing sharply in the last few years. Although the proportion of instrumental violence as a cause of homicide related death is by far the largest among young women, these crimes are overwhelmingly sexual crimes, not those committed for material benefit. The number of homicides connected with sexual crimes has been stable in Estonia since the 1960s. On the other hand, instrumental violence directed against old women mainly results from material motives, and their death rate has been rising rapidly. The sharp increase in homicides directed against middle-aged women does not, however, seem to support unreservedly the conclusion that the level of domestic violence has remained stable. Still, it is to be taken into consideration that the percentage of homicides related to family quarrels does not rise above 40 percent in any age group. Because no material is available on the types of homicide directed against women from earlier years, direct comparisons have not been possible. If the level of domestic violence is nevertheless supposed to have remained stable, as may be surmised on the basis of both the present motive structure of homicides in Estonia and the recent changes in the age distribution of female offenders, even the rise in the homicide death rate for middle-aged women indicates a rapid increase in murders committed with motives for material profit in the course of the 1990s.

The shift in homicide rates has again been most radical in East Virumaa and smallest in western Estonia (see fig. 3.32 and tables 3.12 and 3.13).[54] It would seem that whatever the reasons for the changes in violent crime statistics are at any given time and no matter how they are reflected in the structure of homicide, the consequences will, as a rule, be felt strongest in East Virumaa and least in western Estonia.

The social conditions of East Virumaa evidently include factors which contribute to an accentuation of the changes in violent crime. On the other hand, in the western provinces and on the islands, the local culture seems to be in this respect rather resistant to change. One of the factors is no doubt the proportion of immigrants in the total population, but that cannot account for the differences between the provinces of western and eastern Estonia. Thus, even the

Table 3.12. Recorded Homicides (including attempts) in Estonia, 1983–96, by Region (per 100,000 inhabitants per year)

	1983–87	*1988–96*	*Change (%)*
Estonia	5.3	14.8	+179
Tallinn area	5.5	14.4	+162
East Virumaa	7.3	25.8	+253
The islands	0.4	3.2	+700
Western Estonia	4.2	8.7	+107
Eastern Estonia	4.3	10.2	+137

Source: Politseiameti Teabebüroo.
Note: See table 3.8.

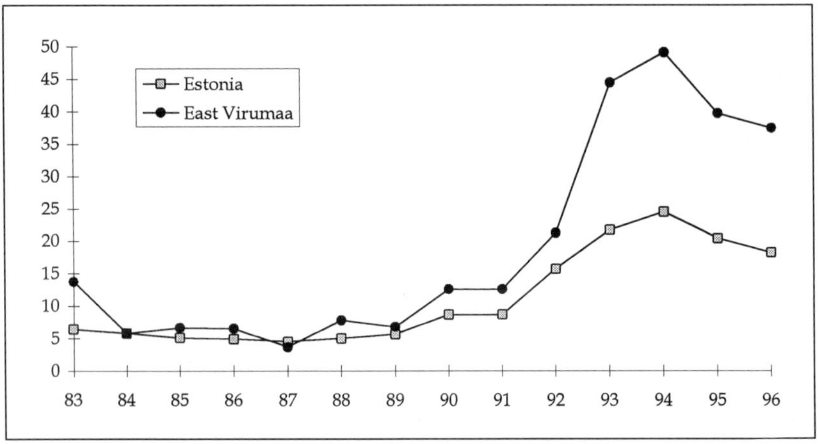

Fig. 3.32. Recorded homicides (including attempts) per 100,000 inhabitants in East Virumaa and Estonia, 1983–96. *Source:* Politseiameti Teabebüroo.

local culture of violence in Estonia seems to have major regional differences. Although the provinces of the Estonian mainland are relatively identical in their structures of population and habitation both in the west and in the east, the changes in violent crime were regularly more pronounced in the east during the last quarter of a century.[55]

It is not probable that the economic and political developments were continually different in western and eastern Estonia; at least during the last ten years this has not been the case.

Table 3.13. Recorded Homicides (including attempts) in Estonia, 1970–96, by Region (per 100,000 inhabitants per year)

	1970–74	*1975–79*	*1980–84*	*1985–89*	*1990–96*
Tallinn area	3.6	4.8	5.4	5.5	16.9
East Virumaa	4.7	10.6	10.6	6.3	31.0
The islands	0.8	1.2	1.2	2.0	3.0
Western Estonia	3.1	3.2	5.1	4.0	10.2
Eastern Estonia	2.9	4.1	6.1	3.9	11.8

Source: Politseiameti Teabebüroo.
Note: See table 3.8.

The Constant and Changing Traits of Estonian Homicide Trends

In the twentieth century it has been characteristic of homicide rates in Estonia to be relatively high in European context. Together with Finland, the other Baltic countries, as well as Hungary, Italy, and most countries in the Balkan Peninsula, it has belonged to a zone where the long-term homicide level is two to three times greater than in Western Europe but, on the other hand, only one half of the level in Russia. The reasons for the violent features in the national cultures of these countries (especially those of the Baltic region and those of the Mediterranean) are sure to differ in part, but they appear to be relatively constant in character, independent of short-term economic and social developments. On the other hand, it is more probable than improbable that the main factors behind the extreme violence in the cultures of Estonia, Finland, other Baltic countries, and even northwestern Russia are the same to a large extent, although it is possible and even probable that the large number of homicides in these countries is the sum of various factors and that in the course of the last two or three hundred years the reasons behind the general level of violent crime have changed, perhaps even several times.[56]

Corresponding to its own tradition of violence, the homicide level in Estonia has been made to rise significantly since the 1960s by mass immigration, chiefly from Russia, Belarus, and Ukraine.[57] With this immigration the structure of the population of the country has radically changed in a very short time, especially in northern Estonia. Since the early 1970s the homicide rates of the non-Estonian population have been about threefold compared with Estonians. The reasons are partly the younger age structure and the higher level of urbanization of the immigrants, partly their immigrant status with consequent phenomena, but also evidently the different tradition of violence of the mostly Russian immigrant population. The effects of immigration on the regional differences in Estonia's homicide statistics are most evident at the extreme ends. On the islands of western Estonia, where immigration was practically nonexistent in 1960–90, the level of violent crime has been the lowest in the country and very stable. In East Virumaa, where the proportion of first-, second-, and third-generation immigrants is more than 80 percent of the total population, the level of violence has been exceptionally high even by Estonian standards; the changes of the level especially have been extremely sharp, upwards as well as downwards.[58] Immigration would, however, not seem to be the only factor accounting for the regional differences in the homicide rates; on the contrary, the level of violent crime in the eastern and western provinces of the Estonian mainland has been (at least since the 1960s) to some extent different despite the similar structure of settlement and population.[59]

The great regional differences raise the question how sensible it is, on the whole, to use the all-Estonian homicide rate as the basis for international comparisons. Based solely on the volume of homicide, it is at present difficult to find two areas in Europe more sharply differing from each other than East Virumaa and the western Estonian islands. However, this problem is not unique to Estonia, though it occurs in other European countries in somewhat less radical dimensions.

The sharp rise in homicide rates beginning in 1978 in Estonia is divided into two distinct parts. In the years 1978–87 the structure of homicides remained traditional, even if the annual number of crimes rose by more than 60 percent compared with the period of 1960–77. Impulsive crimes, connected with family and drinking quarrels, comprised 70–80 percent of all homicides. The changes took place mostly in the number of crimes related to drinking quarrels and were centered in East Virumaa. As the number of homicides in 1978–82 averaged twenty-five crimes a year greater than during the previous ten years, 44 percent of these additional homicides were committed in East Virumaa.

The increase in homicide rates since 1988 differs from that of the late 1970s not only because of its turbulence but also because of structural changes. Sixty percent of the increase has occurred in instrumental homicide: in murders committed for material profit and criminals' mutual violence. On the other hand, the level of impulsive crimes has also increased, being in 1994–96 higher than in the late 1970s. Even if the increase which has taken place in instrumental violence had been omitted altogether, the homicide level in Estonia in 1994–96 would nevertheless have been about 10 crimes a year per 100,000 inhabitants, i.e., more than 50 percent higher than during the previous wave of violence in 1978–82.[60]

The changes in violent crime in the late 1970s, as well as again in the 1990s, coincide with a profound social crisis. It is difficult to prove this, though, because the statistical material describing economic and social processes for the years before 1992 is to a great extent entirely unusable, at least without considerable revision. In the following, the changes in homicide rates are compared to two measures of social disintegration: the level of property crimes and that of alcohol consumption.

Surveying the developments of the interwar period, a relatively similar trend of homicide and property crime until the early 1930s can be seen. During the Depression there was a sharp increase in reported larcenies, which, however, had no effect on homicide rates. Correspondingly, the relatively rapid increase in the number of homicides in 1935–38 was not accompanied by a similar growth in property crime or total criminality (see fig. 3.33). The homicide wave of the late 1930s coincides exactly with the years following Prime Minister Konstantin Päts's coup d'état and the prohibition of the right-wing Vapsi Movement and the suppression of the political ambitions of its members. It is therefore possible that the rise in homicide rates was at least in part connected with these political events. The proposition for constitutional reform backed by the Vapsi Movement received more than 416,000 votes in the 1933 referendum; although its active membership was considerably smaller, in the Estonia of the early 1930s it represented a substantial political force.[61] The movement recruited its members from circles supporting the prevailing social system, albeit not the political one. Thus, it may be assumed that forcing the members into social isolation and political oblivion gave rise to aggressions that found an outlet particularly in violence, but not in any other kind of unlawfulness. To determine whether this was the case, it would be necessary to find out what kind of crimes were increasing in the late 1930s and by whom they were committed.

The relation of violent crime to other developments in criminality in postwar Estonia is extremely difficult to determine accurately. This is because the crime statistics of the Soviet era reflect the prevalent ideas of the level of ideologically acceptable criminality rather than the actual incidents reported to the police. However, in the period of 1973–96 the trends in property crime and in homicide have been remarkably similar (see fig. 3.34). Crimes of theft recorded in statistics started to increase about the same time as homicides, since the year 1979. At that stage the increase could hardly be explained by an improvement in the reliability and accuracy of the crime statistics, which has later on been offered as an explanation (and certainly, at least partly, with good reason) of the sharp increase in property crimes in 1982–83 as well as in 1988–89.[62] The increase in recorded crimes of theft as early as in the late 1970s is the more

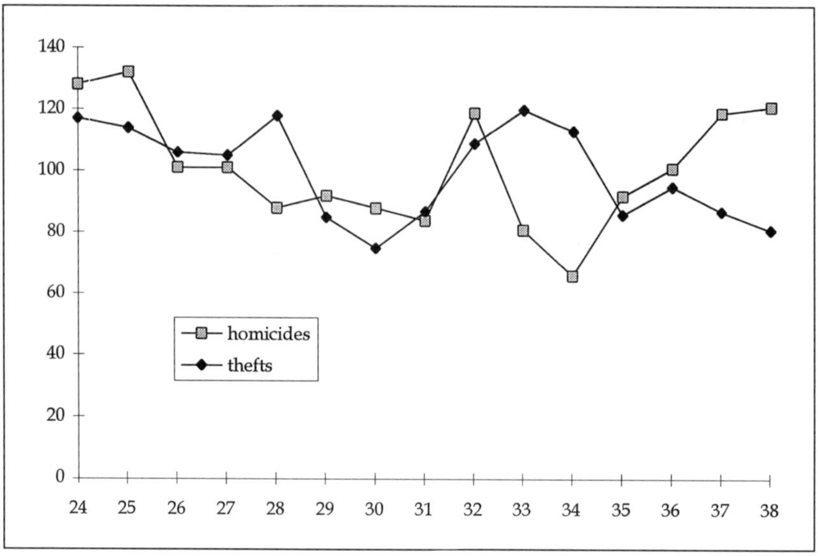

Fig. 3.33. Recorded homicides (excluding attempts) and crimes of theft per 100,000 inhabitants in Estonia, 1924–38 (1924–38 average = 100). *Source:* Tõnismägi 1995, appendix 1.

noteworthy because revealing any growth in criminality usually had negative consequences for the police authorities. Thus, the increase in reported crime must have been noticeable since it also found its way partly into the statistics. Even the rapid increase in homicides after 1988 has been connected with a corresponding development in property crime.

The increase in homicide both in 1978–82 and in 1988–94 has been connected with a strong simultaneous increase in deaths resulting from alcohol poisoning. At the end of the 1970s the rapid growth in the consumption of alcohol seems to have started even a few years before the homicide rates began to rise. The number of cases of alcohol poisoning steadily increased every year throughout the 1970s (see fig. 3.35).

This development in Estonia would superficially seem to fit (as far as the forces behind the growth of violence are concerned) the wave of violence model which Heikki Ylikangas has developed on the basis of the period of high violence in the 1800s in northwestern Finland, the so-called knife fighter (*puukkojunkkari*) period, applying theories of anomaly (which have been applied and tested also by Koskivirta, Pajuoja and Sirén, among others, in their research work in the history of Finnish criminality).[63] The fact is that the end of the

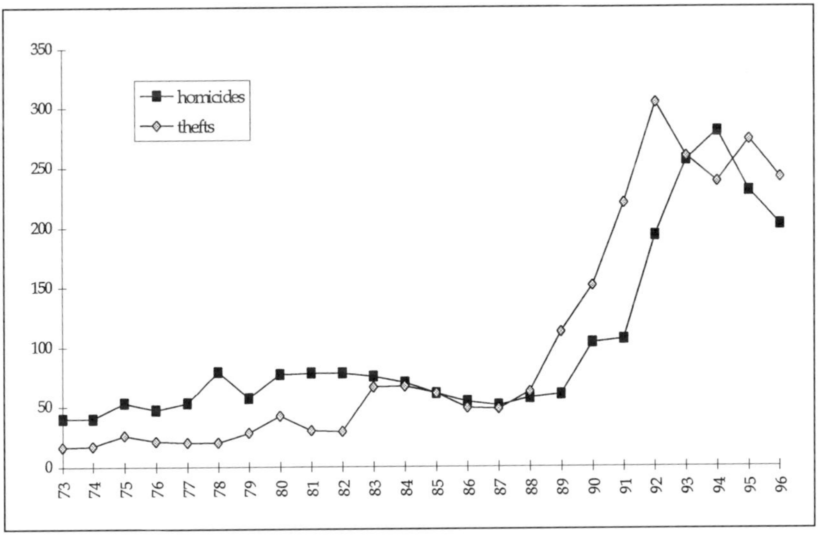

Fig. 3.34. Recorded homicides (excluding attempts) and crimes of theft (including larceny, grand larceny, and burglary, directed toward both private property and state property) per 100,000 inhabitants in Estonia, 1973–96 (1973–96 average = 100).

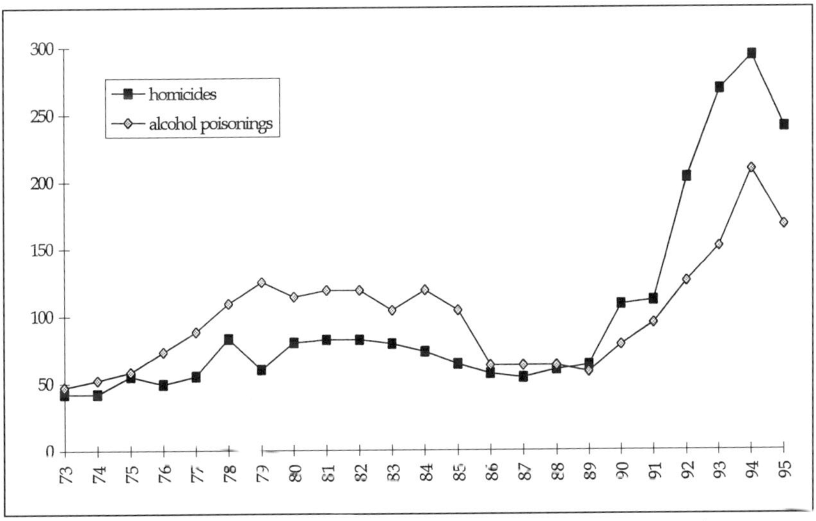

Fig. 3.35. Recorded homicides (excluding attempts) and deaths caused by alcohol poisoning per 100,000 inhabitants in Estonia, 1973–95 (1973–95 average = 100).

1970s as well as the 1990s have been characterized in Estonia by a high proportion of negative expectations about the future among a very large part of the population; and the changes in crime can at least in part be explained by the frustrations caused by that disproportion and by the corresponding rise in the level of aggression in society.

The differences in the motive structure and crime level, on the one hand in 1978–82, on the other hand in 1988–96, are partly to be accounted for simply by the possibilities offered by the surrounding society. In the totalitarian state of the 1970s, where the state had an unquestioned monopoly on violence, the control over the citizens was strict and the material resources were rather equally divided between different population groups (with the exception of the small elite living behind the wall of their monopoly of violence), the opportunities for rational, instrumental violence were small and the increase in aggressiveness showed itself mainly as impulsive deeds. Instead, the present society of the transition period, which is characterized by a relatively weak central authority, nonexistent control over the citizens, and very unequally divided possibilities and wealth, is offering plenty of chances for rational violence. Increased aggressiveness this time is being expressed partly in impulsive deeds (older age groups), but partly also in instrumental violence (youngsters).

Homicide Trends in the Former Soviet Republics and in Eastern Central Europe

The trends in recorded property crime in Eastern Central Europe in the course of the last ten years have been rather similar to those in the former Soviet republics (especially if it is noted that the starting level in the crime statistics of the former socialist countries in Central Europe was less distorted than the one in the Soviet Union). However, an exactly similar social and economic development in the 1990s has not found expression in a corresponding rise in violent crime in the countries of Eastern Central Europe as in the Soviet successor states.

One factor which might account for this, and by which it has sometimes been explained,[64] is the deeper social and especially administrative crises in the Soviet successor states, which have given the shadow economy and organized crime better conditions for activity. This explanation, however, contains some weaknesses.

First there is the question about the significance of organized crime in the increase in homicide rates in Estonia and other former Soviet republics. The bulk of instrumental homicides in Estonia in 1994–96 were more or less unorganized and often even relatively unplanned in character, and thus can be linked

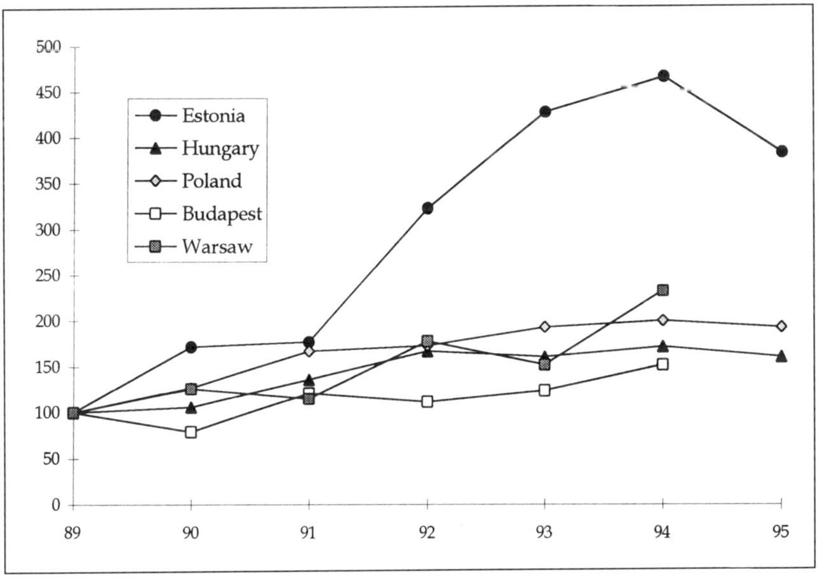

Fig. 3.36. Recorded homicides per 100,000 inhabitants in Estonia, Hungary, Poland, Budapest, and Warsaw, 1989–95 (1989 = 100).

with society's becoming more violent in general. Part of the violence was, however, a consequence of the activity and power exercised by the shadow economy with its systems of solving conflicts (or more precisely the lack of them) and by organized crime. The roots of these phenomena go far back into the history of Soviet society and its schizophrenic economic system. They cannot therefore be considered as creations of today's social changes; rather, the changes have forced the shadow economy and the criminal groups to revise their strategy. The foundation of their power was earlier based mainly on the exploitation of the corrupt state machinery, whereas now they have been forced to replace this method to a great extent with direct violence—a tactic that shows immediately in the crime statistics. On the other hand, although the homicide trends in the Baltic countries and in Russia have been almost identical during the last few years, the relative proportion of the shadow economy of the total GNP is at the moment, for instance in Estonia, considerably smaller than in Russia, and the activity of organized crime is far more restricted.[65] At least so far, it has not been proved either that the activity of the shadow economy or that of organized crime is much more extensive in the Baltic countries than, for example, in Poland or Hungary.[66]

The information obtained on Estonian homicides in 1994–96 does not make it possible to explain the difference between the current crime levels of Estonia and the Central European countries as being due only to crimes connected with the activity of organized crime or the shadow economy. The sources do not permit an exhaustive distinction of organized violence from other instrumental violence. However, on the basis of the information obtained, one can estimate that the proportion of homicides connected with organized crime and the shadow economy is about 10–20 percent of all homicides in Estonia at the moment, making up about 25 percent (at the most) of the rise in crime of the last few years.

Although the rise in organized violence cannot explain the difference in homicide trends between the Eastern European countries and the former Soviet republics, the exceptionally sharp rise in instrumental violence in the Soviet successor states could. The explanation might be the discrepancies between the moral atmospheres of the societies combined with the deeper crises in the state machinery (i.e., the weakness of the police authorities and their efficiency) in the former Soviet republics.

The rapid growth in instrumental violence in Estonia has, no doubt, been encouraged by the vacuum of values left behind by the collapse of the Soviet ideology. In the former socialist countries of Central Europe the influence of the Communist ideology on civil society was not equally extensive as in the Soviet Union, and the moral system internalized by the citizens was more independent of the state ideology. Thus, the common people's values did not experience the same kind of upheaval, and the spreading of nihilism has not been equally intensive. If this observation is valid, instrumental violence ought to have increased in the Central European countries in the last few years far more slowly than in Estonia, although the opportunities for rational violence as well as the factors involved in the process of social change which produce violence have been very similar.[67]

A third factor accounting for the discrepancy could be the intensive internal immigration in the Soviet Union, which affected not only the Baltic countries but also Russia. As a result of this policy, a great number of communities more or less like the towns in East Virumaa have sprung up all over the former Soviet Union. The social structure of these communities seems to encourage high levels of violent crime, as well as to sharpen the changes taking place in those levels. The countries of Eastern Central Europe were to a large extent spared from the creation of such centers of violence. If the reasons for the discrepancy are found in the structure of settlement, in particular, the structural changes in homicides that have taken place in Estonia should in principle have occurred as such in the countries of Central Europe as well.

Notes

1. In this article, only the crimes referred to in n. 37 are regarded as homicides. However, the pre-1945 figures include cases of infanticide only when explicitly mentioned.

2. The tables (with exact numerical information) on which the figures in this article are based are to be found in Lehti 1997.

3. Leps 1991, 55–68.

4. Verkko 1949, 54–55.

5. Archer and Gartner 1984, 79–81, 92–95.

6. The NKVD (Narodnyi Komitet Vnutrennyh Del, i.e., People's Commissariat of Internal Affairs) was the Soviet security service in 1934–46. In 1943 it was divided into two parts: the NKVD and the NKGB.

7. Strods 1996, 112–17.

8. Strods 1996, 122–45, 148–52.

9. In Hungary the homicide level in 1904–13 averaged 2.4 crimes a year per 100,000 inhabitants or approximately the same as in the 1920s (Archer and Gartner 1984, appendix). However, it is unclear whether Archer and Gartner's information from before 1920 refers to the whole of Hungary or only to the area of present-day Hungary.

10. Ylikangas and Pajuoja have explained the wave of violence in the 1920s and 1930s as resulting from social conflicts caused by the civil war. The pattern corresponds with the high level of violence during the entire period between the wars, but it doesn't explain the timing of the peak in 1927–33 (Ylikangas 1973, 320–21; Pajuoja 1987, 173–82). Verkko, on the other hand, thought that the wave was caused mainly by the exceptionally free access to alcohol during prohibition, together with politically unstable conditions (Verkko 1949, 52–53). Even this theory cannot, however, explain the sharp change in criminality in the mid-1920s.

11. Pajuoja 1987, 174–75.

12. Tõnismägi 1995, appendix 1.

13. This is interpreted from crime statistics. It is difficult to define the exact trends of homicide in Estonia during the 1920s and 1930s because the data of the crime statistics differ significantly from those of the cause-of-death statistics. According to the latter, the homicide rates in Estonia increased between 1923 and 1932 and decreased very sharply after 1932. Both the published crime statistics and cause-of-death statistics classify different crimes of homicide very accurately and with the same categories. Thus, there should be no problems with their comparability. Unfortunately, their information differs not only concerning the annual number of the crimes (which is normal) but also when referring to the long-term trends. The description of the homicide trends in Estonia in the 1920s and 1930s given in this article is based on crime statistics.

14. Strods 1996, 148–52.

15. Tammaru 1997, 1661.

16. In 1981, 60 percent of those found guilty of homicides were non-Estonians (Heiman and Svaiko n.d., 7), and between 1990 and 1995, the percentage was exactly the same. Altogether, between 1979 and 1990, an average of 4 Estonians and 10 non-Estonians per 100,000 inhabitants were found guilty of homicides in Estonia every year. Non-Estonians were thus responsible for more than 60 percent of all homicides committed during that period (Leps 1991, 128).

17. When not explicitly otherwise mentioned, the words *nationality, Estonian, Russian, non-Estonian,* etc., in this article refer to ethnicity, not to citizenship.

18. Urvaste 1996, 136–37.

19. On the many-sided effects of immigration on violent criminality, see Ferracuti 1968, 207–12.

20. Of those convicted of murders in 1995 in Latvia, 43 percent were Latvians, 54 percent were Russians, and 3 percent were other nationalities.

21. In crimes where the victim is picked out at random, the likelihood of the victim belonging to the main population group increases in direct proportion to the relative size of the group. On the other hand, in places where the national minority is small, the likelihood that the circle of acquaintances belonging to the minority group also includes people representing the main population is greater than in areas where the minority and the majority group are about identical in size.

22. Gilinskiy 1994, 207–9; Pietarinen 1996.

23. Ylikangas 1973, 315, 321.

24. Franke 1994, 90–93. Instrumental violence–impulsive violence is a pair of concepts used by Franke to describe the two main categories of violence. He defines instrumental violence as the use of violence to acquire material profit illegally, and impulsive violence as the use of violence in daily intercourse between people. In this article the division is applied with two modifications: both homicides related to sexual crimes and homicides related to the mutual violence of criminals and criminal groups are regarded as instrumental violence.

25. Klebba 1975, 202; *Violent Crime,* 2–3.

26. Franke 1994, 91–93; Klebba 1975, 198–202.

27. It is true, however, that, for example, in the Netherlands this is a relatively late phenomenon; there, as late as the 1960s the level of crime in urban areas and in the countryside was still identical (Franke 1994, 82–83).

28. However, in sixteenth- and seventeenth-century Finland the homicide rate was significantly higher in cities than in rural areas. The current situation has existed since the early 1800s (Karonen 1996, 78–80).

29. The information is based on the files of the Keskuurimisbüroo concerning homicides in the years 1994–96. The division of crimes between cities and rural communes is the same as that in the crime statistics of the Politseiameti Teabebüroo. The data used here cover about 60 percent of all the crimes, both urban and rural, registered by the police in 1994–96.

30. The division is based on victimization surveys showing considerable differences between the violent crime levels of the eastern and western provinces (Aromaa and Ahven 1995, 7–11).

31. Franke 1994, 90–93; Pajuoja 1995, 183–85.

32. Heiman and Svaiko n.d., 3.

33. The proportion of crimes committed by women out of all homicides corresponds in Estonia to the pattern Verkko developed in the 1920s; nevertheless, the prompt tendency of the volume of women's crimes to parallel the recent general rise in homicides deviates from his theory. (One has to take into account, though, that the fall in the clearance rate may make the current relative proportion of women's crime somewhat larger than it is in reality.) On the other hand, women's homicide in present-day Estonia is far more impulsive by nature than it seems to have been in the society described by Verkko's patterns (Verkko 1949, 57–66).

34. Urvaste 1995, 3.

35. Including also crimes with unknown motives. The proportion of homicides related to family quarrels accounted for as much as 30 percent of crimes whose motives were known.

36. Especially since one can suppose that also the low clearance rate for homicides involving young victims is related to the high proportion of instrumental violence.

37. The Estonian Criminal Code of today recognizes seven intentional crimes of homicide (*kriminaalkoodeks* §§ 100–104 and § 106). The basic crime is murder (*tahtlik tapmine;* § 100), for which the punishment inflicted is from five to ten years in prison. An aggravated murder (*tahtlik tapmine raskendavail asjaoludel;* § 101) is considered to be a crime that was committed (1) with motives of material profit, (2) with hooligan motives, (3) to cover up or promote another crime or in connection with rape, (4) to kill two or more people, (5) to kill an old person, a child, or a pregnant woman, (6) in an especially cruel way or in a way causing general danger, or (7) by a person who had already earlier been found guilty of intentional homicide. The punishment will be from eight to fifteen years in prison, imprisonment for life, or the death sentence.

Paragraph 102 pertains to infanticide (*ema poolt oma vastsündinud lapse tapmine*) and § 103 to murder committed under extenuating circumstances (*tapmine hingelise erutuse seisundis*). The latter pertains to violent attack or gross insult directed at the perpetrator by the victim and having led to the deed. In both crimes the punishment is a maximum of four years in prison.

Furthermore, intentional homicides also include excessive self-defense (*tapmine hädakaitse piiride ületamisel;* § 104) and enticing or forcing somebody into suicide (*enesetapmisele viimine;* § 106). In the former case the scale of punishment is detention (arrest) or a maximum of two years in prison, in the latter from three to eight years in prison.

38. In Finland, on the contrary, the concept seems to have become steadily broader in the postwar period; in the 1950s there were 30 percent attempts out of all registered intentional homicides, in the 1960s 31 percent, in the 1970s 46 percent, but in the 1980s as much as 64 percent and in 1990–96 67 percent.

39. In the course of the last ten years, the proportion of fatal assaults out of all intentional homicides has been 19 percent in Finland. In Estonia the classification of fatal violent crimes either as assaults or as homicides depended in the past rather directly on the amount of time that had elapsed between the deed and the death. If the death occurred within fifteen minutes after the assault, the deed was regarded as a homicide; if after twenty-four hours or longer, it was regarded as an aggravated assault. In crimes where death followed from a quarter of an hour to twenty-four hours after the assault, the classification depended on the estimation of the authorities involved, but most of these cases were tried as assaults (Leps 1991, 104–6).

40. Heiman and Svaiko n.d., 1–8.

41. Heiman and Svaiko n.d.; Värnik 1997, 37. Although the number of deaths caused by alcohol poisoning does not directly describe the total volume of the consumption of alcohol, the changes in the death rate indicate similar changes in consumption rates.

42. Värnik 1997, 44.

43. Leps 1991, 67.

44. Gorbachev 1997, 179–90; Susiluoto 1996, 49. The onset of the decrease in the homicide rate coincides also with a radical decrease in the number of suicides in Estonia in 1982–83. Värnik (1997, 45) thinks the latter is a consequence of an anti-alcohol campaign at that time in Estonia. However, the mortality statistics related to alcohol poisonings don't confirm the suggestion that there was any decrease in alcohol consumption in the country at that time (see fig. 3.21).

45. Värnik 1997, 45.

46. In percentages, the change was greatest on the islands, but involved very small absolute numbers of crimes (from nil to two per year), so the changes may well be attributable to random factors.

47. The prefectures of East Virumaa and Narva.

48. The prefectures of Harjumaa, West Virumaa, and Tallinn. In Tallinn the clearance rate was also on average 58 percent. In Harjumaa it was one of the lowest in the country, 46 percent.

49. If the preliminary investigation does not solve the crime in a relatively short time (in two to six months) and the investigator deems that it is not possible to find any additional evidence in the case, the preliminary investigation will be interrupted (*peatada*) until some new evidence appears.

50. This information was obtained from Jüri Kosenkranius, a leading homicide investigator in the Keskuurimisbüroo.

51. The minimum is obtained if we estimate that none of the unsolved crimes belongs to this group, the maximum by regarding all unsolved homicides as murders for profit.

52. The impulsive crimes making up the bulk of the homicides of middle-aged people are, in principle, solved more easily than profit-motivated crimes, which are often directed at victims previously unknown to the perpetrators.

53. Kirs 1995. In 1994, 83 percent of the people reported missing were found, 70 percent alive and 12 percent dead. Only a minority of those found dead were victims of crime.

54. As for the islands, very small absolute numbers are involved, from one to three homicides a year, and thus the change may also be attributed to random factors.

55. In the past few years, the reason has in fact been mainly the impact of the city of Tartu for the figures of eastern Estonia, but Tartu doesn't explain the whole of the difference in the 1990s and even less so in the 1970s and 1980s.

56. For explanations of the high violent crime in Finland, see Ylikangas 1996, 7–9. In the areas of high homicide in Finland between 1750 and 1825, the basic reasons for crime seem to have varied considerably by area (Koskivirta 1996, 153–56; Ylikangas 1973, 273–324).

57. In 1990–96 by 58 percent on average.

58. In this respect the regional distribution of crime is to some degree similar to that experienced in Finland between World Wars I and II (Pajuoja 1987, 173–78). Nevertheless, immigration does not seem to account for the sharp rise in violent crime that started in Estonia in 1978 and again in the 1990s, but it has been raising the homicide rates steadily and slowly.

59. The higher level of violent crime in the eastern provinces has been observed also in the victimization surveys carried out during the 1990s (Aromaa and Ahven 1995, 10).

60. In reality, the homicide level in 1994–96 was on average 21 crimes a year per 100,000 inhabitants, fully 220 percent higher than in 1978–82.

61. Tomingas 1992, 348.

62. Leps 1991, 67.

63. Ylikangas 1973, 311–27; Koskivirta 1996; Pajuoja 1987; Sirén 1996.

64. See, e.g., *Nacionala drosiba*, 78.

65. Aromaa and Lehti 1996, 9–20, 27–32.

66. The surveys of business security carried out in the Baltic countries in 1995–97 did not suggest this kind of discrepancy (Aromaa and Lehti 1997; cf. Árvay and Vértes 1993).

67. No information on the types of homicide in the 1990s in the former socialist countries in Central Europe was available for this article.

References

Archer, Dane, and Rosemary Gartner. 1984. *Violence and Crime in Cross-National Perspective*. New Haven, Conn.

Aromaa, Kauko, and Andri Ahven. 1995. *Victims of Crime in a Time of Change: Estonia, 1993 and 1995*. National Research Institute of Legal Policy Research Communications 19. Helsinki.

Aromaa, Kauko, and Martti Lehti. 1996. *Foreign Companies and Crime in Eastern Europe*. National Research Institute of Legal Policy Publication 135. Helsinki.

———. 1997. *Ulkomaalaiset yritykset ja lähialueiden rikollisuus. Suomalaisyrittäjien kokemuksia Latviassa, Pietarissa ja Virossa 1994–96*. National Research Institute of Legal Policy Research Communications 31. Helsinki.

Árvay, János, and András Vértes. 1993. *Size of the Hidden Economy in Hungary: Research Work on the Assessment of the Real Performance of the Private Sector in Hungary*. Preliminary report, pt. 2. Budapest.

Eesti Arvudes, 1920–35. Tallinn, 1937.

Ferracuti, Franco. 1968. "European Migration and Crime: Crime and Culture." In *Essays in Honor of Thorsten Sellin*, ed. Marvin E. Wolfgang. New York.

Franke, Herman. 1994. "Violent Crime in the Netherlands: A Historical-Sociological Analysis." *Crime, Law, and Social Change* 21.

Gilinskiy, Yakov. 1994. "Crime in St. Petersburg." In *Petersburg in the Early Nineties: Crazy, Cold, Cruel* . . . St. Petersburg.

Gorbachev, Mikhail. 1997. *Memoirs*. Reading, England.

Heiman, B., and V. Svaiko. n.d. "Õiend eriti ohtlike isikuvastaste kuritegude dünamiika ja nende kuritegude toimepanemise põhjuste analüüsist." Unpublished ms. Tallinn.

Home Office crime statistics. England and Wales, 1994. London, 1995.

Karonen, Petri. 1996. "Pohjolan vaarallisimmat asuinpaikat." In *Laittomuuden laitatiellä. Rikos Suomessa 1500-luvulta nykypäiviin*, ed. Sari Forsström. Helsingin yliopiston historian laitoksen julkaisuja 1/1996. Helsinki.

Kirs, Alar. 1995. "Eestis 1992–1995 toime pandud tahtlike tapmiste statistiline võrdlev analüüs." Unpublished ms. Tallinn.

Klebba, Joan A. 1975. "Homicide Trends in the United States, 1900–74." *Public Health Reports* 90.

Koskivirta, Anu. 1996. "Omankädenoikeutta itärajalla. Kymenkartanon ja Savon läänin henkirikollisuus 1748–1774; Suomen ja Skandinavian historian tutkielma." Master's thesis, Department of History, Helsinki University.

Lehti, Martti. 1997. *Viron henkirikollisuus 1990-luvulla*. National Research Institute of Legal Policy Publication 148. Helsinki.

Leps, Ando. 1991. *Kuritegevus Eestis*. Tartu.

Nacionala drosiba: Kriminologiskas un socialas problemas. 1995. Kriminologiskais biletens 25. Riga.

Pajuoja, Jussi. 1987. "Suomalaisen väkivallanaallon huippu 1920- ja 1930-luvulla." In *Oikeutta ja historiaa. Heikki Ylikankaan 50-vuotisjuhlakirja*. Juva.

———. 1995. *Väkivalta ja mielentila. Oikeussosiologinen tutkimus syyntakeisuussäännöksistä ja mielentilatutkimuksista*. Suomalaisen lakimiesyhdistyksen julkaisuja Asarja 201. Helsinki.

Pietarinen, Juha. 1996. "Raportti poliisin yhdysmiestoiminnasta Venäjällä 2/1996." Unpublished ms.

Sirén, Kirsi. 1996. "Korkean rikollisuuden alueet Suomessa 1700-luvun lopulla ja 1800-luvun alussa." In *Laittomuuden laitatiellä—Rikos Suomessa 1500-luvulta nykypäiviin,* ed. Sari Forsström. Helsingin yliopiston historian laitoksen julkaisuja 1/1996. Helsinki.

Sourcebook of Criminal Justice Statistics 1989. 1990. Washington, D.C.

Strods, Heinrihs. 1996. *Latvijas nacionalo partizanu kars 1944–1956.* Riga.

Susiluoto, Ilmari. 1996. "Historian raskas taakka." In *Venäjä-jättiläinen tuuliajolla,* ed. Anne Sailas, Ilmari Susiluoto, and Matti Valkonen. Helsinki.

Svalastoga, Kaare. 1982. *On Deadly Violence.* Oslo.

Tammaru, Tiit. 1997. "Venelased Eestis: Ränne ja kohanemine." *Akadeemia* 8.

Tomingas, William. 1992. *Mälestused: Vaikiv ajastu Eestis.* Tallinn.

Tõnismägi, Heino. 1995. "Ajalooline ülevaade Eesti Vabariigi kuritegevusest (1919–38.a.)." Unpublished ms. Tallinn.

Urvaste, Heino. 1995. "Ülevaade tahtlikest tapmistest." Unpublished ms. Tallinn.

———. 1996. "Aastal toime pandud kuriteod statistikas." *Juridica* 3.

Värnik, Airi. 1997. *Enesetapud Eestis 1965–1995.* Tallinn.

Verkko, Veli. 1949. *Lähimmäisen ja oma henki. Sosiaalipatologisia tutkimuksia Suomen kansasta.* Suomalaisen lakimiesyhdistyksen julkaisuja B 33. Jyväskylä.

Violent Crime: Bureau of Justice Statistics Selected Findings. 1994. April. Washington, D.C.

World Health Statistics Annual, 1994–95. 1995–96. Geneva.

Ylikangas, Heikki. 1973. *Väkivallanaallon synty. Puukkojunkkari-kauden alku Etelä-Pohjanmaalla.* Helsingin yliopiston historian laitoksen julkaisuja 3. Helsinki.

———. 1996. "Ongelmakohtia väkivaltarikollisuuden kehityksessä Suomessa." In *Laittomuuden laitatiellä—Rikos Suomessa 1500-luvulta nykypäiviin,* ed. Sari Forsström. Helsingin yliopiston historian laitoksen julkaisuja 1/1996. Helsinki.

Index

THE HISTORY OF CRIME AND CRIMINAL JUSTICE SERIES

David R. Johnson and Jeffrey S. Adler, *Series Editors*

The series explores the history of crime and criminality, violence, criminal justice, and legal systems without restrictions as to chronological scope, geographical focus, or methodological approach.

Controlling Vice: *Regulating Brothel Prostitution in St. Paul, 1865–1883*
Joel Best

Prostitution and the State in Italy, 1860–1915, *Second Edition*
Mary Gibson

Murder in America: *A History*
Roger Lane

Violent Death in the City: *Suicide, Accident, and Murder in Nineteenth-Century Philadelphia, Second Edition*
Roger Lane

Cops and Bobbies: *Police Authority in New York and London, 1830–1870, Second Edition*
Wilbur R. Miller

Race, Labor, and Punishment in the New South
Martha A. Myers

Homicide North and South
H. V. Redfield

Men and Violence: *Gender, Honor, and Rituals in Modern Europe and America*
Edited by Pieter Spierenburg

Rethinking Southern Violence: *Homicides in Post–Civil War Louisiana, 1866–1884*
Gilles Vandal